BUSHWHACKED

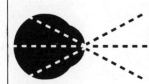

This Large Print Book carries the
Seal of Approval of N.A.V.H.

BUSHWHACKED

Life in
GEORGE W. BUSH'S
AMERICA

MOLLY IVINS AND LOU DUBOSE

Thorndike Press • Waterville, Maine

Published in 2004 by arrangement with
Random House, Inc.

Thorndike Press® Large Print Basic.

The tree indicium is a trademark of Thorndike Press.

The text of this Large Print edition is unabridged.
Other aspects of the book may vary from the original edition.

Set in 16 pt. Plantin.

Printed in the United States on permanent paper.

Library of Congress Cataloging-in-Publication Data

Ivins, Molly.
    Bushwhacked : life in George W. Bush's America /
Molly Ivins and Lou Dubose.
        p. cm.
    Originally published: 1st ed. New York :
Random House, c2003.
    ISBN 0-7862-6243-5 (lg. print : hc : alk. paper)
    1. United States — Politics and government — 2001–
2. Bush, George W. (George Walker), 1946– — Ethics.
3. Political corruption — United States.   4. United States
— Economic conditions — 2001–   5. United States —
Social conditions — 1980–   6. Large type books.
I. Dubose, Lou.   II. Title.
E902.I95 2004
    973.931—dc22   2003070271

This book is dedicated to the memory of six great and wonderfully nonconformist Texans. They all persisted in the good fight to make our state and our country a better place. They were not well behaved.

To John Henry Faulk,
freedom fighter, died 1990

To Bob Eckhardt,
congressman, scholar, and cartoonist, died 2001

To Billie Carr,
political organizer, died 2002

To Warren Burnett,
trial lawyer, died 2002

To Maury Maverick,
lawyer, writer, and curmudgeon, died 2003

To Malcolm McGregor,
legislator, bibliophile, and pilot, died 2003

We loved them all. It was the grandest privilege to know them.

As the Founder/CEO of NAVH, the only national health agency solely devoted to those who, although not totally blind, have an eye disease which could lead to serious visual impairment, I am pleased to recognize Thorndike Press* as one of the leading publishers in the large print field.

Founded in 1954 in San Francisco to prepare large print textbooks for partially seeing children, NAVH became the pioneer and standard setting agency in the preparation of large type.

Today, those publishers who meet our standards carry the prestigious "Seal of Approval" indicating high quality large print. We are delighted that Thorndike Press is one of the publishers whose titles meet these standards. We are also pleased to recognize the significant contribution Thorndike Press is making in this important and growing field.

Lorraine H. Marchi, L.H.D.
Founder/CEO
NAVH

* Thorndike Press encompasses the following imprints: Thorndike, Wheeler, Walker and Large Pr int Press.

• CONTENTS •

CONTENTS

• INTRODUCTION •

This book is about the connections between what happens in people's lives and the decisions made by often obscure parts of the federal government. Some concept, eh? Policy matters; stop the presses. There was a time when explaining how what the government does affects "ordinary people" was considered political reporting. But reporters somehow became more fixated on the polls, the consultants, the horse race, and the partisan bickering; ordinary people pretty much fell off the screen. We're still here. The difference between one underassistant secretary and another assistant undersecretary is still turning people's lives upside down; indeed, it can be the difference between life and death.

While the Washington press corps, ever more courtierlike, focuses on the White House, we found that starting at the other end, with "average citizens," provides a much clearer view of what is happening in America.

The good news is that nothing will cheer you up more about this country than getting out and talking to the people in it. We were prepared to a play a dirge on our literary violin for the hapless victims of various misbegotten and mean-spirited policies. Unfortunately for our purposes, we kept finding Americans who are tough, funny, sassy, brave, smart, and full of fight. They get pissed-off, they endure, they fight like hell, they start all over — whatever it takes. They don't waste time feeling sorry for themselves. Still, it's remarkable how easy it is for some casual, not necessarily malicious, but not-very-well-thought-through change in a policy, made by some clueless citizen in Washington, can simply wreck people's lives.

We found heroes all over hell and gone. Most of them are "ordinary people," some of them are government bureaucrats, and a few of them are even politicians.

More or less in the "duh" category, we found that government no longer works for most of the people of this country. It works for big corporations, it works for big campaign donors, but it works less and less for "average" Americans. While talk of Christian compassion wafts through Washington, people are not only getting screwed — losing their life savings, their pensions, their health insurance, their jobs, and

10

unemployment comp — they're also getting sick, getting hurt, and even dying because the people's interest now takes second place to that of big-money contributors. A government of big corporations, by big corporations, and for big corporations has thousands of ramifications for the people, few of them good. As the acolytes of large corporations increasingly take over the various regulatory agencies that are supposed to keep corporate power in check — a process now so far advanced it's faintly comical — the results veer between infuriating and frightening.

After more than two years of George W. Bush's administration, it is becoming clearer that we are looking at people with an agenda driven by ideology. They believe the free market can solve all problems, that government is generally bad, that we should privatize everything we possibly can, that there is no such thing as global warming, that the environment is unimportant, and that worker safety will be protected by benign employers. We have seen a serious degradation of civil liberties matched by an equally remarkable increase in property rights. And in the middle of all this came that tragic spanner-in-the-works, September 11.

All this abstract, ideological, the-free-

11

market-is-God, Ayn Rand piffle is doing cruel things to real people. This book is about them.

We are, as always, optimistic to the point of idiocy, and although not much given to Simple Solutions, we consider public campaign financing the necessary first step, the sine qua non, as they rarely say in Lubbock, for fixing this deal.

Our biggest problem with the Bush administration is that for us it's déjà vu all over again. We spent six years watching the man as governor of Texas, the basis for our 1999 book, *Shrub*. We were tempted to begin this book by observing, "If y'all had've read the first book, we wouldn't've had to write this one." Cooler heads prevailed.

In Texas we have been dealing with postpartum blues since George W. left for Washington. He left us with tax breaks for the rich that make it impossible for government to provide basic services for working people. With bills written by energy lobbyists working the cash-and-carry model of government perfected here in Texas. He eliminated the most basic workplace protections. Those of us who knew the president when he was governor of a low-tax, low-service, no-regulation state are very seriously not amazed by what he has

12

done in Washington.

Terry Allen, a great songwriter out of Lubbock, penned one called "Lubbock on Everything." Kind of feels to us like the Bush years are "Texas on Everything."

Texas has a lot of things suitable for export. The songs of the Flatlanders or the Dixie Chicks come to mind; ruby-red grapefruit from the Rio Grande Valley, boots from El Paso, sweet crude from Odessa, and brown shrimp from Corpus Christi. But public policy stamped MADE IN TEXAS is like Hungarian wine — it does not travel well. In fact, it ought to be embargoed. Very few laws passed east of the Sabine or south of the Red River are safe for national consumption.

As president, Bush had his first big legislative victory in a tax cut that turned a $127 billion surplus into a $288 billion deficit. Been there. As governor, Bush inherited a $6 billion surplus, pushed through two major tax breaks for property owners, and promised they would "grow the economy" so much the state would never even miss the money. Two years after he left we're looking at a $10 billion deficit, and rising.

Pay-to-play energy policy. Done that. When Bush's own appointees to our state environmental-protection agency warned that the public was demanding a cleanup of the most contaminated air in the country, Governor Bush secretly turned the job over to the presidents of the Marathon and Exxon oil companies. Every jot and tittle of the governor's 1999 bill to "clean up refineries" was written by an oil-company lobbyist. Only under the threat of a lawsuit did Texans find out who wrote the law that "encouraged" polluters to "volunteer" to reduce emissions. (Bush had two voluntary emissions-control programs here in Texas. One involved polluting industries. The other was directed at adolescent males, who were encouraged to "try abstinence." Only 3 of our 8,645 most obnoxiously polluting refineries actually volunteered to cut back on their toxic emissions. Numbers on teenage boys are not yet in.) No one in Houston, Dallas, or San Antonio was shocked to see Vice President Cheney turn the nation's energy policy over to the oil companies and then refuse to turn over the records of those meetings to the public. Seen that.

Killing regulations put in place to protect working people from job injuries? Old news in Texas. When workers in our Panhandle meatpacking factories won lawsuits against the world's biggest kill-cut-and-wrap company, Governor Bush pushed through "tort reform," legislation that made it almost impossible for workers to sue their employers. Then a Bush appointee to the Texas Supreme Court* made it flat impossible — he ruled that any employee "consulting" a lawyer about workplace hazards could be fired. See a lawyer? Lose your job. Bush vetoed so many labor bills down here that one Houston legislator still swears the governor vetoed a worker-protection bill that was actually defeated on the house floor by the governor's staff.

Not only is Texas not surprised. For a change, we're ahead of the country. After Bush left, we had us a little spate of what we call ree-form. The 2001 session of the Texas Legislature had to clean up some of the mess Governor Bush left behind. A conservative Republican senator from Dallas introduced a bill to rescind the $2.9 billion tax cut Bush passed. The voluntary-emissions law written by an industry lobbyist was replaced by a law that compels polluting industries to clean up. A hate-crimes bill

*Greg Abbott was a Karl Rove candidate for the Supreme Court and has now moved on to the office of attorney general, where he promises even more tort reform.

that includes protections for gays and lesbians (that was the deal-buster for Bush) passed both houses and was signed by the Republican who took over as governor here after the Supreme Court appointed Bush president. Roadblocks to Medicaid, in a state with the nation's highest percentage of poverty, were eliminated by the hard work of a Hispanic senator from South Texas and an African-American house member from Houston. The Great State's Legislature even passed a law that would have ended execution of the mentally retarded. But that one was too much for Bush's designated successor. Governor Goodhair* Perry vetoed the bill because he finds that executing people who lack the wits to understand either crime or punishment is a matter of Christian duty.

The 2000 presidential campaign focused so much attention on the state of the Great State that it has actually done us good. The good news is that the first post-Bush session of the Texas Legislature almost made our mock license-plate motto "Texas: Mississippi with Good

---

*That man has a head of hair every Texan can be proud of, regardless of party. There is a difference of opinion over whether it is his only accomplishment.

Roads" obsolete.* We're no longer a Third World state. The bad news is, to borrow a line from a Texas boogie band, "We're Bad, We're Nationwide." The worst public policy created in Texas has gone national. "I'd like to have the opportunity to show Washington how to handle a budget surplus," our Republican governor said in 1999. And has he ever.

Here's the kicker. Six months after that speech, when one of the boys on the bus asked him about the fiscal crisis Texas was facing in the legislative session ahead, candidate Bush said, "I hope I'm not around to deal with it."

He's not.

He was our governor.

Now he's your president.

---

*The 2003 session, when the Republican right seized control of both houses of the Ledge and ruled with callous disregard for the public interest and the rules of the House and Senate, was serious backsliding in the direction of the old Bush League Texas. Things got so bad that fifty-three Democrats in the House slipped across the Red River into Oklahoma to deny a quorum for Republican speaker Tom Craddick — a man possessed of Bob Dole's charm and Tom DeLay's hardass, hard-right agenda.

•1•

ALOHA, HARKEN

In the long run, there is no capitalism without conscience; there is no wealth without character.
— GEORGE W. BUSH ON
WALL STREET, JULY 9, 2001

In the long run, we are all dead.
— JOHN MAYNARD KEYNES ON
THE LONG RUN, 1924

There he was. On the Tuesday after a long Fourth of July weekend. In the ballroom of an ornate Wall Street hotel that once housed the New York Merchants Exchange. Standing in front of a blue-and-white backdrop with the words CORPORATE RESPONSIBILITY printed over and over on it, in case you should miss the point. Promising us "a new ethic" for American business. Our president, Scourge of Corporate Misbehavior.

It was like watching a whore pretend to

be dean of Southern Methodist University's School of Theology. But as Luther said, hypocrisy has ample wages.

"Harken," said the Bush camp over and over, "was nothing like Enron." Interestingly enough, it was exactly like Enron in each and every feature of corporate misbehavior, except a lot smaller. A perfect miniature Enron.

By the summer of 2002, it had long been known that twelve years earlier Bush made a pile by selling his stock in Harken Energy Corporation just before it tanked. At the time, he was serving both on Harken's board and on a special audit committee looking at the company's financial health. As he spoke on Wall Street, stories were surfacing about Harken's sham sale of a subsidiary to a group of company insiders. The acquisition was financed by an $11 million loan guaranteed by the seller, Harken Energy. In other words, a fake asset swap to punch up Harken's annual profit-and-loss statement.

The "sale" of Aloha Petroleum, from Harken to Harken, was again Enron writ small and so outrageous that the SEC stepped in, declared the accounting unacceptable, and forced the company to restate its earnings. Bush unquestionably knew about the deal.

Even if he had convinced the public that earlier stories about his $848,560 insider trade, his failure to report it to the SEC, his low-interest loans from Harken to buy company stock (a practice he particularly denounced in his Wall Street speech, as though he had never heard of such an unseemly scam before), and the Enron-esque sale of Aloha Petroleum were all what he described as "recycled stuff," he was still surrounded by bad stories about to break. Enron was ripe for federal prosecution; Bush and Enron's CEO, Ken Lay, his single largest campaign contributor, had been tight for years. Halliburton was being investigated by the feds for fraudulent accounting practices put in place when Dick Cheney was CEO. Congress was investigating the secretary of the Army for his role in the collapse of Enron, in the fleecing of electricity customers in California, and for his failure to divest himself of Enron stock in a timely manner.

SEC chief Harvey Pitt had so many previous business connections with the firms he was now regulating, he had already had to recuse himself in twenty-nine cases being pursued by the SEC. Bush's hard-nosed, hard-assed political adviser, Karl

2000 or because Al Gore failed to raise the issue, the press started to notice Bush's business pattern only in the wake of the wrecks of Enron, Tyco, WorldCom, Adelphia, etc. As the economy contracted and stock values plummeted in mid-2002, reporters began to focus on Bush's M.O.

Bush walked away from the Texas "awl bidness" in 1990 with almost a million in cash — after a career during which he lost more than $3 million of other people's money. Here he was advocating "a new ethic" on Wall Street despite his own business dealings, which couldn't even pass the "old ethic" test. The earlier dealings had been the subject of a pro forma investigation directed by the man President Bush the Elder appointed head of the SEC, and the investigation itself was conducted by a man who had worked as GeeDubya's personal lawyer before joining the SEC. A few of GeeDubya's deals, particularly a series of critical bailouts of his ever-sinking oil-field ventures, are truly astonishing — not just because of the volume of dollars flowing out of Northeastern banks and disappearing in Texas but because the transactions made little or no economic sense.

A company balance sheet can be misleading. There was leaseholds, there was momentum.
— CANDIDATE GEORGE W. BUSH ON PHILIP UZIELLI'S $1 MILLION BAILOUT OF ARBUSTO

One of Bush's white knights, a friend of the Bush family consigliere* James Baker III, is so interesting that to leave him out is the journalistic equivalent of a breach of fiduciary responsibility. Philip Uzielli's $1 million cash-for-trash deal in 1982 allowed GeeDubya to keep his company alive long enough to sell it to Spectrum 7, then to sell the again-sinking Spectrum 7 to Harken and then to unload his sinking Harken stock — just before the bad news became public — for a large enough profit to buy 2 percent of the ownership of a baseball franchise that made him $15 million in less than nine years. Philip Uzielli ("Uzi" to GeeDubya) is a Panamanian businessman and Princeton classmate of James Baker. In 1982 he was listed as CEO of Panama's Executive Resources and as a director of

---

*Maureen Dowd, columnist for *The New York Times*, was apparently the first journalist to use the word *consigliere* to describe Baker's role in the Bush family.

Harrow Corporation and Leigh Products. As we reported in *Shrub*, when GeeDubya's company, Arbusto, was in a terminal cash crunch, Uzi showed up and paid $1 million for 10 percent of a failing company valued at $382,376, according to the company's financial statements. In other words, Uzielli paid $1 million for $38,200 in equity. Bush had changed the name of Arbusto to Bush Exploration after his father became vice president. (GeeDubya says *arbusto* is the Spanish word for "bush," although *Cassell's Spanish/English Dictionary* translates it as "shrub," the source of one of GeeDubya's nicknames.) By the time of the corporate name change, Arbusto had drilled so many dry holes that West Texas oilmen called it "are-busted." Mr. Uzielli lost his entire $1 million investment but later told reporters he didn't regret it. He described his investment with Bush as "a losing wicket" but said "it was great fun." What a sport.

Arbusto was not an oil company so much as it was a tax write-off company, taking advantage of the IRS tax-code provision that allowed investors to deduct up to 75 percent of their losses in the oil business. Bush didn't strike oil, he struck money from friends of his daddy. After the Uzielli bailout Bush Exploration was acquired by Spectrum 7. Spectrum 7 was owned by William DeWitt, Jr., son of the owner of the Cincinnati Reds. DeWitt couldn't pay Bush for what remained of Bush Exploration, so he sort of took him in, made him CEO and a director, paid him $75,000 a year and $120,000 in consulting fees, and gave him 1.1 million shares of Spectrum 7 stock.

Two years later Spectrum 7 had lost $400,000 in six months and was $3 million in debt. So Harken stepped in. The Texas-based company bought Spectrum 7 for $2 million in Harken stock. Of the $2 million, $224,000 in shares went to Bush, along with options to purchase more.

There was no malfeeance [sic], *nor attempt to hide anything. In the corporate world, sometimes things aren't exactly black and white when it comes to accounting procedures.*
— PRESIDENT GEORGE W. BUSH, JULY 8, 2002, ON ABSENCE OF "MALFEEANCE" IN THE ALOHA SALE

"His name was George Bush," said Harken's founder, Phil Kendrick. "That was worth the money they paid him." Oil-field losses followed GeeDubya the way that cloud of dirt used to follow Pig Pen in

"Peanuts." By 1989 Harken was booking big losses but Daddy was president. In February 1990 the company's CEO, Mikel Faulkner, warned board members that a failed deal the previous year left the company "with little cash flow flexibility." In the months that followed, Harken's memos and board minutes should have been written in red ink. So the management team devised a scheme to obscure these losses.

See if you can follow this bouncing ball. Harken masked its 1989 losses by selling 80 percent of a subsidiary, Aloha Petroleum, to a partnership of Harken insiders called International Marketing & Resources for $12 million. Of that sum, $11 million came from a note held by Harken. Aloha was a small chain of gas stations and convenience stores in Hawaii, originally started by J. Paul Getty and acquired by Harken in a package deal in 1986.

When Harken sold Aloha in 1989, here's how it did the accounting. Since Harken carried an $11 million note on the $12 million sale, the only money it got up front was the first $1 million. But Harken booked $7.9 million, using the mark-to-market accounting that Enron made so fashionable in the late nineties. In January

1990, IMR in turn sold its stake in Aloha to a privately held company called Advance Petroleum Marketing, and the Harken loan was effectively transferred to Advance.

In brief, Harken insiders borrowed money from their own company to buy a subsidiary at an inflated price. Then they booked sales revenue that didn't exist as profit. Then they got rid of the loan that had provided the revenue that never really existed. This is the kind of deal that made Enron famous. It allowed Harken to declare a modest loss of $3.3 million on its 1989 annual report, and as a result the company's shareholders had no clue how bad things were. And we all thought the smart guys at Enron invented those clever transactions.

By 1990 Harken's management realized that the accounting in their sale of Aloha wasn't quite right. Their thinking on the subject had been clarified after what they described as "discussions" with the SEC. Actually, the SEC flatly declared the sale bogus. When Harken applied the standard "cost recovery" method of accounting required by the SEC, its 1988 losses suddenly became $12.57 million. It is remarkable what can be achieved by just a little attention from a federal regulatory agency. The same standard accounting practices applied to

1989 showed the company had lost $3.3 million over the first three quarters, whereas the "aggressive accounting" originally applied by Harken gave them a $4.6 million profit for the period. Harken's accounting firm was Arthur Andersen.

Any time an officer of a publicly held corporation sells stock, we ought to know within two days. We ought to know. We being shareholders and employees.
— GEORGE W. BUSH ON WALL STREET, JULY 9, 2002

Harken's sham sale of Aloha was a shameful violation of shareholder trust, but it kept Harken's share value up long enough to let Bush sell his stock before the corrected profit-and-loss statements were released in August. The press seemed to prefer the stock-sale story because it is easier to explain than the Aloha deal. As reporters began to press harder on the issue, even the unflappable Ari Fleischer began to flap. "The SEC has been well aware of the issue and the SEC has concluded that this is not anything that's actionable," said Fleischer in early July. Bush too became testy, telling reporters that if they wanted more information they should get the minutes of

Harken's board of directors' meetings. Harken refused to release the minutes. The story might have stalled there had it not been for the work of Charles Lewis and the Center for Public Integrity. The Washington, D.C.–based public-interest group obtained Harken board minutes and correspondence through a Freedom of Information Act request to the SEC. Then they did what both President Bush and his SEC chairman, Harvey Pitt, had refused to do: they made the documents public by putting them on the center's website (www.publici.org).

You don't need an accountant to interpret the Harken documents. The company was in desperate trouble. At a May 1990 meeting attended by Bush, board members discussed a stock offering they hoped would bring in enough money to keep the company solvent. Bush was named to the board's "Fairness Committee," which was to measure the effects of bankruptcy on small stockholders. Ever the populist, GeeDubya said at this meeting "that inherent in these principles must be the interests and preservation of value for the small shareholder of the company." A month later Bush left the small shareholders holding the bag; he dumped $848,560 of the stock without disclosing the sale to the SEC. The purpose of the SEC's disclosure rule is precisely to inform all shareholders that something may be wrong — by letting them know when someone with inside information sells a large block of stock.

The Harken memos show just how much Bush knew about the company's dicey finances. By late May 1990, internal company memos warned that there was no other source of immediate financing, that a cash crunch was only days away, and that loans were slipping "out of compliance." Banks were demanding guarantees of sufficient equity to cover the notes. As chairman of the audit committee actually working with the accounting consultants called in by the board, Bush knew exactly how grim their conclusions were. He was warned, along with other directors, in a May 25 memo that it would be illegal to dump his stock. He sold in June to a private purchaser who has never been identified.

The company was kept afloat by investments from a small liberal-arts college in Cambridge, Massachusetts. This news was revealed only after a group of dogged and enterprising Harvard students at the nonprofit HarvardWatch dug into records there and turned their findings over to *The Wall Street Journal* in 2002.

Harvard's Harken bailout helped salvage Bush's last shaky oil company, at one time setting up a Harvard-Harken venture that moved $20 million in liabilities off Harken's books. It also cost the university's endowment more money than the young Bush ever earned in West Texas. Hooking up with Harken contributed to a record $200 million write-down for Harvard Management in 1991. Why did Harvard do it? Let us count the ways. Harvard Management exec Michael Eisenson sat on Harken's board with Dubya Bush. George Herbert Walker Bush was vice president of the United States — and a Skull and Bones Yalie. His son held a Harvard Business School M.B.A. — and was a Skull and Bones Yalie. After Poppy became president and tiny Harken somehow secured a huge drilling contract in Bahrain, Harvard kept pouring millions into the little Texas oil company in '89, '90, and '91.*

*Here's how the student/alumni investigators described Harvard's bailout of Bush. In late 1990, at a point when Bush held three high-level positions at Harken Energy, Harken and its largest shareholder, Harvard University, created the Harken Anadarko Partnership (HAP). According to minutes of Harken's August 29, 1990, board meeting, Bush gave the deal his personal approval. Over the

In July 2002 the White House offered three explanations for Bush's failure to report his own Harken stock sale. The first was that the filing of the disclosure form was "the corporation's responsibility." A letter from Harken's general counsel dated October 5, 1989, gently reminds Bush that he had failed to file the same Form 4 when he exercised his director's option to buy 25,000 shares of Harken stock exactly one year before he unloaded it in June 1990. The "Dear George" letter from Harken's general counsel, Larry Cummings, made it clear to Bush that company lawyers or accountants couldn't file the forms because they required his signature.

Turns out Bush regularly failed to report insider dealings to the SEC. On two occasions before his June 1990 stock dump, Bush had sold as a board member and failed to file the disclosure forms.

---

next two years the partnership allowed Harvard to bail out Harken's struggling business by effectively shouldering a large percentage of the company's loss-generating assets and debts in the Anadarko region of Texas and Oklahoma. This maneuver transformed the public perception of Harken's financial state; the company's reported losses and liabilities were drastically reduced over the next two years.

There are countless subjects on which George W. Bush might have pleaded ignorance in 1990, but a failing oil business was not one of them. At the end of 1989 Harken president Mikel Faulkner told a reporter at the *Petroleum Review* that Harken would book more than $6 million in end-of-the-year profits. On August 22, 1990, Harken's second-quarter report predicted $23.2 million in losses. Once the news hit the street, the stock sank immediately from $4 to $2.37; it later bottomed out at twenty-two cents a share.

Eight and a half months later *The Wall Street Journal* reported that the president's son was under investigation for failure to report the stock sales. The chairman of the SEC was Richard Breeden, who had worked for Poppy Bush as an economic adviser. The walls of Breeden's office were so plastered with photos of Poppy and Barbara Bush that a *New York Times* reporter observed, "George Bush is Breeden's Mao." The general counsel at the SEC was James Doty, the same James Doty of the Baker Botts law firm, who represented GeeDubya when he bought his 2 percent interest in the Texas Rangers with the money he got from dumping his Harken stock. The Houston law firm was founded by the great-grandfather of James Baker III, secretary of state under Bush the Elder and the point man for Bush the Younger in Florida after the disputed 2000 election.

Breeden and Doty never asked for an interview with the subject of their investigation. Since 1993 Breeden, Doty, and other partners of Baker Botts have contributed $210,621 to GeeDubya's political campaigns, making the firm the president's number-fourteen career patron. They were beaten out for the number-thirteen spot by Arthur Andersen, at $220,557.

In a letter regarding "George W. Bush Jr.'s [*sic*] Filings," SEC investigators observed that Bush was familiar with the SEC's filing deadlines, having met them when he filed reports of dealings with three other companies in which he owned stock. But with Harken, Bush filed "four late Forms 4 reporting four separate transactions, totaling $1,028,935." During his first campaign for governor of Texas, Bush repeatedly told reporters he had been "exonerated" by the SEC, and Fleischer repeated the same line in the summer of '02. But the report issued by the SEC's enforcement division in 1993 specifically says the investigation "must in no way be construed as indicating that the party has been exonerated."

Just as Harken was selling itself its own subsidiary in Hawaii, it set up another corporation on another island. Harken Bahrain Oil company registered in the Cayman Islands in September 1989. The Caymans, like Bermuda, are a convenient offshore address for U.S. companies that want to do business at home but prefer not to pay U.S. taxes. After the furor over tax-dodging corporations broke, Bush made this ringing statement in August 2002: "We ought to look at people who are trying to avoid U.S. taxes as a problem." Corporate tax dodgers now cost the country seventy billion dollars annually, according to the IRS, all of which has to be made up by average citizens who can't acquire a mail drop in the Caymans. The Scourge of Corporate Misbehavior even daringly urged corporate tax-dodgers to "pay taxes and be good citizens." Then the White House had to acknowledge that Harken Energy had set up an offshore subsidiary to avoid taxes. Bad timing.

Harken was not Enron, but it was certainly Enron in the making. What Bush took out of Harken was also twenty times as much as Bill and Hillary Clinton lost in a crummy Arkansas real estate deal that cost American taxpayers seventy million dollars to investigate. By the time Bush signed the Corporate Responsibility Act, Harken was selling at forty-one cents a share. Don't put your Social Security money in it.

So who are the "regular folks" who have been affected here, and what have those effects been? In this chapter, you, dear readers, are the regular folks. Americans lost $6 trillion when the stock market collapsed after Enron, WorldCom, and Tyco. It's your 401(k) that's the subject here, your pension, your Social Security, your investments, your savings, and your jobs. You.

Of course George W. Bush and his petty self-dealing at Harken did not cause the collapse of Enron et al. What we are looking at is not causation but connection. If one wanted to paint with a broad brush, surely Bill Clinton, president during the enormous stock market boom of the second half of the nineties, has more responsibility for the eventual collapse than does George W., president for only eighteen months when it happened.

But an even broader brush shows a different pattern. Starting in 1980 with the presidency of Ronald Reagan (or even the 1978 deregulation of the airlines, if you'd like to include Jimmy Carter), this country has been going through a deregulatory mania. Supply-siders, Milton Friedman, free-marketeers of all stripes, "movement conservatives," *The Wall Street Journal*'s editorial page — not to mention a motley assortment of anti-government cranks from militias to Republican candidates — have been trying to persuade us that government can't do a damn thing right and that free markets are the answer to absolutely everything. There's a true-believerism about the free-marketeers that is genuinely unsettling, as though it were a cult or a religion in which certain fundamental assumptions are never questioned. All you have to do to believe is ignore history and experience.

Capitalism is a marvelous system for creating wealth. On the other hand, unregulated capitalism creates hideous social injustice and promptly destroys itself with greed. A marketplace needs rules. From the very beginning, capitalism has required careful regulation. In the market towns of medieval England there were as many as twenty or thirty laws governing just the balance scales, and whether you could put your thumb or any other digit on the scale. Mostly what we've learned from the American experiment is that competition is good, but we need rules because people cheat.

And there are some natural monopolies that need regulation or they end up in cartels that rip everybody off.

Government regulation and the much-maligned trial lawyers are the two instruments by which we control corporate greed. It seems to me government is neither good nor bad but simply a tool, like a hammer. You can use a hammer to build with, or you can use a hammer to destroy with. The virtue of the hammer depends on the purposes to which it is put and the skill with which it is used.

Of course government regulation is burdensome and often absurd. One famous federal form required employers to "list your employees broken down by sex." "None," read one reply. "Alcohol is our problem."

What has changed in this country over the course of the past twenty-some years is that government has served less and less as a brake on corporate behavior and more and more as a corporate auxiliary, because of the corrupting effects of the system of legalized bribery we call "campaign financing."

And here we find the root cause of the stock market collapse. During the nineties the SEC was increasingly starved for funds by the Republican Congress on the grounds that regulation is bad, and so it suffered a tremendous erosion of its authority. While the press was telling the Enron disaster story and CEOs were stepping forward like Baptists at an altar call to restate their companies' earnings, Bush fought for a bare-bones SEC budget, recommending $576 million in July 2002. (The House authorization at the time was $776 million.) Clinton's SEC appointee, Arthur Levitt, had struggled valiantly for such obvious reforms as expensing stock options and monitoring accounting firms, but the politicians paid no attention during the years of go-go and the all-absorbing crisis over the president's sex life.

Phil and Wendy Gramm made a significant husband-and-wife contribution to the mess. In 1992, just a few days after Bill Clinton's election, Wendy Gramm, in her last days as the lame-duck chair of the Commodity Futures Trading Corporation (which was short two of its five members), pushed through a federal rule that exempted energy-derivatives contracts from federal regulation (because regulation is bad).* Energy deriv-

---

*The commission rule became known as the Enron exemption when it was passed into law in 2001, advanced by (Mr. Wendy) Phil Gramm, who chaired the Senate Banking Committee.

atives were just then becoming one of Enron's most profitable lines. According to Robert Bryce's book on Enron, *Pipe Dreams*, this key piece of deregulation is what allowed Enron to become a giant in the derivatives business. The exemption not only prevented federal oversight, exempting the companies from the CFTC's authority, it even exempted them if the contracts they were selling were designed to defraud or mislead buyers. Five weeks later Enron announced it was hiring Mrs. Gramm as a member of the Enron board, a job that eventually paid her about $1 million in salary, attendance fees, stock-option sales, and dividends. Senator Phil Gramm's Banking Reform Act formally repealed the long-standing prohibition (which grew out of the stock crash of '29) against merging banks, brokerage houses, and insurance companies. Then the IRS was emasculated by Gingrich Republicans on the grounds that collecting taxes is tantamount to fascism.

The whole dizzying array of corporate clout-wielders in Washington — powerful lobbyists who leave no fingerprints on curious little exemptions and special provisions that apply to only one company — gets larger and more brazen by the year.

George W. Bush didn't invent any of

this. His role is to pretty much embody it. He is what people mean when they speak of "crony capitalism." His administration is what we mean by the cliché "setting the fox to guard the hen coop." (Raccoons are actually far more dangerous to chickens — take our word for it.) Bush is not motivated by greed — he honestly believes government should be an adjunct of corporate America and that we'll all be better off if it is. Thus his role has been to build upon, to extend, to exaggerate, to further privatize, to cheerlead for, to evangelize about all that the free-marketeers have been preaching over the years.

The odd thing about Bush at midterm is that most of the Washington press corps has yet to recognize just how extreme his ideology is. As governor of Texas he tried to privatize the state welfare system and considered privatizing the University of Texas; he fought for "voluntary compliance" with environmental regulations. With the power of large corporations in this country already grossly disproportionate because of their influence over politicians through money, government is the last effective check on corporate greed. To put a man in charge of the government who basically doesn't believe it should play a role is folly.

The tragedy of having him in office at this time is that the man is congenitally incapable of checking the excesses of capitalism. No sooner was the Sarbanes bill passed than Bush's man at the SEC, Harvey Pitt, busily began undermining it. Pitt's claim to the title of biggest raccoon in the henhouse is rivaled only by the perfectly ludicrous appointment Bush made to the board assigned to implement the new McCain-Feingold campaign-finance reforms — a man vehemently opposed to campaign-finance reform. There are contenders at Interior, Labor, and EPA as well, but Pitt probably deserves the prize. Pitt wanted to appoint Judge William Webster to head the new accounting firm oversight board set up by the Sarbanes bill. Webster turned out to have corporate conflicts of interest out the wazoo, and Pitt himself was fired as a result. However, he remained on the job and by January 2003 had managed to actually *weaken* the rules that had been in effect *before* the corporate scandals broke. So many fundamental reforms have not been addressed — the failure to count stock options as a business expense, which gives CEOs an incentive to run up stock prices with tricky accounting; out-of-control hedge funds; derivatives; directors with conflicts of interest; the list goes on. Less than nothing has been done about any of it, so one can guarantee this whole corporate-fraud fiasco is going to happen again.

George W. Bush should declare himself a conscientious objector in his own war on corporate crime.

• 2 •

JULIA JEFFCOAT'S JOBLESS RECOVERY

*When America works, America prospers.
So my economic security plan can be
summed up in one word: jobs.*
— GEORGE W. BUSH, STATE OF THE
UNION ADDRESS, JANUARY 29, 2002

*This should bring some comfort to those of our
fellow citizens who need extra help during the
time in which they try to find a job.*
— GEORGE W. BUSH, AT THE SIGNING
OF THE UNEMPLOYMENT BILL,
JANUARY 8, 2003

I'm exhausted.
— JULIA JEFFCOAT, JANUARY 15, 2003

Julia Jeffcoat was telling the story of the last
ten years of her life as a city bus wended its
way north out of downtown Philadelphia.
The bus was a luxury. Julia usually walks the
six miles between her "home" and the

46

Center City office of the Philadelphia Unemployment Project. But the temperature was stuck below 20 degrees F., the wind blowing in hard gusts from the south. The Delaware and the Schuylkill Rivers were frozen over, and a New York publishing house was springing for the $1.10 bus token.

"I walked this morning," Jeffcoat said. "It's good exercise." The exercise has kept Jeffcoat trim and youthful, but this engaging African-American woman with the generous, easy-to-read face is incapable of even a small lie for pride. "I don't have money for the bus," she confessed quietly.

The forty-three-year-old single mother gets none of the comfort promised by her president when he finally signed the bill authorizing extended benefits for the chronically unemployed on January 8, 2003. Her unemployment is too chronic by six months. She's one of more than a million American workers not covered by the bill Bush signed after having ignored the unemployed for a year. By that time Julia and a million people like her had already fallen through a crack the size of the Grand Canyon. Another 1.2 million people were about to run out of benefits before Bush got the message that he'd be in trouble politically if he didn't do something about it.

Who knows what finally moved Bush off the dime? Could have been the midterm elections that put Republicans in control of both houses of Congress, even though 2.2 million workers had lost their jobs since the 2000 election. Perhaps he realized his $337 billion dividend tax break for big investors would be a hard sell while the families of two million unemployed Americans couldn't even find a faith-based soup kitchen. A Senate staffer who was working on unemployment issues back when Dubya Bush was running for governor of Texas says the unemployed had to wait: "It was the elections. The president couldn't say a word about how bad the economy was until after the election."

Whatever the reason, as Christmas 2002 approached, he at last addressed the problem. His delivery was flat, but when Bush got around to noticing the unemployed in his December 14 weekly radio address, his words sounded like Samuel Gompers'. "These Americans rely on their unemployment benefits to pay for the mortgage or rent, food, and other critical bills. They need our assistance in these difficult times and we cannot let them down." By George, he'd noticed at last.

Too late for Julia Jeffcoat and a million

other Americans waiting for the economic security Bush promised them.

Julia had lost her job as a security guard in December 2002. She got the twenty-six weeks of unemployment benefits most states provide. That's $500 a month, but we can assure you it did not put Bush's tax cuts at risk because it comes from a state trust funded by taxes paid by employers. Then Julia got a thirteen-week extension. When Julia says she is "exhausted," she is not whining about walking to town to look for work. She means her unemployment benefits are exhausted.

When that happens during periods of high unemployment, the federal government usually steps in with extended benefits provided through temporary emergency unemployment-compensation laws. In the recession of the mid-seventies, benefit extensions allowed workers to collect unemployment for sixty-four weeks. During the Poppy Bush recession of the early nineties — after two vetoes — the first President Bush grudgingly agreed to an extension of twenty-six weeks.

But this is 2003. Times are tough. Dubya Bush is suddenly confronted with bigger deficits than his Poppy inherited from Ronald Reagan. Of course, Junior

Bush does deserve credit for stepping on his own dick, as they say in San Angelo. For once he didn't inherit, he created most of his own deficit with his 2001 tax cuts for the wealthy. Not just tough times in 2003, but a tough Republican Congress as well. Even before the midterm elections returned control of the Senate to the Republicans, Tom DeLay, the hard-ass congressman from Texas, stood in the way of any senator wimpy enough to turn the federal treasury over to the unemployed.

Ted Kennedy started the fight in the Senate, filing a bill in August 2002 to give unemployed workers an extension and to save Jeffcoat and the other one million American workers who ultimately lost their benefits. Then the late Paul Wellstone of Minnesota introduced a bill to extend benefits and save "exhausted workers." Hillary Clinton joined Kennedy and Wellstone in a compromise bill. Clinton and Oklahoma Republican Don Nickles finally passed a watered-down bill. DeLay wasn't even buying the Nickles-Clinton compromise. The most powerful member of the U.S. House believes unemployed workers are deadbeats waiting for a handout. He warned that "they would have unlimited unemployment compensation" so they could "stay out of work for the rest of their lives." The "people's House" refused to act.

Not only did Dubya Bush say nothing. He did nothing. "None of the Senate bills had any backing from the White House," said a Kennedy staffer. "We even called the Department of Labor for help and got no response. The fact is that had the White House weighed in, this would have been taken care of before December."

The fact is that until December the administration let the House have its way. Our compassionately conservative president gave Tom DeLay the hit-away sign, and Julia Jeffcoat got clobbered.

Jeffcoat is a buoyant woman, optimistic, full of nervous energy she burns up by talking a lot. It's evident she's not the hottest hire in the Philadelphia job market. Since her first child was born twenty-five years ago, she has moved from one low-paying job to another — never earning more than $6.80 an hour. But she managed to patch together enough work to survive, until she lost her job as a security guard at Philadelphia's Veterans Stadium. That was about the time the city's unemployment rate hit 7 percent.

You wouldn't want Jeffcoat's résumé any

more than you would want her luck. "I first started out at Bryn Mawr," Jeffcoat said, without cracking a smile. No joke. She worked at the elite women's college just outside Philly. "I was serving food to rich kids. They're really rich over there. I was in food preparation." She was sixteen and stayed on at Bryn Mawr until she was nineteen, when her daughter was born. Then she tried door-to-door sales and took a stab at returning to school while working an eleven-to-seven night shift as a nurse's aide. She worked as a street vendor, then, in the mid-nineties, she met someone who hooked her up with security work at "the Vet."

She worked Eagles and Phillies games, she worked concerts. In December 2002 the stadium's security firm, Contemporary Services, laid her off. She had been working for $6.75 an hour — $14,000 a year, assuming she got in forty hours a week. When you work events, it's hard to get your forty hours, she said. None of the jobs she held ever provided quite enough money to support her daughter or the two sons born after she left Bryn Mawr. The children ended up living with their father. When her unemployment checks stopped, Jeffcoat was evicted from her one-bedroom apartment. She's out of work, out of money, and out of luck.

Her sixteen-year-old lives with friends. She lives with relatives. Jeffcoat works two days a week cleaning and stocking a small store for which she earns $60 — under the table. But the "job" is actually Muslim compassion disguised as employment; call it "faith-based" unemployment compensation. The store is owned by an Egyptian couple and is so small they can easily manage it themselves. "They are real good people," said Julia. Her son gets most of the money. "He's got to have something to live on," she said. "He's on his own and I'm the only one supporting him."

Jeffcoat was embarrassed when she opened her large purse and her clothes and makeup kit fell out. "That's the way it is when you stay with relatives," she said. "You got to be ready to move."

"I go to church," she said. "Things will get better." The president too believes in providence.

John Dodds has worked for the Philadelphia Unemployment Project for twenty-five years. PUP is a nonprofit mix of an advocacy group and an employment-placement office. Computers provide connections to job postings. Phones are available for job applicants. A counselor advises groups and individuals looking for work. On this January morning, in the low-tech end of the placement center, the chalkboard postings were for temporary data-entry jobs at the local Internal Revenue Service office. Dodds and his small staff also work with legislators in Harrisburg and Washington. He refuses to guess what the "real" unemployment rate is when the Department of Labor is reporting 8 percent in Philadelphia. "I don't want to get into those calculations about the undercounted unemployed. If you add in the discouraged workers who have stopped looking, the underemployed, the uncounted, it might be higher. But eight percent is high."

Dodds is a realist. He notes that the federal tab for unemployment when state benefits run out is a big-ticket item. "It was $7.5 billion," he said. "And who wants to raise taxes for the unemployed?" It is also unpopular with employers, since high unemployment rates tend to drive down wages by forcing workers to compete for jobs. So emergency federal unemployment benefits are a hard sell. Few members of Congress see any political payback for voting to extend unemployment benefits.

Although the $7.5 billion in federal benefits go to no one who will make a political contribution to the 2004 election — helping win what Karl Rove calls the "money primary" — it is still real economic stimulus. "That money goes right into the economy," Dodds said. "And it goes to areas of high unemployment. Julia Jeffcoat will take every penny she gets in unemployment and spend it by the end of the week she got it. And she will the next week and the next week until she gets a job. Then whatever income she gets, she'll spend all that. She is a raging machine for the economy. She's popping everything she has right back into it."

When you have no discretionary income, you spend everything you have.

Unemployment insurance was a New Deal program, created in 1935. Even then everyone understood that it served two purposes. Soft-hearted liberals celebrate the first: it provides income support for jobless workers and their families. Clear-eyed businesspeople celebrate the second: it props up the economy by keeping consumer spending alive during economic slowdowns. Those dollars flow right through the hands of the unemployed working class and into the bank accounts of the owning class. The dirty secret of the New Deal is what a giveaway it was to businesses big and small.

Here's where you've got to recognize the genius of the Bushies. While the country is dragging through a recession, they come up with a way to put money directly into the pockets of big bidness, bypassing both workers and small businesses. (We told you in *Shrub* the guy is not dumb; Dubya Bush himself warns us about "misunderestimating" him.) Buoyed by the midterm elections, Bush surprised even his most ardent supporters with a $337 billion dividend tax giveaway to people who have enough stock to live off dividends. And he did it while he was stiffing the unemployed.

If you want a real déjà voodoo economic experience, read *The New York Times*. High unemployment. Growing deficits. War with Iraq sinking the economy. House members complaining that unemployment causes real pain "in my neighborhood," and filing a bill that "will provide relief for unemployed Americans whose benefits have been exhausted."

That was *The New York Times* of January 1992.

The reporter was *Times* veteran Adam

Clymer — the man Dubya Bush once called "a major-league asshole." We hope Clymer saved his old, outdated, floppy disks so he won't have to completely rewrite the second Bush war-and-recession story. He could have an intern do it. Drop the "Herbert" but not the "Walker." Substitute "repeal the tax on dividends" for "repeal the capital gains tax" (done that). Cut all the flaccid Poppy Bush lines: "Message: I care" and "vision thing," and you've got a perfectly recyclable, up-to-date *Times* dispatch for 2003.

As with Clymer, this is Dodds' second Bush recession. It turns out that Bush *père*, the New England gentleman steeped in noblesse oblige, was a worse hard-ass than his blustery Texas son when it came to dealing with unemployed workers. Poppy vetoed an extension bill because he said there was no money to fund it.

"In the last recession, we had to fight like hell," Dodds said. "In July 1991 we turned out twenty-five hundred people. Then in August we went to Washington. We had a big rally. Then we visited every member of Congress. We didn't send people to meet with just their own congressman. They went into every office. They went in and said, 'We're the lobbyists

57

for the unemployed.' Within a week, Congress passed a bill.

"Bush vetoed it," Dodds said. "Then he headed out to Kennebunkport for a vacation."

To be fair, President Bush I didn't veto the bill. He actually signed it before leaving for vacation and *then* he refused to sign the emergency funding provision to provide the money for worker benefits. It was a shiftier "Texas Sidestep" than the one the governor dances in *The Best Little Whorehouse in Texas.* You can almost get nostalgic when you think back to Poppy standing on the lush green lawn of his Walkers Point compound in Maine — tan and relaxed, sports coat, no tie, casual slacks and topsiders — telling the press pack why the nation could not afford an extension for jobless workers: "Yes, we're coming through some tough economic times in the state of Maine, and other states as well. But it's my view that we're coming out of the recession."

Poppy could make you smile. "Cutting the capital gains tax would create jobs instantly. [It didn't.] It would be tremendous." He was even cute in dismissing rumors that his chief of staff, John Sununu, was about to join the unemployed. "It's a funny season down there in Washington. Kind of not too much happening down there. Congress is out. President's gone. So you've got a lot of tick-tock stories going — who's up and who's down."

Unemployed workers, who kind of figured they were in the "who's down" category, joined Poppy and Barbara on their Maine vacation. What the hell, they were out of work anyway and figured the Bush family compound would provide them with good visuals. The Philadelphia Unemployment Project provided the buses and vans. It was all so unseemly. Poppy and the family trying to enjoy an afternoon in the speedboat while the unemployed and unwashed from Philadelphia and from all over Maine chased reporters all over town. MESSAGE: BUSH DON'T CARE read the sign one protestor carried to a press conference at the Shawmut Inn. An editorial cartoonist captured the spirit of the whole affair with a sketch of a golf ball sitting on the forehead of a prostrate and exhausted unemployed man. Above him stood Poppy, golf club in hand, ready to swing, but asking: "Do you mind if I play through?"

It took months after that for the unemployed to win, but before the end of the year Congress had passed the Emergency

Unemployment Compensation Act of 1991. The senior Bush reluctantly signed it.

At least Bush II signed the bill the first time it was presented to him. Dubya Bush may not be the class act his old man was, but he dances a better Texas sidestep. As governor of Texas, Bush (and Karl Rove) did some of their best work through surrogates. "No Bush fingerprints," was the way one senator described the killing of a bill back in the Texas Senate Judiciary Committee. "But ya know he did it," he added with a wry smile.

The U.S. House and Senate fought over the extension of unemployment benefits for the last six months of 2002. Bush was nowhere to be seen on the issue, even though Senator Don Nickles later startled the troops by announcing that the president had supported the bill all along. "That was the first time anybody had heard that," said a Senate staffer who worked on the bill. "And try to find it in the *Record*. It's not there." Members of Congress are a lot dumber than they make themselves sound in the *Congressional Record*. They routinely edit what appears there, mostly to clean up their grammar and syntax. Nickles' line about "the administration" supporting the benefits bill was "redacted" from the *Record*.

(To observers of the legislative process in Austin, the fight over the federal unemployment bill was remarkably similar to the time in 1999 when Bush killed the James Byrd Jr. Hate Crimes bill in Texas. Several Bush surrogates in the Texas Senate worked to kill that bill. For Bush it wasn't about race, it was a religious-right litmus deal; he would have let it pass if gays and lesbians had not been included under the protections in the act. After the bill was safely deader than Monty Python's parrot, a Republican senator popped up to announce that the governor had been for it all along.)

While Bush avoided the nation's unemployed, pressure for extending benefits continued to mount throughout 2002. The lame-duck Congress reported for duty in January 2003, and the extension was passed in one day with the president's approval. That was when Oklahoma's Senator Nickles popped up to deliver the president's ex post facto endorsement of a bill he had never lifted a finger to support. "The president was very interested in having this thing passed," said Nickles. "And really, I think he was interested in having it passed earlier rather than later." Earlier would have been, uh, earlier. In time for Julia Jeffcoat.

She would have gotten additional benefits if Congress had passed a bill earlier, or included a reach-back provision picking up the million unemployed workers who had already exhausted their benefits. That would have required nothing more than a wink and a nod from the president and a muzzle for Tom DeLay. Yes, it would have cost an additional $3.4 billion, according to Jessica Goldberg of the Center on Budget Policy Priorities. "Less than four tenths of one percent of the president's 'stimulus package,'" Goldberg said. "And there was twenty-five billion dollars in the federal Unemployment Trust Fund, which can be spent on nothing else."

OK, so Dubya did better than his old man and signed a bill that got some help to workers. But in January 2003 he was still promoting his $337 billion dividend tax giveback to rich investors. Two million jobs had disappeared since he took office two years earlier. The unemployment rate in Philadelphia was 8 percent. A million workers had exhausted their benefits while there was $25 billion in the trust fund set aside to cover them.

And Julia Jeffcoat was walking south on Broad Street, her face set hard against the wind, with no idea where to find her next meal.

•3•

CLASS WAR

*It is easier for a camel to go through
the eye of a needle, than for a rich man
to enter into the kingdom of God.*
— MATTHEW 19:24

*Too many young people today do not have
the same hope for the future that I did
when I was growing up. When I was
a child, I was full of hope and expectation.
Today, there are far too many children in
this country who feel trapped in hopeless
poverty. They have no expectations.*
— B RAPOPORT

*Everybody does better when
everybody does better.*
— W. F. "HIGH" HIGHTOWER,
DENISON, TEXAS

OK, so Bernard Rapoport is not an "average
American." Just for starters, he's the only

Jewish, socialist insurance millionaire in Waco, Texas. He's worth a few units — that's Texan for a hundred mil. Just to give you an idea, he's lost at least a unit since the stock market started tanking, and while he ain't exactly enthusiastic about the result, except for wishing he still had the money for his foundation, he says, "I don't notice it."

"B," as everybody calls him, is above average in income, energy, brains, age, height, citizenship, generosity, spoken words per minute, and ability to cuss out selfish bastards. He also scores high on enjoyment of life, devotion to family, and books read (the man reads books as though he were eating popcorn). Talking with him is kind of like getting hit by a tidal wave.* He's the only eighty-four-year-old we know who lives life at 95 mph. The reason we're using him in this chapter on class warfare is to demonstrate not only what Bush's economic and tax policies are doing to you but what they are doing for people in B's income bracket.

Here's the way he looks at it. "You make

*If you would like to know more about Rapoport, he has an as-told-to autobiography out: *Being Rapoport, Capitalist with a Conscience*, University of Texas Press, 2002.

fifty thousand dollars a year, you pay nine thousand in income taxes — that doesn't put you in the poorhouse, but it sure as hell tightens your budget. I make a million dollars a year, I pay four hundred thousand in income taxes — that leaves me six hundred thousand to live on. That doesn't cramp my lifestyle. I'm still rich. You gonna feel sorry for me?"

Rapoport does not put his money in offshore banks to avoid paying taxes. His daddy escaped from a Siberian prison camp in 1905, and B proudly keeps his father's membership certificate in the Socialist Party of America on his office wall. David Rapoport worked as a peddler, selling blankets off a cart in the poor "Mexican" neighborhoods of San Antonio (the Mexicans having been there a lot longer than the Anglos, of course). He never made more than $4,000 a year. "Yes, we were poor!" says B, in his usual explosive style. (You have to envision an exclamation point at the end of all of his sentences.) "But we didn't know we were poor! We were rich in everything that counted! We had books and education, and we listened to opera on the Victrola, and people would come over almost every night and talk about the state of the country and the world!"

B went to public schools in San Antonio, then, in the depths of the Depression, to the University of Texas. Tuition was $25 a semester. "I paid three hundred sixty dollars a year, for room, board, books, everything. I worked six days a week and I never saw a football game. I love football." B, a former chairman of the university's board of regents, now sits on the fifty-yard line at UT football games.

B's great desire was to be a college professor, but he dropped out of graduate school in economics and worked in a jewelry store in order to help send his sister to Columbia. In 1942 he met Audre Newman on a blind date and proposed to her over breakfast the next morning. They started a jewelry store in Waco but were soon sidetracked by Homer Rainey's campaign for governor. Rainey had been president of the University of Texas until he was fired by a spectacularly know-nothing board of regents. In 1946 Rainey ran for governor in one of the most memorable campaigns in Texas history. B and Audre put all their savings, $2,000, into the campaign and then borrowed another $3,000. They campaigned tirelessly while trying to keep the jewelry store going. Rainey carried McLennan County (Waco) but lost the election, leaving B and

Audre heartbroken, disillusioned, and hellaciously broke. B drifted into selling insurance and turned out to have a knack for it. With help from Audre's uncle, B started his own company, American Income Life Insurance. He still gets up at five every morning, reads, plays tennis, and is at the office before everyone else.

OK, so he makes all this money — what's he going to do with it? He has a nice house, but it's no mansion. This is Waco, for God's sake: it's a fifties ranch-style. Good news! His wife of fifty-five years loves good clothes and jewelry and dresses beautifully. Alas for conspicuous consumption, Audre is one of the great bargain shoppers of all time. She would consider it an absolute scandal to pay full price for anything, and she finds the most gorgeous stuff for ten, twelve bucks. It's an art, it's a science. She shops Loehmann's and Filene's Basement ("back in the days when it was really good," she specified). Last Call, the Neiman-Marcus markdown shop, and the outlet malls south of San Marcos also make her list. In the early days of their marriage Audre made her own clothes, buying remnants from literal fire sales for twenty-five cents a yard and then cutting off the burned parts. The habit of thrift stuck, as does her unpretentiousness; she is shrewd, gorgeous, and sensible, and puts up with B nobly. When asked if she wants another house — Aspen? The Riviera? — Audre said, "I already clean enough bathrooms."

The Rapoports have one son, whom they adore. Alas for the purposes of inherited wealth, they raised him so well, he won't take B's money either. Ronnie is a professor of political science at the College of William and Mary. His mother and father are so proud of him, and so crazy about his daughters, Abby and Emily, it almost makes your heart hurt with happiness to hear them talk about the family.

So here's B, a workaholic with a passion for social justice and a ton of money. What to do? Put both the money and his energy back into this country, of course. This country gave him the opportunity to get rich — you think he's going to forget that? How did he get rich? First, he got a free education. B and Audre fully fund a charter school for disadvantaged kids in Waco ("where the teachers can by-God hug the kids!"). He has given untold amounts to the University of Texas over the years and served as chairman of the board of regents when Ann Richards was governor. He gives money to politicians at local, state, and national levels who demonstrate concern for economic justice. One wall of his old office at American Income Life used to be covered with signed pictures to B from famous folk — think of any liberal politician of the past fifty years, and there was a picture on B's wall. Presidents, senators, congressmen, statehouse pols. He absolutely adored the late Paul Wellstone.

B didn't just support them when they were in office; when some broken-down pol, felled in electoral combat or even tainted by scandal, came adrift into private life, B Rapoport was there, a foul-weather friend. He has hired so many demoralized Democrats who were forced to leave office one way or another, it's amazing he could keep the insurance company running.*

In one of the more comical capers of his career, when Bill Clinton's old buddy Webb Hubbell was being investigated by the absurd Kenneth Starr, B got hauled in

---

*It was always a slightly eccentric company. Everybody's desk was covered with pictures of family, plants, birthday balloons, none of that "neat desk" stuff. Some underling once raced in to tell B one of the salesmen was gay. "How much business does he write?" asked B.

front of a grand jury in Little Rock to explain why he had thrown a six-month consulting contract Hubbell's way. He did it because a guy he knows named Truman Arnold, an oilman in Texarkana, called him one day and said Hubbell was a good guy and asked B for the favor. B does favors for friends — what are you gonna do? Shoot him? (Keep in mind, Texas is still a state where multimillion-dollar deals are done on a handshake. In order to do this, you have to know the people you deal with.) B reports that the grand jurors looked like mushrooms from having been kept in the windowless basement of the courthouse for so long. The prosecutor asked him, "What is your name?"

The response ran, approximately, "My name is Bernard Rapoport, and if you dumb sons of bitches don't understand why someone would help a guy who is down and being kicked, you are contemptible! I don't know what your Christian religion demands of you, but this poor bastard never would have gotten into trouble if he hadn't been a friend of Bill Clinton's, and I have helped at least a hundred guys who have been through some version of this same political hanging, and I tell you I have a right to help any down-and-out son of a bitch who needs it!" The prosecutors barely got another question in edgewise. Then they dismissed him. As he left, one grand juror said to another, "He must be innocent. He sure wasn't nervous."

To this day, B will occasionally muse on what "Papa" would have said about where his son is today. (Papa didn't have much use for the rich; he used to roust his son out of bed in the morning with "Workers of the world, unite!") Like most American Jews of his generation and wealth, B has been a generous supporter of Israel, but the current impasse in the Middle East leaves him as close to despair as the normally up-beat Rapoport is capable of getting. "I don't like Jewish fascists any better than I like Christian fascists, or Muslim fascists, or any other kind of fascist," he has been known to snarl. B was crazy about Teddy Kollek, the longtime mayor of Jerusalem. Kollek asked, B gave; but always with the proviso that it should be as much for the Palestinians as for the Jews.

B Rapoport doesn't actually like money and he doesn't want things like big houses and fancy cars. But he's good at making money, and, frankly, after he sold his insurance company, he had it coming out of his ears. What do you do when you have a couple of hundred million and your wife won't spend it and your son won't take it? B is giving it away as fast as he can, and what's left over when he and Audre are gone will go to their foundation, mostly to support education. He is a firm believer in the estate tax and considers its abolition both mean and stupid. "A progressive income tax is the only fair form of taxation known to man. Of course we need to redistribute income in this country from the wealthy to the poor. And right now these Republicans are redistributing it from you to me." Aside from the chance to do more good works, the last thing in the world he needs is more money. What a friend he has in George W. Bush.

If you want to see Bernard Rapoport explode — and that's damn good entertainment value for the dollar — get him started on rich people who not only don't give anything back to this country but who don't even have the decency to pay the taxes they owe. The rich and corporations that buy mail-drop addresses in the Caymans or the Bahamas disgust him. His contempt for their greed is magnificent, even biblical (Old Testament, of course). He can put the principle in both biblical and Marxist terms — remember, we're dealing with one of the best-read people in America. The idea that those who have more owe more is so ingrained in him that he cannot begin to comprehend the silly bastards who don't get it. That anyone who has become as rich as Rapoport could still be indifferent to the obligation to create opportunity for others is to him an impenetrable mystery and a source of galling fury. "Taxes, for God's sake," he raged, "are what support education!"

Suggest to B that social needs should be met by private charity, as George W. Bush maintains, and you are met with an avalanche of statistics, facts, numbers (not for nothing, all those years in insurance), ending with an abrupt and devastating damning of anyone who could be so criminally stupid as to think that will work. This student of history will take you back to the nineteenth-century poorhouses of England to demonstrate why it is a monstrous idea.

Funnel government money through religious charities? Rapoport is an eighty-four-year-old Jew who lives in Waco, the Vatican City of the Baptist Church.* The

---

*As the great William Brann once observed, "The trouble with our Texas Baptists is that we do not hold them under water long enough."

man grew up in Texas eighty years ago. He knows from anti-Semitism. The wisdom of putting a wall of separation between church and state is more than slightly clear to him.

Like any other businessman, B Rapoport can entertain with stories about the idiotic requirements of government paperwork, but if you wanted to fix that, you'd put a B Rapoport in charge of it. He didn't get rich by wasting his time or anyone else's. He also understands that government, properly used, is the great engine of social justice; that without it, the capitalist system, under which he himself has so richly benefitted and which he wholeheartedly supports, will simply run haywire from greed and unfairness.

B is an old man now. He's been working for social justice for a long time, for a system that will let more of the sons of pushcart peddlers in the barrios become multimillionaires. One hesitates to use the word, *dis-couraged,* about B Rapoport. Let us say rather that his righteous rage is larger than it was a few years ago.

How has Bush II affected him? Let us count the ways. In the first round of Bush tax cuts, 40 percent of the cut went to the richest 1 percent of the population, those

74

making over $373,000 a year. Since B makes quite a bit more than that $373K, he got way more than the average cut for that group, which was $53,123. With the second Bush tax cut, which was passed by Congress in 2003, B will get a break of $92,000, and that's on income alone. The average working family will get $256, and almost half of all taxpayers will get a cut of less than $100. It's not going to turn their lives around. B does not need the $92K. Let's assume B has two units invested prudently and is earning 4 percent. If Bush ever gets the divided tax completely repealed (and these guys always get their whole loaf half at a time), B will get an additional $3,441,729 to spend annually. Good news for B: how much will you get out of it?

According to White House numbers, the second round of tax cuts would leave us with greatly increased deficits indefinitely. Bush said during his 2003 State of the Union address, "We will not deny, we will not ignore, we will not pass along our problems to other Congresses, to other presidents and other generations."

Let's do a little exercise. Polls show that 90 percent of all Americans consider themselves middle-class. About 70 percent of Americans make less than $50,000 a year. In 2001, 1.3 million more Americans slipped below the federal poverty line, set at $18,100 a year for a family of four. That's 33 million Americans at risk of hunger, including 13 million children. Nearly 8.5 million people, including 2.9 million children, live in homes where they have to skip meals or have too little to eat, sometimes going a whole day without food. Those 33 million people are 11.7 percent of the population, up for the first time since 1993. Median income in this country is $44,000 a year for a family of four. *Median* means half the people in this country live on less than that, many of them on a whole hell of a lot less.

The median is a much more meaningful number than "average" when it comes to discussing income, because the rich in this country are so much richer than the rest of us. As *The New Yorker* put it, if Bill Gates walks into a soup kitchen where two nuns are feeding thirty-eight homeless people, the average income of the people in that room is $1 billion per person. But it's still thirty-eight penniless people, two nuns, and Bill Gates. Of course, half of us make more than the median, but what's amazing is how many of us make just a little more and how few make so much more.

This means the quintiles — the population divided by the bottom 20 percent, next 20 percent, etc. — flatten out pretty fast. If you could see a drawing of the way income is split up among the population of this country, it's like a profile of a chimney half-built into a wall, like a New Mexican *kiva*. There's a sort of bulb at the base, which juts out a little bit more at the top than at the bottom (because more of us are middle class than are poor), and then suddenly the thing starts to stretch up, and up and up and up. That's your top 5 percent, your top 1 percent, so far above where most Americans are that you can barely see them. If it were really a chimney, the stack would go up past the rooftop to about twenty-five stories, getting thinner all the way.

But there at the very tippy top, among a tiny fraction of the people, is where most of the country's money is concentrated. The top 1 percent has almost twenty-five times as much as does everybody in the bottom fifth. This is not a normal condition in America, although as Kevin Phillips points out, there have been three periods of extreme division by income — the Gilded Age, the 1920s, and now. By the beginning of the new century, the gap between the rich and everyone else had escalated to levels not seen since the twenties. The rich got a lot richer and the poor got poorer — and so did everybody in the middle.

The middle-class "average" American has been slipping behind financially since 1973. The most reliable numbers one can use to measure what's happening are "real wages," the inflation-adjusted purchasing power of our paychecks. The wages paid at the median of the scale declined between 1973 and 1996, shifted up again between 1997 and 1999, and have been going down again since. This is not the function of some "invisible hand" or law of capitalism. It's the result of a series of political decisions made by politicians who are increasingly owned by their rich donors. Paul Krugman of *The New York Times* reports, "Most of the gains of the past 30 years were actually to the top 1 percent [of the highest 10 percent], rather than to the next 9 percent. In 1998, the top 1 percent started at $230,000. In turn, 60 percent of the gains of the top 1 percent went to the top 0.1 percent, those with incomes of more than $790,000. And almost half of those gains went to a mere 13,000 taxpayers, the 0.01 percent, who had an income of at least $3.6 million and an average income of $17 million."

According to the Congressional Budget Office, between 1979 and 1997 the income of those in the middle quintile rose from $41,400 to $45,100, adjusting for inflation. That was a 9 percent increase. The income of families in the top 1 percent rose from $420,200 to $1.016 million, a 140 percent increase. Another way to look at it is, in 1979 the richest families were ten times richer than the middle clump of us. By 1997 they were twenty-three times as rich and rising fast. In 1998 the top 1 percent had more income than the 100 million in the bottom 40 percent.

In the Eisenhower era, corporations paid an average of 25 percent of the federal tax bill. In 2000, they paid only 10 percent, and by 2001, only 7 percent. In 1960 corporations paid an effective tax rate on corporate income of 47 percent. Today it is 35 percent. As we all know, many, many corporations have paid zero in income taxes for years, despite hefty balance sheets, à la Enron, and have indeed worked themselves into a position where the U.S. government owes these flagrant tax-cheaters money. Returning to the 1960 rate and closing the most glaringly obvious loopholes would increase annual tax revenues by $110 billion. American corporations taking tax shelters on offshore islands are now estimated to cost the treasury $70 billion a year. In *The Cheating of America* by Charles Lewis and Bill Allison of the Center for Public Integrity is an amusing history of tax cheating by the rich. They report, "In 1933, average Americans were shocked to learn that all twenty partners of J. P. Morgan & Company, the giant Wall Street banking firm, had paid no income taxes for the previous two years. Newspapers of the day trumpeted the disclosure as tax evasion by the firm's partners, although they had broken no law. J. Pierpont Morgan, Jr., the son of the firm's founder and his successor at its helm, later remarked, 'Congress should know how to levy taxes, and if it doesn't know how to collect them, then a man is a fool to pay the taxes. If stupid mistakes are made, it is up to Congress to rectify them and not for us taxpayers to do so.'" The old boy speaks for many today.

You don't have to acquire a mailbox in Bermuda to cheat on taxes. Lewis and Allison report that in 1995, eighty-four millionaires who were still here filed tax returns on which they owed no income tax. Some 13,630 tax returns were filed by individuals who earned more than $200,000 but paid taxes at an effective rate of under 10 percent. And 17 percent of the roughly 7,500 corporations with assets of over $250 million filed returns claiming they owed no income tax.

Meanwhile, the IRS was being slowly starved to death by successive Republican Congresses, the same way they did with the Securities and Exchange Commission. Under Newt Gingrich, Congress held grand-inquisitor hearings in which the IRS was denounced for "Gestapo tactics." The R's then passed a "tax reform" act that should have been called the Let's Hamstring the IRS So It Can't Make Rich People Pay Act. The result is that since 1995, the IRS has focused most of its tax-fraud investigations on the working poor, those who qualify for the Earned Income Tax Credit, the only good idea Ronald Reagan ever had. Treasury secretary Paul O'Neill blamed the situation squarely on Congress. "We've been directed by Congress to examine the devil out of such returns," he told a congressional committee. "You think I like that? I hate that." O'Neill was later fired by Bush. In April 2003 the IRS announced it would be auditing more of the working poor.

The decline in auditing rich people and corporations actually started fourteen years ago. In 2001 audits of the working poor increased by 48.6 percent. Those applying for the EITC have a 1 in 47 chance of getting audited, while those making more than $100,000 have a 1 in 208 chance of getting audited. In 1988 that number for those over $100,000 was 1 in 9, according to the Institute for Public Affairs.

Supreme Court Justice Louis Brandeis wrote, "We can have democracy in this country or we can have great concentrated wealth in the hands of a few. We cannot have both." Progressive taxation and the estate tax were both results of the backlash against the Gilded Age. By calling the estate tax "the death tax," as though it were a tax on passing on rather than a tax on estates of more than $2.5 million, the Bush administration succeeded in repealing it through a gradual phaseout and increasing the exemption to $7 million. The repeal of the estate tax is a lovely example of just how much political clout the very rich have in this country. Some rich people in Southern California hired a lobbyist, who in turn hired the well-wired Patton Boggs law firm. The group was backed by the Mars family and the Gallo wine folks.

Another group of rich folks in Alabama joined the fray and the nexus of right-wing think tanks and interrelated lobbying groups took it up. Combine repeal of the estate tax with the flat tax, also popular on the Republican right, and we're back to the McKinley era.

This is not an enchanting portrait of America. Since Bush became president, the stock markets have lost more than $6.5 trillion in value, unemployment is up more than 40 percent, and our projected surplus under Clinton has disappeared into a growing deficit. Bush is the only president in at least 140 years (and probably ever, reports *Newsweek*'s Allan Sloan) to suggest cutting taxes as we were heading into a war. The controversial heart of Bush's second tax-cut plan is to eliminate taxes on stock dividends, which are unearned income, directly benefitting people in B's bracket.

More depressing numbers: Paul Krugman reports that over the past thirty years the average annual salary of Americans has increased by 10 percent, adjusted for inflation. The income of the top 1 percent rose by 157 percent in the same period. Over the same period, the average annual pay package of the top 100 CEOs increased from thirty-nine times the pay of an average worker to more than one thousand times the pay of an average worker.

Now, all that is merely about income. The figures get worse when it comes to accumulated wealth, how much the people at the top pile up over the years and the generations. Kevin Phillips reports in his excellent book, *Wealth and Democracy*, the net worth, including home equity, of the middle quintile of Americans *declined* by 10 percent between 1983 and 1995, then rose again in 1998 and 1999, and slipped right back down in 2000–2001. The top 1 percent, over a million people, saw their net worth grow by 75 percent. According to the *Federal Reserve Bulletin*, between 1983 and 1997 only the top 5 percent saw an increase in their net worth, while wealth declined for everyone else. Eighty percent of the nation's property — land, stocks, bonds — is now in the hands of 10 percent of the people: the 13,000 richest families have a net worth equivalent to the assets owned by the poorest 20 million people. This is a shocking change from the largely middle-class America of forty years ago.

An amazing fact of economic life in America: a rising tide for the rich does not, in fact, lift all boats. What we are seeing is trickle-up economic policies. Add the fact that worker benefits are shrinking, particularly health-care coverage, and that Americans are working longer hours. According to the Bureau of Labor Statistics, by 1999, over one decade, the average work year has expanded by 184 hours. The typical American worked 350 hours more per year than the average European. Kevin Phillips writes, "Buffeted by these downcurrents — longer work hours, two-earner households, personal strain, and the increasing cultural and philosophic subordination of median households — the broad U.S. quality of life indexes began to decline in the 1970s. Until the seventies, social health and progress indicators in the United States had climbed upward alongside the gross domestic product. But once having turned, they continued to fall, continuing on a downslope in the eighties and most of the nineties as federal policy remained preoccupied with capital rather than with workers or social conditions."

You want to know why? Because B Rapoport is one unusual millionaire. He gives money to politicians who care more about the people than they do about their rich donors. Most political contributors are in it for the money, and they are richly repaid with special tax breaks, anti-competitive measures, and government subsidies — at the expense of those who don't contribute, don't pay attention, and don't vote.

There's an old adage about government, that there are only three questions: (1) Who benefits, who profits? (2) Who rules the rulers? And (3) What the hell will they do to us next?

Those who rule the rulers are those who give large campaign contributions. Thomas Frank, the passionate populist and author of *One Market Under God: Extreme Capitalism, Market Populism, and the End of Economic Democracy*, once started an essay with a quote from *The New York Times*:

> *Despite this, many economists still*
> *think that electricity deregulation will work.*
> *A product is a product, they say,*
> *and competition always works better*
> *than state control.*
> *"I believe in that premise as a matter*
> *of religious faith," said Philip J. Romero,*
> *dean of the business school at the*
> *University of Oregon and one of the*
> *architects of California's deregulation plan.*
> *— THE NEW YORK TIMES,*
> FEBRUARY 4, 2001

Time was, the only place a guy could

expound the mumbo jumbo of the free market was the country club locker room or the pages of *Reader's Digest*. Spout off about it anywhere else and you'd be taken for a Bircher or some new strain of Jehovah's Witness. After all, in the America of 1968, when the great backlash began, the average citizen, whether housewife or hard hat or salary-man, still had an all-too-vivid recollection of the Depression. Not to mention a fairly clear understanding of what social class was all about. Pushing laissez-faire ideology back then had all the prestige and credibility of hosting a Tupperware party.

But thirty-odd years of culture war have changed all that. Mention "elites" these days and nobody thinks of factory owners or gated-community dwellers. Instead they assume that what you're mad as hell about is the liberal media, or the pro-criminal judiciary, or the tenured radicals, or the know-it-all bureaucrats.

For the guys down at the country club, all these inverted forms of class war worked spectacularly well. That is not to say the right-wing culture warriors ever outsmarted the liberal college professors or shut down the Hollywood studios or repealed rock 'n' roll. Shout though they might, they never quite got cultural history to stop. But what they did win was far more important: political power, a free hand to turn back the clock on such non-glamorous issues as welfare, taxes, OSHA, even the bankruptcy laws, for chrissake. Assuring their millionaire clients that culture war got the deregulatory job done, they simply averted their eyes as bizarre backlash variants flowered in the burned-over districts of conservatism: Posses Comitatus, backyard Confederacies mounting mini-secessions, crusades against Darwin.

Populists, as opposed to liberals, do not get particularly excited about culture wars. We do not believe the important differences in this country are about smokers versus nonsmokers or wine versus beer drinkers. This fight is not about yoga and vegetarianism. It is not about lifestyles. It is not about religion. Keep your eye on the shell with the pea under it. It is about who's getting screwed, and about who's doing the screwing. And anybody who tells you different is lying for money.

Tom Frank says the free-market fundamentalists are "puffed up by a sense of historical righteousness so cocksure it might have been lifted from *The God That Failed*, that old book written by ex-Communists disavowing their former convictions." The free-market fundamentalists and "movement conservatives" are just as blinded by ideology as the old Communists. They worship at the altar of the free market, blind to a country where the government is redistributing resources from the poor and the middle class to the rich. This is open class warfare. This country is not working for most of the people in it. The health-care system is falling apart, the social safety net has been shredded, the Bushies want to privatize Social Security and the schools. These are the same ideological geniuses who brought you the savings-and-loan scandals, $2 trillion in deficits, the California electricity crisis, Enron, WorldCom — in fact, it's the same loser laissez-faire ideology that produced the Great Depression. The free market is a wonderful thing — but it functions well only within a nest of law and regulation. When those who are regulated by the government buy the government, the people get screwed.

Taxes, of course, are only one half of the

perpetual struggle in government, the other being spending. Very simple under Bush. The military and homeland security get more, everything else gets cut. The term *compassionate conservative* is a bitter joke. Try this one: the late Paul Wellstone sponsored a bill that said no government contracts related to homeland security could go to companies that use foreign tax havens to avoid U.S. taxes. Sayonara, sucker. C'mon, what do you think these campaign contributions buy? That bill was deader than same-sex marriage in the Texas Legislature.

This administration has put in new eligibility requirements that make it more difficult for low-income families to obtain a range of government benefits, including housing programs, Medicaid, the school-lunch program, education, preschool programs (let's hear it for the Education President), foreign aid, the EPA, veterans — hey, I hate when that happens. Meal programs for seniors: 36,000 cut off. Home heating: 532,000 cut off. Homeless kids cut off education programs: 8,000. Kids cut off after-school programs: 50,000. Kids cut off child care: 33,000. Good thing the country is being run by compassionate Christians, eh?

According to the White House itself, the total cost of the second round of Bush tax cuts is at least $50 billion a year for the next decade. That is enough to pay for a prescription-drug plan under Medicare, enough to provide health insurance to every child in America, and more than enough to pass every major homeland-security proposal made by experts in the field, according to Representative David Obey.

B Rapoport swept an interviewer off to the Rapoport Academy, the charter school run by their foundation. Charter schools were a pet project of Governor George W. Bush. Unfortunately, since Bush is not interested in policy, the original law was so carelessly written and contained so little oversight (because government regulation is always bad), we had a series of disasters in which people who were incompetent and/or crooked took huge chunks of the state's money to start schools that either never opened, couldn't educate a Labrador retriever, or wound up in some fantastic fiscal flameout. It took a liberal to make the idea work.

This is a magical place. The school has 150 students, chosen by lottery from the poorest kids in Waco. They are almost all black. The average family income of the students is $6,000 a year. A few are special-ed kids with physical handicaps; some others have mental handicaps. They arrive at the school with no academic skills and no social skills; some have never eaten a meal at table before.

These 150 kids are checking fifteen hundred books a month out of the school library. Many of the fifth-graders read at the ninth-grade level. One hundred percent of the fourth-graders passed the state's TAAS test in reading; 92.5 percent passed math. The kids are poised, articulate, and stunningly polite. They are getting the rigorous Core Knowledge curriculum developed by E. D. Hirsch at the University of Virginia. The school works with the parents through an astonishing array of outreach programs. It also has a special science-education curriculum where the kids all do original experiments and then parents come to hear them explained. Classical music is part of the deal. A third-grader with silver beads in her braided 'do was asked what the music was. "Oh, that's the 'Moonlight Sonata,' " she replied. "It's by Beethoven."

To send these kids to the Rapoport Academy costs $20,000 a year per child, some provided by the state and the rest by the Rapoport Foundation. The principal, Nancy Grayson, not only believes but knows that these kids can make it. B is convinced she's one of the thirty-seven secret saints of the Jewish tradition who are doing the Lord's work on earth. B and Audre come here frequently to read to the kids. A few years ago they brought Hillary Clinton to the school to read, and she said to the kids, "I am the First Lady of our country. Do you know who the First Man is?"

"Yes," chorused the otherwise well-educated children. "Mr. Rapoport!"

When B comes to the school, all the kids know him: "That's my girlfriend!" he carols to one in the fourth-grade line, who beams back at him. But the first-graders are not so well trained, so when B appears, they drop what they're doing and run to hug him, four, five, six little kids trying to climb over one another to kiss him. He puts his long arms around all of them and says to himself as he hugs them, "I am so rich. Oh, God, I am so rich." (Yeah, we know, we should have found some repellent, tax-dodging, selfish rich guy for this chapter, but what could we do? B is the only rich guy we know.)

• 4 •

The Blues in Belzoni

*I know how hard it is for you to
put food on your families.*
— George W. Bush, January 27, 2000

*Eugene Scalia would be a dedicated
advocate to the policies of the
Department of Labor.*
— Ari Fleischer, Spokesman for
George W. Bush, December 14, 2001

*The first duty of government is to protect the
powerless against the powerful.*
— The Code of Hammurabi, the
World's Oldest Legal Code, 1700 b.c.

The disconnect (a word that has mysteriously replaced *disconnection*) between the government of this country and the people in it has been the subject of complaint for the length of our history. This is a report on the specific disconnect between Washington, D.C.,

94

under George W. Bush, and some women in Belzoni, Mississippi.

Eugene Scalia, meet the workers of the Mississippi Delta's catfish houses. But please, shake their hands gently; many of them are in pain. The lumps on their wrists and the fingers that look as though they have been twisted into a bunch of twigs by rheumatoid arthritis are the consequence of what you have so dismissively dubbed "junk science." Please, shake their twisted hands very gently.

Eugene Scalia describes himself as a labor lawyer, which is true, in a sense — the same way it's true that the late Colonel Sanders was a big advocate for chickens. Scalia *fils* is the son of Justice Antonin Scalia. The younger Scalia, thirty-seven, was a partner in the law firm that represented George W. Bush in his case before the Supreme Court, the one that made him president and billed his backers $892,000 for the legal work.

Gene Scalia kept his distance from that case so no one could claim the high court's decision to name Bush president was tainted by nepotism. *Gore v. Bush* was not the sort of case the younger Scalia would have argued or briefed, even if his father weren't on the Supreme Court. At his firm, Gibson, Dunn & Crutcher, the big constitutional questions — affirmative action, school vouchers, did Monica Lewinsky go down on Bill Clinton — were left to Ted Olson. Scalia had other interests. While Olson was working on right-wing publisher Richard Mellon Scaife's $2.5 million investigation of Bill Clinton's past in Arkansas, Scalia was becoming the godfather of the anti-ergonomics movement.

Admittedly, an obscure field of law.

Scalia believes ergonomics — the shop-floor science that aims to make heavy and repetitive production-line work less destructive to workers' bodies — is a threat to American business. He has been very well paid to make that argument. As Upton Sinclair, the great muckraker, once observed, "It is difficult to get a man to understand something when his salary depends on his not understanding it."

Scalia worked with another Gibson, Dunn lawyer, Baruch Fellner, but Scalia was the star. The king of denial of bad backs. Wherever there was an attempt to address ergonomic injuries — at a House subcommittee meeting, a Department of Labor hearing, a courtroom in D.C., California, North Carolina, or Washington State — Gene Scalia was there. The terror of wimps claiming repetitive-stress injuries. Any bureaucrat writing rules to protect the men and women who move the nation's freight, build its buildings, type its memos, and process its foods would first have to get past Gene Scalia.

For big bidness, Scalia was the go-to guy in the fight against ergonomics regulation. In 1988 B.C. (Before Clinton), Elizabeth Dole, not normally considered a commie, ordered the Labor Department to write a set of rules to protect workers from debilitating injuries. She had been appointed labor secretary by George the First and was succeeded in 1991 by Lynn Martin, who continued the work on the "ergo" rules, as did Clinton's labor secretaries Robert Reich and Alexis Herman.

It took twelve years to get ergonomics regulation through the bureaucratic process. The Commerce and State Departments can rewrite the rules for export-import bank lending in a few weeks. Writing rules to protect the backs, shoulders, and wrists of working people takes longer. More than one thousand witnesses testified either for or against the proposed rules; seven thousand written comments were submitted to the Department of Labor; and hearings were held all over the country. Everybody got input, everybody got to sit at the table — company reps, flaks, union guys, big bidness, small bidness, chiropractors, disabled workers — you name the interested party, they were there. Gene Scalia was always there.

In March 2000, in its boxy, modern office building on Constitution Avenue, the Labor Department began its final forty-seven days of ergonomics hearings, the end of the process started in 1988. As the first session began, an OSHA panelist warned that anyone sitting in the front row was in danger of "getting run over by an attorney rushing to the podium." Eugene Scalia provided the punch line for that joke; he was the first witness of the day and literally sprinted to the front of the chamber, set up his flip chart like someone on speed, and was so aggressive he seemed to frighten himself. Dark features, thinning hair, cut-the-bullshit attitude. Scalia ignored the Labor Department judge and the chair of the panel to shoot his questions at individual members. "I haven't got much time up here," he said. When the judge warned him to let a witness complete his answer, Scalia complained the long responses were a waste of his time. When a bureaucrat said a question was unclear, Scalia fired back,

"Why don't you just answer the question?"

At the end of the day Scalia got another chance to perform and challenged rules to protect pregnant women in the workplace. He complained that under the proposed rules, employers would have to consider obesity and height in workplace assignments, clearly a task he considers beyond human ingenuity. Worse, he suggested, perfectly healthy workers could "claim that they are injured in order to avoid work and obtain benefits."

Just as there are Puritans among us who are deeply distressed by the idea that someone, somewhere might be having fun, there is a certain kind of conservative obsessed with the idea that some malingering worker somewhere might be getting away with something. One does occasionally find a case of a worker on disability who appears to be able to lift his bass boat off the trailer without difficulty, but in fact those few cases are so savagely outweighed that American workplaces are regularly scenes of carnage. About six thousand people are killed at work every year, twice as many as died on September 11, but government pays little attention. In addition, 165 people die of occupational diseases every day.

A weary Judge Joseph Vittone granted

Scalia an additional five minutes to complete his questions — but only if he promised not to come back again. After two days and eight hundred pages of testimony, Scalia was back, this time complaining about the department's bias, lecturing the judge, and laying the groundwork for a legal challenge of the worker protections. "He's like a little bulldog," says AFL-CIO safety and health director Peg Seminario.

Clients pay their lawyers for tenacity, and Scalia qualifies as a pit bull. He so zealously believes in the anti-ergonomics cause that he took his fight to op-ed pages and right-wing foundation bulletins, sources of much of the right's culture wars and ideology. Ergonomics regulation, he claimed in a 1997 article, is a union scam that would "reduce the pace of work, thereby pleasing current members." It would also require companies to hire more workers and "union membership (and dues) would increase, thereby pleasing union leaders." Ergonomics measures, he wrote, were merely aimed at making the workplace "more comfortable." Heaven forfend. In an article for the Cato Institute, Scalia ridiculed an OSHA investigation of complaints by workers at Pepperidge Farm. Could workers be injured by "lifting the top of a sandwich cookie from one assembly line and placing it on top of the bottom of the cookie on another assembly line, flicking a paper cup onto a conveyor belt with the thumb and placing a cookie in the cup?" He failed to mention that the high-speed production line requires those same repetitive motions thousands of times every hour, day after day, week after week, year after year. In a National Legal Center white paper, Scalia again scoffed at the government's case against Pepperidge Farm. The biggest workplace risks workers faced on the cookie-production line, he claimed, were "boredom or compulsive snacking."

Scalia did not represent Pepperidge Farm in its fight with OSHA, but he couldn't leave the case alone. In a piece for the op-ed page of *The Wall Street Journal*, not noted for its blue-collar readership, Scalia was more concerned about the "delightful Milano cookie" than the workers who make it. His description of OSHA's Pepperidge complaint made it appear Washington bureaucrats are so far from reality they actually claim flicking and cupping cookies can cause "death or serious physical harm." He did not explain that without the ergonomics rules he was seeking to defeat, OSHA's only recourse was to invoke the cumbersome "general duty clause," which requires employers to protect workers from death or serious physical harm. "Hard work is tiresome and sometimes uncomfortable," concluded Scalia, the Connecticut Avenue lawyer, sententiously. "Work less and you'll feel better. Why, I've experienced the very thing myself!"

It is a cultural imperative that business will oppose any government effort to regulate the workplace. "It's almost a knee-jerk reaction," said a labor lobbyist who has devoted most of her career to ergonomics. "But what Gene did was turn the usual business response, which we deal with all the time, into a philosophical opposition. It was not an opposition to the rule, it was opposition to ergonomics."

Scalia created opposition by redefining the debate. Labor advocates were no longer defending the proposed rules, they were defending ergonomics itself. The ghastly possibility that some cookie flipper might claim he or she was injured just to avoid work and obtain benefits — the horror, the horror.

"Like a cruise through Disney World's Pirates of the Caribbean, to survey ergonomists' theories is to glimpse the exotic and the absurd, occasionally amusing, and some grisly," Scalia claimed in 1994. For seven years he didn't let up: ergonomics is founded on "junk science." Repetitive-stress injuries might not exist at all. Heavy lifting does not cause back strain. Reported increases in repetitive-motion injuries are caused by feeding frenzies created by doctors, reporters, and hysterical workers, a form of mass hysteria. Scalia even managed to popularize (in limited circles) an obscure word from the Greek, *iatrogenesis,* meaning a disorder caused by the diagnosis or treatment of a physician. What's wrong with workers is not their wrists, backs, shoulders, or hands — it's in their heads, he claimed. And it's put there by "the medical and legal professions, by management, unions, governments and the media." A veritable cabal of suspect institutions, all joined in league to protect larcenous cookie flippers.

Sherry Durst* is not, like Scalia, a graduate of the University of Chicago Law School. She graduated high school in Tchula, a town of two thousand in the Mississippi Delta. She has never heard the word

---

*Name changed to protect the identity of the subject.

iatrogenesis, but she's smart enough, as Lyndon used to say, to tell chicken shit from chicken salad.

Durst is a small, attractive twenty-two-year-old, with large eyes and a generous smile. While Eugene Scalia was the solicitor general of the Labor Department, Sherry Durst was one of the people he was supposed to be working for.

On the same March morning in 2000 when lawyer/lobbyist Eugene Scalia raced to the front of the Department of Labor hearing room to take the lead in the industry fight against ergonomics protection for workers, Durst got up and took her three-year-old son to the neighbor who takes care of him while she works. She then drove twenty miles to the Freshwater Farms catfish processing plant, just east of the Yazoo River in Belzoni. She put on an apron, a hair net, special latex gloves, and a pair of rubber boots. She walked into the refrigerated plant and took her station on the thin black rubber mat next to the conveyor belt. At the start of the conveyor belt, live catfish spilled out of holding tanks and began to move in Durst's direction.

By the time the judge made his opening remarks and Scalia finished his first twenty minutes of testimony, Sherry Durst had skinned one thousand catfish. For eight to ten hours a day, Durst grabs a catfish off the conveyor belt, presses one of its sides against a set of blades mounted on a high-speed rotor, then flips the fish and repeats the process. Then she grabs another, and another, and another. If the line was running fast on March 13, 2000, Durst would have skinned twelve hundred fish before Scalia completed his brief morning testimony.

By the time Judge Vittone adjourned the ergonomics hearing at noon and the lawyers and lobbyists scrambled for cabs to make their lunches at the Red Sage or Olives, Durst had skinned between thirty-six hundred and four thousand catfish. Moments before each live fish arrives at the skinning station, it is stunned by electric shock, beheaded by one woman, and eviscerated by another, who jams each fish's intestinal cavity against a stationary vacuum pipe called a "long gun." In order to keep her job at Freshwater Farms, Durst has to skin a minimum of twelve fish a minute. At times, a white supervisor stands behind her with a stopwatch, calculating minutes and catfish. Durst never falls below fifteen, at times hits twenty, and has skinned more than twenty-five catfish a minute.

"It's hard work," she said. "You stand on

the floor, sometimes eight to ten hours a day. You can imagine how it feels. When the line is moving fast, all you can do is grab the fishes as fast as you can and turn them over on one side and then the other. You lose count." Workers get a morning break from ten to ten-fifteen — "where we have a little break room and have our little snack, or some people go outside and smoke." Lunch is from twelve to twelve-thirty, and there is an afternoon break from three to three-fifteen. "That little break be over before you know it," said Durst.

With the exception of the time she is allowed to be off the line, Durst spends her entire day standing and grabbing catfish — twelve to twenty-five a minute. "You have a group leader working with you," she explains matter-of-factly. "You have to obey her, everything she tell you. You ask her when you need to go to the bathroom."

That March 13, the Department of Labor's Judge Vittone adjourned the hearing at 6:30 p.m. Assuming the cut-and-gut line at Freshwater's Belzoni plant ran ten hours that day, and factoring in the two breaks and lunch, Sherry Durst skinned between 8,100 and 10,800 catfish. If she went to the bathroom once, the count dropped by 120.

Going to the bathroom is a problem. While a worker is in the rest room, the line continues to move, fish pile up, supervisors get angry. In 1990 rest-room breaks were the central issue in the strike at the neighboring Delta Pride catfish factory. Sarah White was a worker at the plant in Belzoni, where she is now the United Food and Commercial Workers Union's local rep. She recalled the strike's hidden issue: "It came down to rest-room breaks," she said in her small office across the street from the county courthouse. "We got another five or six cents an hour, but the strike centered on bathroom rights."

The company opened with an offer of six bathroom visits a week (have you ever taken a road trip with a pregnant woman?). When the union rejected the fixed number, the company's position hardened. "They told us they gave us six breaks, but since we said no, we were going to have to go once a day — at lunchtime," said White. "They added five minutes to our lunch break and said we would have to go then. We couldn't abide it. We tired of it. The workers couldn't abide it anymore."

The Mississippi Delta is full of stories about women who decide they can't abide it anymore. The late Fannie Lou Hamer said, "I'm sick and tired of being sick and tired." The civil rights leader was from Ruleville, sixty miles north of Belzoni. The workers at the catfish plants know just how she felt. In addition to the fixed number of bathroom breaks, there were other forms of degradation. Male supervisors would walk into the women's rest rooms and tell women to get up off the toilet and go to work. "I've had a supervisor walk into the rest room and tell me, 'Get up, Sarah. You've been sitting there too long.' That don't happen no more. The civil rights movement changed a lot of things." (Those of you who think the civil rights movement ended in the 1960s haven't been to Belzoni lately.)

Jazz artist Cassandra Wilson, another daughter of the Delta, said Mississippi women "will be as nice as possible until you cross the line." In 1990 Delta Pride crossed the line. "They told us go on, go on out on strike," said White. When the workers struck, the company brought in replacements and stopped negotiating with the union. "The company brought in scabs from Greenville and Cleveland, but they were too slow," White said. Production slowed to a crawl. Black activist-comedian Dick Gregory joined the strikers for a day.

The congressional Black Caucus supported them. Jesse Jackson came to help. Workers survived on sixty dollars a week in strike pay and a fifty-pound weekly ration package of rice, beans, and peas provided by the union. Supporters across the country prepared to travel to Indianola for a "civil rights/workers' rights" march from downtown to Delta Pride's Indianola plant.

The company blinked first. The three-year-old local, made up of mostly African-American women, won concessions from a catfish co-op made up of the most powerful white men in the region. They won the right to privacy in the rest room, a reasonable lunch-break policy, an hourly wage increase, and overtime pay that kicked in at the end of each eight-hour day, rather than at the end of a forty-hour week.

"Wages could be higher," said White. For a forty-hour week skinning fifty thousand to sixty thousand catfish, Sherry Durst earns $240, an annual income that keeps her and her son $540 above the federal poverty level. "They tax us so hard, we keep only about $160 or $170 each week," Durst said. Eugene Scalia and Baruch Fellner could spend that much on dinner at the Red Sage. "You got to decide if you are going to buy a car, pay your house rent, or buy your food," said another Freshwater employee.

Sherry Durst manages, as Bush once said, "to put food on her family." She says she hasn't been treated for carpal tunnel problems or tendonitis, but her hands do hurt at night. She plans to leave before the serious problems set in. "A catfish house is not a place for a young person to spend the rest of their life," she said. "I want a job sitting behind a desk, like white folks." Durst is young, smart, eloquent, and determined. But the unemployment rate in Humphreys County is 12 percent. The average income for households where the women are the breadwinners is $15,833.

The commercial catfish business — like the plantation system to which it is sometimes compared — is feudal in structure. Workers and their bosses are bound together and locked in place in a relationship defined by land ownership. Up and down the Mississippi Delta the landowners have moved from cotton to catfish, but land ownership still shapes the social hierarchy. The more ponds a landholder owns, the larger his share in the local catfish co-op. At the bottom of the feudal pyramid are the African-American men who work in the catfish ponds and the African-American women who work in the processing houses.

"You can go to a chicken house, but there's not much else you can do around here," said Carrie Ann Lewis. Lewis, like Durst, went to work in a catfish-processing plant when she was in her early twenties. For four years in the late 1980s she worked at Delta Pride. Today she is physically worn out. Each of her wrists has a large prominent knob on top. "Gangliatic cysts," said Dr. Ron Myers. He is standing in the crowded space that doubles as a bedroom–living room in the four-hundred-square-foot house Lewis shares with her two children.

Lewis was a "long gunner." She spent her days grabbing fish off the conveyor belt and thrusting them into the vacuum "gun barrel" that sucks out the intestines. "Sometimes so many of those fishes go by you see fishes in your sleep," she said. Within a year Lewis began to develop tingling and numbness in her hands. Pains in her shoulder joints were diagnosed as tendonitis. At night her hands ached. If the pain lasted all night, she was unable to sleep. She agreed to an operation on one wrist and it provided some relief, so she had the same operation on the other wrist.

She was out on workers' compensation for six months. When she returned to the plant she asked to be assigned to something other than the long gun. "The supervisor told me, 'You can go back to the long gun or you can go home.'" She went home and has been there ever since. A local lawyer, whose ad is on the back of the forty-seven-page Belzoni phone book, got her a $2,000 settlement. At twenty-nine, she was finished. She has other health problems and lives on a $545 monthly disability check. Carrie Ann Lewis reached her highest lifetime earnings, $3.45 an hour, in 1989, the year she left Delta Pride. It's not likely she will ever make that much again. According to Dr. Myers, she can never work on a cut-and-gut line in any of the half-dozen catfish-processing plants that surround Belzoni.

Ron Myers grew up in Chicago and graduated from medical school in Wisconsin — a place as far from the Delta in culture as it is in miles. His great-great-grandfather had been enslaved on a plantation one hundred miles from Belzoni. Myers, who is also an ordained minister, left the Midwest to open a clinic in Mississippi when a congregation in Wisconsin agreed to support his work. "I began to see twenty-four-, twenty-five-, twenty-six-year-old ladies with the arthritic wrists of sixty-year-olds," Myers said. He advised them to follow the least intrusive and most prudent course of treatment — rest. It was advice managers in the catfish plants couldn't buy. The local plants now keep Dr. Myers off the list of physicians approved by their health-care plans. "These women are operated on, sent back to work too soon, but never allowed to take enough time off to rest," said Myers.

He became an outspoken critic of the catfish industry. It would not exist without the women who do the processing work, he said. Yet the women are ignored. There is no place for them in the town's catfish museum. And they were discouraged from setting up a booth at Belzoni's annual World Catfish Festival. Denise LaSalle, a black R&B singer who had moved on from Belzoni to the big time, was turned down by the catfish festival's entertainment committee. So Myers organized an annual African-American Heritage Buffalo Fish Festival, scheduled on the same day that Belzoni holds its catfish festival. Buffalo is a carp that is not raised commercially. Pollution in the Mississippi has made local buffalo fish hazardous to eat, so Myers has the fish for the festival brought in from Louisiana.

In April 2002 Belzoni's two fish festivals were as divided as the black and white neighborhoods in the town that calls itself the Heart of the Delta. At the white folks' World Catfish Festival, fifteen thousand people wandered the downtown streets. In the course of a day thousands lined up for catfish and hush puppies. Crafts were sold from booths. On the steps of the Humphreys County courthouse, which serve as a stage for local talent, a couple of white guys fronting a big jazz ensemble offered up something that was supposed to be the blues. The crowd swelled when an entrant in the talent contest began to sing the "Dixie" variation in Mickey Newbury's "American Trilogy." The entire downtown was given over to this local celebration of the catfish. But the festival — with its funnel-cake booths, craft sales, and children's games — was whiter than Brigadoon. There was hardly an African-American face to be seen.

They were all three blocks away, where Belzoni's African-American community was gathered in front of a stage made of two-by-fours and plywood, listening to hip-hop contestants, local musicians with bad amplification, and other contests and readings organized by "the Doc." Late in the afternoon Denise LaSalle's touring coach pulled up at the makeshift stage and the local-girl-made-good led her band through an R&B show that made the white bluesmen on the courthouse steps sound like the Carpenters. She closed with a gospel number — "because when I left Zion Rock Church in Belzoni, Mississippi, I took God along with me." She came back for the Buffalo festival because "Doc asked me and because of the women working up in those catfish houses."

The doctor, a beatifically sweet man who weighs close to three hundred pounds and runs on adrenaline, returned to a theme he'd been working all day. He has organized carpal tunnel workshops, fried buffalo, directed traffic, served as an emcee. Onstage, he got back on-message. "They brought our ancestors here to chop cotton; now we chop catfish for six-fifty an hour," he told the all-black crowd gathered on the vacant lot beside his small clinic. (Actually, nonunion companies pay less than $6 an hour, and even union workers don't start at $6.50. Sherry Durst started at Freshwater Farms at $5.95. Many of the line workers at Delta Pride top out at $7.30 after fifteen years.)

Labor unions can help with wages and some working conditions, but only the federal government has the muscle to protect workers' bodies in the Third World pockets of this country, places like the Mississippi Delta, the Rio Grande Valley of Texas, and Appalachia.

As the clock ran out on Bill Clinton's second term, it looked as though the federal government wouldn't be coming to the aid of the tens of thousands of women cutting catfish in the Mississippi Delta. The corporate coalition that had hired Scalia to block ergonomics regulation was close to achieving a goal they had been working toward for years. They had almost busted the worker protections once before, when the Newt Gingrich House cut off all funding for writing such rules in the mid-nineties. But Clinton's Labor Department managed to keep the process alive. When Judge Vittone gaveled the Department of Labor ergo hearings to an end, the twelve-year process was over and the rules could be implemented. But Bill Clinton had little time left in office, and the rules had to be listed in the *Federal Register*. It seemed that big business had stalled long enough to kill the ergo rules.

Bill Clinton stepped in and saved them.

While he waited for the Supreme Court to decide who would follow him into the White House, Clinton took the final step in the bureaucratic process. He ordered the rules posted in the *Federal Register*. Within a few weeks there finally would be federal protection from the kind of repetitive physical labor that has left Carrie Ann Lewis with "the arthritic wrists of a sixty-year-old." The business community reacted as though ergonomics rules were something Clinton had thought up while he was packing up his files. Gene Scalia returned to the op-ed pages. The National Coalition on Ergonomics — a creation of Scalia's that is funded by big corporate interests — cranked up its "grassroots" operation. As they say in Amarillo, big bidness went "balls to the wall" fighting the new rules.

"They really wanted this," said a member of the late Senator Paul Wellstone's staff. "We heard they had a bill drafted before the session began. It didn't take long to see how determined they were." All the business community needed was a signal from the White House. As soon as Karl Rove moved into Hillary Clinton's old office, they got it. "These regulations would cost employers, large and small, billions of dollars annually while providing uncertain benefits," said a White House press release. "If implemented, they would require employers to establish burdensome and costly new systems to track, prevent and provide compensation for an extremely broad class of injuries, whose cause is subject to considerable dispute." The press release was business-lobby boilerplate straight from the National Coalition on Ergonomics.

You have to give Eugene Scalia credit for making it possible for the White House (or anyone) to claim that the very idea of repetitive-motion injuries in the workplace is "subject to considerable dispute." The Department of Labor reports that there are 1.8 million American workers disabled by injuries caused by physical stress on the job each year. Those workers had been waiting a decade for the rules. Whether the injuries are called musculoskeletal disorders, carpal tunnel syndrome, or repetitive-motion injuries, the cause is not under "dispute" by those who are not in the pay of big business. The National Academy of Science had already done two studies, ordered by Congress, on the connection between types of work and workplace injuries. (A second study was necessary because conservative members of Congress didn't agree with the conclusions of the first study they had commissioned. They didn't agree with the conclusions of the second one either, but since a third would only have confirmed numbers one and two, they gave up.)

With the backing of the business community and the Bush administration, the House moved to kill the ergo rules. House whip Tom DeLay — also known as "the Hammer" and "Tom DeReg" — hasn't found a government regulation he liked since he gave up killing bugs in Sugar Land. In fact, the former exterminator still stands foursquare for bringing back DDT. Just the man to kill ergo in the House.

In the Senate the late Paul Wellstone and Ted Kennedy were still standing for the democratic wing of the Democratic Party and were willing to filibuster any attempt to bust the ergo regs. Beyond Kennedy and Wellstone, a number of Democrats still retain some quaint attachment to working people — or at least they worry that organized labor will fail to support them in the next election. A few Republicans — Arlen Specter of Pennsylvania and Lincoln Chaffee of Rhode Island — also pay attention to the labor constituencies in their states. So according to political math, the Senate should have been a stopper.

But the Republicans had a secret weapon: the Congressional Review Act, an obscure law passed during the Gingrich Revolution. The CRA allows Congress to overturn any executive order that has been on the books for fewer than sixty days. It also limits debate to ten hours in each chamber and prohibits amendments and filibusters. Once DeLay had rounded up his votes in the House, all the business lobby needed was ten hours and fifty senators. (In case of a tie, there was no doubt how Vice President Cheney would vote.)

As Senate debate began, Chris Dodd of Connecticut emphasized how painstaking the ergonomics rule-making process had been. OSHA had extended its time period on the regulations and had held nine weeks of public hearings. Dodd even suggested that one thousand witnesses and seven thousand written comments might be sufficient.

For workers sitting in the gallery and watching, the debate was almost as painful as a carpal tunnel injury. "So after twelve years of work . . . in ten hours of debate, we are going to wipe all this out," Dodd said. Kennedy pleaded with Senator Don Nickles of Oklahoma, the Senate sponsor of the CRA bill, to hold off for sixty to ninety days to allow time to meet with Bush and discuss his objections. But the business lobby just wanted to bury it.

"They were in a full-court press," said Peg Seminario, the AFL-CIO's health and safety director who had worked on the rules for years. "Once Bush was elected, it was clear he was going after the rules. With Bush in office and [Elaine] Chao at Labor, they could have used the legislative process to modify the rules or change them. It was even reviewable in court. Business could have challenged the rules in court, but there was so much process, there was such a record, so much evidence and testimony on both sides, they could only have made minor changes. But they knew that once you are into those processes, you will have rules, no matter how you change them. So they had to get Congress to do it. They had to go the CRA route to try to kill it forever."

The Bushies insisted they only wanted better rules. Secretary Chao wrote a letter to senators promising to go to work on new ergonomics standards. That was all the ass-cover six conservative Democrats needed. After ten hours of debate, the Senate voted 56–44 to kill the rules twelve years in the making. Republican moderates

Specter and Chaffee voted with the Democrats, but Zell Miller of Georgia, Blanche Lambert Lincoln of Arkansas, Fritz Hollings of South Carolina, Max Baucus of Montana, and John Breaux and Mary Landrieu of Louisiana — all Democrats from states carried by Bush — voted with the Republicans.

Kennedy sent the Labor Department a formal request for documents, trying to find a paper trail on who had made the decision to kill ergonomics regulation. "He got nothing," said a Senate staff member. "Nothing worth having. Probably because there was nothing. This all had to be done through private meetings with the White House staff. With Karl Rove, the president and vice president talking to Chao or her staff."

The House vote was a done deal but still brought on an offensive drive by the lobby, the likes of which has rarely been seen since the happy days of the Gingrich Revolution six years earlier, when Newt Gingrich and Tom DeLay turned their office fax and copy machines over to the business lobbyists. The usual suspects from the K Street firms were joined by a large number of corporate CEOs, and many of them stuck around for the celebratory press conference after the 223–206 vote. Sixteen House Democrats joined the Republicans to kill protection for workers. It was a great day for UPS, one of Scalia's old employers. The company had given 85 percent of its $1.3 million in political contributions to Republicans the previous year. Killing off the ergo regs was a good return on that investment.

When Tom DeLay called to thank the president for his support, Bush said he'd done nothing. DeLay told *The New York Times* that he had had to explain to the president that "the very fact that he was in the White House had helped" because it bucked up Republican senators from states with big labor constituencies.

Bush, Rove, DeLay, and Scalia won and won big. The CRA also prohibits any federal agency from writing rules similar to those killed by the legislative process. Ergonomic Protection for Workers, RIP.

"The good companies make their workplaces safe for their employees," said Jackie Nowell, who lobbied on ergonomics for the United Food and Commercial Workers. "People are going to be hurt by the bad companies." The only reason regulation is ever necessary is because of bad companies. One bad company was the subject of a devastating series in *The New*

York Times in early January 2003: McWane Inc.'s Tyler Pipe plant in the president's home state is so callous about its workers the series was sickening to read. There are also entire industries with miserable records — beef packing among the most notorious. Every bad company operating in the country got a nod and wink from the White House when President Bush joined forces with Eugene Scalia to kill the ergonomics guidelines that began in the White House of the first President Bush.

Seven months after he signed the death warrant on ergonomics regulation, President Bush, who has never held a job involving physical labor, appointed Eugene Scalia solicitor of labor. The appointment put Scalia in charge of the federal government's labor-law firm: five hundred attorneys responsible for enforcing 180 federal laws covering everything from workplace safety to child labor. The laws protect the worker, but there's a catch. The worker can't hire a lawyer to enforce them. There are many federal workplace protections that can only be enforced by the Department of Labor. "A worker has no individual cause of action with these laws," explained a Senate staffer. "They are enforced by the solicitor of labor." Sherry Durst, meet your lawyer:

Gene Scalia. The president had decided that decisions whether to file suit against an employer for breaking workplace-safety laws, child-labor laws, or hundreds of other federal protections for workers would be made by an anti-worker zealot.

The Democrats never saw the Scalia nomination coming. Despite repeated campaign promises of a bipartisan approach to Congress — "the way politics is practiced in Texas" — Bush never consulted them. "He wasn't looking for any Bob Bullocks on this one," said a Democratic staffer, referring to the late lieutenant governor of Texas, who theoretically favored bipartisanship. (Actually, he favored his own control over everything.) "On their big issues, we never hear from them."

By the fall of 2001, Bush and Rove had already driven Vermont senator Jim Jeffords out of the Republican Party and Democrats controlled the Senate, so confirming Scalia was not going to be as easy as killing the ergonomics regs. A Democratic Senate majority meant that Kennedy chaired the Health, Education and Labor Committee. "The senator was furious about the Scalia appointment," said a committee staff member. Senator John Edwards of North Carolina, whose daddy had worked in a mill for thirty-seven years, asked, "Just out of curiosity, have you yourself ever had any personal experience working in a manufacturing plant or the kind of poultry facility that Senator Wellstone was asking about?" Scalia replied, "No, I have not worked in a facility like that." Kennedy pressured his committee members to vote no, but Jeffords "reluctantly" cast the deciding vote to support the nomination.

Kennedy admits Scalia is a skilled lawyer, qualified to do many things. But to serve as an advocate for the nation's workers? Kennedy's staff discovered that Scalia had once actually represented workers — a group suing their own union after they had crossed a picket line. Kennedy decided to filibuster. Tom Daschle, then Senate majority leader, took his time scheduling a vote, predicting Scalia would lose whenever it happened. Bush realized it had been a lot easier to be "bipartisan" when the Republicans controlled both houses of Congress. So the president "recessed" Scalia in, installing him in office while Congress was adjourned. A recess appointment is basically an "up yours" to the Senate. It is something presidents rarely do, but it allowed Eugene Scalia to slip past the Senate.

Thirteen months after Secretary Chao

wrote senators promising she would "improve" ergonomics regs, the Bush administration announced its grand new plan for worker protection. To wit, OSHA announced that in six months it would publish a set of voluntary guidelines companies might choose to use to protect workers.

In one of those little protocol tiffs that absorb so much energy in Washington, the White House even stiffed Democratic senators with the release of the plan on the voluntary workplace guidelines. "They came over and briefed the Republican senators," a Senate committee staff member said. "Then they made the Democrats go over to the Labor Department for their briefing. And they didn't even have enough information packets for the Democrats who showed up." Readers of Washington tea leaves noted the new "voluntary rules" were announced on a Thursday — bad news is always released at the end of the weekly news cycle.

A month later Secretary Chao assured angry members of the Senate Labor Committee that solicitor Scalia would aggressively enforce the voluntary guidelines — as soon as they were written. Chao said she was aware of Scalia's anti-ergonomics work in the past, but that was when he was a lobbyist working for business interests. At the DOL, she promised, Gene Scalia would be different: "He has a new client."*

*Scalia no longer has an opportunity to represent Sherry Durst. After two years he was a victim of an unwritten administration policy (the Rove Rule) that places pragmatic politics above principle. Scalia had assumed he would be going to court to clean up the mess at the United Brotherhood of Carpenters and Joiners. The mess had been made by Douglas McCarron, who had liberally interpreted the union's election rules to get himself elected union president. McCarron was also tainted by his role in an insider-trading scandal involving a union-owned company. All of this made him the perfect target for the solicitor's office. But he is also one of very few friends George W. Bush has in organized labor. He was the only labor guy invited to Bush's big (one-day) economic summit in Waco. And he was expected to endorse Bush in 2004. Secretary of labor Elaine Chao prudently decided that the Labor Department didn't need to take Doug McCarron to court, as *The Wall Street Journal* lamented in an indignant op-ed piece. Working folks will find little comfort in Scalia's replacement: his DOL understudy, Howard M. Radzely. Before signing on at the Labor Department Radzely was a law clerk for Michael Luttig, an arch-conservative from Tyler, Texas, sitting on

The news that there would be no work-place protections and that Eugene Scalia would be their advocate didn't surprise a small group of catfish workers sitting in the living room of a housing project on a Sunday afternoon in Tchula, Mississippi. In this part of the Delta, most news related to work — whether cotton farms, catfish factories, or chicken-processing plants — is bad. "The unions, they might help you a little," said a former "Chili stripper" (Chili's restaurant chain buys tons of catfish every year, cut into small "Chili strips"), "but these companies don't much listen to no union. These companies wear you out, and when you

---

the Fourth Circuit Court of Appeals. Radzely also clerked for Supreme Court justice Antonin Scalia, not exactly the working woman's advocate on the high court. Radzely's appointment might interest Sarah White back in Belzoni. He came into office as the United Food and Commercial Workers Union was leaning on the Department of Labor to enforce rules that provide worker access to rest rooms. Word quickly leaked from the DOL that Radzely's strict constructionist take on the rules would require employers to *provide* adequate rest-room facilities but not require employers to *allow* workers access to the rest rooms.

can't work no more, they tell you good-bye."

She is in her mid-thirties; she doesn't look a day over fifty-five.

•5•

LEAVE NO CHILD BEHIND

*You teach a child to read and he or her
will be able to pass a literacy test.*
— GEORGE W. BUSH, TENNESSEE,
FEBRUARY 21, 2001

*Where did this idea come from —
that everybody deserves free education?
. . . It's like free groceries. It comes
from Moscow. From Russia.
Straight out of the pit of hell.*
— REPRESENTATIVE DEBBIE RIDDLE,
AUSTIN, MARCH 5, 2003

OK, so we're not real partial to public education in Texas.

And we got fooled. Maybe more than twice.

So did you.

Here's how it happened.

Between GeeDubya Bush's second legislative session in 1997 and the official

131

beginning of his run for the presidency in 1999, the state of Texas pissed away much of a $6 billion surplus. A surplus in Austin is like the hundred-year flood in Amarillo: it comes about every eight hundred years. You want to make full use of everything you can get out of it.

Governor Bush made good use of the surplus, at least for his own political purposes. In a state known for low taxes and no income tax, he gave a big chunk of the surplus back to taxpayers. Then he ran for president saying, "I passed the largest tax break in the history of the state of Texas." And why not? The economy was booming. Enron stock was going to hit $100 and split. Streets were filled with trucks laying fiber-optic cable. If you could get a table near the lean and hungry venture capitalists at the Mezzaluna restaurant in downtown Austin, you might hear one of them mention "the next killer ap." Then you could call your broker, sell Agillion, and buy Tivoli. The boom was like Robert Earl Keen's song "The Road Goes on Forever and the Party Never Ends."

Dubya Bush arrived as governor after the party started. By the time it ended, he had ridden the Texas tech boom all the way to the White House. The first big

Austin campaign bash in the summer of 1999 featured bad country music and a stump speech heavy on Bushonomic blather: ". . . the largest tax cut in the history of the state of Texas . . . give tax dollars to the people who earned them . . . ," etc. Bush budget director Albert Hawkins, who had just left the state's payroll to join the campaign, stood at the back of the crowd. Hawkins is a veteran capitol numbers-cruncher who knew better. Asked why none of the record surplus was banked in the state's rainy day fund, Hawkins dismissed the question. The state's finances were in good shape, he said. "We didn't see any need to put any money in the fund."

Then the stock market tanked, the Supreme Court named Bush president, tax revenues disappeared, and Texas went broke. As we write we're looking at a $10 billion deficit in Texas — which will end up being $12 billion because our comptrollers always lie about deficits. Or tell the truth in $300 million increments. It's raining in Texas. Six or seven billion dollars in the Texas rainy day fund would be right useful to legislators slashing programs in a state that's always in a dead heat with Mississippi for last place in government spending. As Bush rolled out his second big tax cut in Washington in 2002, the state he left behind was being ravaged by the deficits he created.

One casualty of the post-Bush budget crash in Texas is the state's public schools. That's how Odell Edwards* — along with all but 8 percent of his African-American classmates at Houston's Phillis Wheatley High School — really got fooled. As Odell started tenth grade, his school district faced a $160 million deficit. His campus was rated as "low-performing." And there was a 92 percent chance that in two years he would fail the "high-stakes" test required by President Bush's "No Child Left Behind" education-reform law.

Odell gets Bushwhacked twice.

Governor Bush's tax cuts in Texas put Odell's school district in a financial bind. President Bush's No Child Left Behind law puts Odell himself in a bind, almost guaranteeing he will be left behind. Sitting in a McDonald's in southeast Houston, this wiry kid full of nervous energy seems unaware of the odds he faces when he gets his first crack at the high school exit exam next year. His odds are bad because the Texas Education Agency has done some-

*Name changed at subject's request.

thing extraordinary. It created a high-stakes exit exam that almost perfectly predicts one thing: race. Edwards is African-American. According to field tests of the Texas Assessment of Knowledge and Skills, he has an 8 percent chance of passing. His grade-point average could be 95 (he admits that it's "mostly B's and C's"), but in a trial run of the test 92 percent of black kids failed. As a result, the test is being tweaked and scores will ultimately be curved. The trial tests predicted a disaster for black kids. And if Odell fails the Texas Assessment of Knowledge and Skills, he doesn't get out of Wheatley High. He gets a couple of re-takes. But what are the odds that a kid officially designated a failure after eleven, then twelve, then twelve and a half years of public education will come back for that third test in the summer after high school?

Odell works twenty-five to thirty hours a week at McDonald's and lives with his mother and stepsister. He'd like to get out of fast food but likes the money. He wants to buy a car and says maybe he'll go to Houston Community College — at a campus that just opened in an abandoned strip mall on Martin Luther King Drive.

It's the American teenage dream, on a modest scale.

Here's a young African-American man of limited means who's always attended public schools where his minority was the majority. He's the guy George Bush must have had in mind when he talked about "the soft bigotry of low expectations." Bush can say what he wants to about ending that invisible bigotry, but he has helped stack the deck against Odell Edwards.* Odell's school faces budget and staff cuts — at the same time that President W.'s education law is demanding much more from Odell.

He'd have a better shot if he lived in Massachusetts. They spend money on public education there. In Texas we do schools on the cheap. "You can't say

---

*Black folks in Houston are used to the system working against them. Around the time young George W. Bush was chilling out in a classroom at the exclusive, private Kincaid School, the public schools in Houston, where summers are like Managua without the breeze, were just getting air-conditioning. After a school-board debate about who gets air-conditioning first, a board member proposed following the alphabet. The city's African-American high school campuses at the time were Wheatley, Worthing, Yates, and Washington.

throwing money at public education won't work," an East Texas senator used to say. "Because we've never tried it."

It's going to take a heroic effort for Odell Edwards to cut loose from fast-food counter culture at McDonald's.

Here's how the rest of you got fooled. You were told the No Child Left Behind law is the Texas model of competency testing gone national. That's not exactly true, and if it were, it wouldn't be good. For decades the Great State has served as the National Laboratory for Bad Policy.

In truth, the No Child Left Behind Act Bush got passed in January 2002 is not the Texas education model imposed on the nation. It's the Texas model with bells added to bring on the far right and whistles added to attract congressional liberals, and insufficient money to pay for any of it. And it was signed into law at a time when our public schools are being slammed by huge state-budget deficits.

As full-time residents of the state that gave you tort reform, H. Ross Perot, and penis-enlargement options on executive health plans, we're obliged to warn you that if Dubya Bush had exported "the Texas Miracle," the country would be in

137

deep shit. In public education there was no Texas miracle. The last Lone Star miracle we know of was the time the face of Jesus appeared on a screen door in Port Neches, and that's been more than thirty years.

Linda McNeil is a professor at Rice University, codirector of the Rice Center for Education, former high school English teacher, a past vice president of the American Educational Research Association, and author of *Contradictions of School Reform* and numerous papers published in scholarly journals. In other words, not the sort of person the Bushies want meddling in public-education policy. After all, she has never published anything advocating phonics, and she has no real ties to the corporate world.

McNeil does use a corporate metaphor when talking about education reform in Texas — in particular when describing the system the Texas Education Agency uses to track progress on the standardized tests our state's kids have been taking for about ten years. This is the system that supposedly authenticated the miracle in Texas public ed. McNeil likens it to a local company housed in a sleek corporate tower a few miles north of the ivory towers at Rice University.

"Enron," she said.

"You've seen newspaper accounts that explain how Enron used a single indicator to show how well the company was performing," McNeil said. She went on to explain that the average scores on Texas' standardized tests are like Enron's stock price — inflated and manipulated. Profits and successes were reflected in stock price. Debts and losses were carried on a different set of books. McNeil believes that placing so much emphasis on kids' scores, and linking the scores to the jobs and cash bonuses of school administrators, corrupted the system. Just as Enron's focus on stock price corrupted the company by encouraging every employee to do everything possible to keep the stock price climbing, school administrators were pressured to use "any means necessary" to pump up text scores. Everything from replacing good curriculum with text practice drills to dumping weak students likely to be a liability to the school's ratings.

McNeil has worked with two other professors. Angela Valenzuela teaches in the College of Education at the University of Texas. Walt Haney is a displaced Texan from Corpus Christi, now on the faculty of Boston College. The three profs are persistent empiricists, always citing statistics about academic performance, always studying the effect of policy on the children in the classroom. (It does seem odd that Bush's first Texas education commissioner, Mike Moses, has taken up with these three education Cassandras, running around the state screaming, "The scores are falling!" Moses is now superintendent of schools in Dallas, a minority school district about to be overwhelmed by the high-stakes test mandated by the education law Bush pushed through Congress.)

Working together, the three professors of education found that bogus test scores are only one of two ugly truths about education reform in Texas. The other, linked to test scores, is the dropout rate — one of the highest in the nation.*

They started by asking why scores on the tests controlled by the Texas Education Agency steadily increased, while scores on national tests not controlled by the agency

---

*Texas excludes students in juvenile detention and students whose whereabouts are unknown from dropout records, along with two dozen other categories of nonschool attenders. It's also one of very few states that count students who pass the GED test as graduating students.

barely moved. If the state's standardized-test scores climbed over ten years, then scores on the Scholastic Aptitude Test (SAT) and the American College Testing Program (ACT) should have increased with them.

They didn't.

Average scores on the state standardized tests showed healthy gains. Average scores on the college-board SAT and ACT showed meager gains. By 2002, after ten years of testing, students in Texas were doing great on the state tests. But they ranked forty-seventh nationally on college-exam scores. (We beat out North Carolina, Georgia, South Carolina, and the District of Columbia.)

The SAT and ACT scores would be even lower if the weakest students didn't drop out of Texas high schools.

"We *disappear* our kids," McNeil said, a usage normally heard in connection with Central American death squads. Many children — far more than 50 percent in the cities — who enroll in the first year of high school in Texas don't make it to graduation. There's an institutional incentive for them to leave. If test scores are low, schools are rated low-performing. In low-performing schools, principals lose their jobs. Tests as a single criterion to evaluate schools provide an incentive for principals to disappear weak students to keep their campus test scores high. (This is not just about job security and money. Most public-school faculties in Texas will jump at the chance to push an incompetent principal out the door, but teachers will also fight a system that drives away dedicated, competent principals working with limited resources and against great odds.)

The low-performing students encouraged to go quietly are mostly Latino, African-American, and students with limited English proficiency (LEP). After they leave, the Texas Education Agency cooks the books. In 2001 the agency released dropout figures — all under 4 percent. But the conservative Manhattan Institute came up with a dropout rate of 52 percent. The Intercultural Development Research Association, a liberal education-advocacy group based in San Antonio, has tracked dropout numbers for ten years. It says the rate is 40 percent, which translates into more than 75,000 teenagers each year. A state senator from Corpus Christi calls the TEA dropout numbers "treasonous." *The Dallas Morning News* reports that the feds threatened to cut dropout-prevention funds because the Texas formula for calculating dropouts is so inaccurate.

McNeil and her Rice University researchers found a Texas Education Agency accounting system that would have done Arthur Andersen proud. Principals desperate to keep kids away from tenth-grade exit exams discovered a Never-Never Land, a special place where kids never make it to the tenth grade and never take standard exams. All they need is a waiver from the state to allow kids who failed one course in the ninth grade to stay there. These "technical ninth-graders" sometimes stay on ninth-grade enrollment ledgers for three years — if they stay in school. Sometimes, McNeil wrote, they're discouraged from taking the course they failed, which would allow them to advance.

In one Houston high school with a student body of 3,000 only 296 kids took the tenth-grade test. Barring fluctuating fertility rates, there should have been between 700 and 750 students in the tenth grade. "All our children will be tested. No one will be excluded," claimed Houston superintendent Rod Paige, the year before Bush named him secretary of education.

The kids who stick around for the tests aren't exactly reading Faulkner and solving quadratic equations. Listen to almost any teacher in the state of Texas and you'll hear a story about valuable classroom time lost to drills that prep students for the test. About art teachers compelled to drill a half hour each day for the test. About English teachers required to start every class with a drill that teaches students to underline the central ideas in short paragraphs. About testing consultants who charge a stiff fee to help principals get campus scores up by telling teachers to focus all their drilling efforts on "the bubble kids" — the ones in the small "bubble" of scores just below passing. (Forget the children at the bottom — you'll never get their scores anywhere close to the magic passing number.) About a small school district spending $20,000 on prep handbooks for the TAAS, the recently replaced Texas Assessment of Academic Skills.

Heard about *Guerrilla TAAS*? A neat little test-attack-skill handbook with a camouflage cover. "Cool," say the kids. "Cami."

There's more.

The guerrilla consultants show up at schools to lead *Guerrilla TAAS* pep rallies. They wear camouflage combat fatigues. Even the principal and assistant principals get to suit out in camouflage — all included in the price of the *Guerrilla TAAS* package.

"Hey, guys, we're going to teach you how to kick this test's butt."

Some miracle, huh?

Is there a papal nuncio in the house?

There was no place for educators like McNeil, Valenzuela, and Haney in the planning of the No Child Left Behind law (isn't it grand how a campaign scripted by a burn-their-crops-and-kill-their-children guy like Karl Rove comes up with such sweet-sounding titles for bad bills?). The Bushies believe education reform is the business of the business community.

The new law is filled with accountability standards and provisions for "sanctions" of underperforming schools. One testing-company CEO told a gathering of Wall Street analysts that Bush's education law "reads like our business plan."

No surprise.

Some critics would say the Bushies believe education law should be written not only by big business but *for* big business. This is not new. Schools have always been profit centers for publishing companies. It's no surprise that the business lobby has a pack of dogs in the education-legislation hunt. But this deal was done Texas-style. *The New Yorker*'s Nicholas Lemann worked in the Great State and understands who's in charge. After he wrote about the education law, Lemann explained Texas political culture to PBS's *Frontline*: "Clearly in Texas, I think more than nationally, business has been the prime mover behind standards. But the context there is, business runs everything in Texas more than it does nationally. I remember once, when I worked at *Texas Monthly* [in the early 1980s], the editor went on vacation, and he asked me to write the editor's column, which was in effect the editorial that month. So I wrote it, and I had some line like, 'The highest purpose of government is to help people who are unable to help themselves.' And the political writer for *Texas Monthly* went insane over that. It was really interesting. He came in and said, 'We can't publish that. We can't publish that.' And I said, 'Why is that?' He said — and this guy is a Democrat — 'Because the highest purpose of government is to help business. Everybody knows that.' "

The business-driven standards-and-accountability movement in public ed is, of course, bigger than Texas. In an article published in *The Nation* shortly after the No Child law passed Congress, Stephen Metcalf wrote that the Bush education revolution "is the culmination of a decade of educational reform spearheaded by conservatives and business leaders." Metcalf compared educational plans drawn up by the boys at the Business Roundtable to the goals Horace Mann and John Dewey defined for public education: "to fashion a common national culture out of a far-flung and often immigrant population, and to prepare young people to be reflective and critical citizens in a democratic society," wrote Mann. The father of modern American public education wanted to develop "self-governance through self-respect; a sense of cultural ownership through participation; and ultimately, freedom from tyranny through rational deliberation."

The father of education reform in Texas was no Horace Mann or John Dewey devotee. Democrats controlled Texas in 1983 when H. Ross Perot was summoned to Austin and asked to make our schools right. Perot was a quirky, data-hustling billionaire from Dallas, ordering his own hired commandos into Iran to get his employees out of trouble. He hadn't developed into the endearing caricature who ran for president in 1992. In his reform effort he did some real good. But his big goal, which he never achieved because he got into a fight with the state's football coaches (always a bad idea in Texas) was to link teacher pay to student performance. That bit of bad policy will also come later — after we field-test it in Texas.

The Perot-led outbreak of reform in Texas, which did do some good by raising standards, was driven by the business community's demand for a basic level of competence in workers. Big bidness was tired of waiting for the public schools to provide it. They wanted results, even though they weren't willing to pay for them. So they began to push for standards. If you buy the big-business plan — and a lot of people do — then you buy into the standards movement.

Our current crop of CEOs is not nearly as much fun in part because they're not charming Texcentrics like Perot. They're all business, guys like IBM chairman Lou Gerstner, who wrote *Reinventing Education: Entrepreneurship in America's Public Schools.* They believe teaching children is like running a business. You have inputs (the dollars you spend on public education) and outputs (test scores). If the test scores are high enough, graduates are ready for jobs in the low end of the labor market. Turn out enough kids with basic literacy and number skills, and the nation is positioned to compete in the global market.

Kids are "human capital," parents are "customers," and teachers are "sellers in a marketplace." The idea is to set up strategic partnerships that involve market penetration in schools. Education is all about business. When Bush invited a group of education leaders to the White House on his first day in office, the guest list read like a *Fortune* 500 CEO's Rolodex. It was an important symbolic moment that not only said, "Education First!" but also said, "We Mean Business!"

To be fair, Dubya Bush has made education his issue; he's *passionate,* as he would say. He ran on it. Made countless speeches about it. His and Rove's favorite photo op is Bush reading to a circle of small, preferably minority children. He was sitting in front of a classroom in the Emma E. Booker Elementary School in Florida when the first plane crashed into the World Trade Center.

Even if the policy experts he brought to the White House looked like the boys from the Bohemian Grove, at least Bush convened an education meeting on day one of

149

his administration. Other than Saddam Hussein and tax cuts for the rich, education reform is the only policy initiative that interests him. But he believes public education is too important to leave in the hands of principals, teachers, school administrators, and local, democratic institutions like school boards.

Read the Business Roundtable position paper *The Nation* turned up, full of warnings that "voices of opposition [to standardized testing] would emanate from parents and teachers." The "leadership and credibility of the business community is needed," say the Roundtablers, to make standardized testing standard practice in public education.

There's grassroots democratic participation in public schools for you.

Aware that his secretary of education was an unlikely candidate to explain education policy to Congress, much less get a bill passed, Bush enlisted Sandy Kress, an attorney who had served on the Dallas school board. "[Education secretary] Rod Paige was never a player," said a Senate staffer about the Rodney Dangerfield of the Bush administration. "He was so far in the background that he was almost irrelevant."*

By the time Paige was stunning senators at his confirmation hearing with a magnificently vapid opening statement and his inability to answer in depth any question about education, his successor as Houston superintendent of schools, Kaye Stripling, was already hard at work cleaning up the mess Paige had left behind. But that's another story. Bush nominates figureheads for domestic-policy positions. If you don't believe this, try to write a book about the influence labor secretary Elaine Chao has had on labor policy, or EPA director Christine Todd Whitman on environmental policy, or education secretary Paige on education policy. Paul O'Neill got serious about fiscal policy and was sent packing.

*In May 2003, Paige distinguished himself for the first time by setting off a controversy about his observations on Christian values. Paige told a reporter, "But, you know, all things being equal, I would prefer to have a child in a school where there's a strong appreciation for values, the kind of values that I think are associated with the Christian communities, and so that this child can be brought up in an environment that teaches them to have strong faith and to understand that there is a force greater than them personally."

Larry Lindsay took a hard look at the cost of going to war in Iraq, came up with $200 billion, and got sacked.

Kress is a devout education-policy reformer and policy wonk, who according to one congressional staffer "exudes so much confidence that he sometimes comes across as arrogant." He has mastered the minutiae of public-education policy. His commitment to education reform is sincere and heartfelt. "Our African-American kids in the fourth grade are doing better in math than African-American kids anywhere in the country," Kress said. "In fact they are doing better than white kids in seven states. That doesn't sound as good as it ought to. But it's better than it ever was in American history. Black kids doing better than white kids." Kress is a skilled negotiator who worked legislators on the congressional committees revising and marking up the public-ed bill. "He knew the issues and spent a lot of time with members from both parties," said a Kennedy aide. Kress had served on the board of one of the most challenging school districts in Texas, where he was far more engaged with policy than most trustees. He's also slicker than greased owl shit. "He was the guy with the plan in his briefcase," said a public-ed lobbyist.

Even so, it's nothing short of remarkable that they pulled it off.

Bush got off to a bad start on education reform when he excluded Ted Kennedy from a meeting of congressional education leaders in Austin before the inauguration. "Somebody on his staff must have thought it would be cute not to invite Kennedy," said a Senate staffer. Then he ignored Senate Health and Education chair Jim Jeffords because he was a Republican who didn't pass Karl Rove's ideological litmus test. Then Bush and Rove appointed the memorably unremarkable secretary of education.

The president's odds of passing an education-reform bill improved when his party lost control of the Senate. When Rove's arrogance drove Jeffords out of the party, Ted Kennedy became chair of Health and Education. "When Kennedy took over, we were dealing with a consummate pol and a great staff," a Bush administration official told *The Washington Post*.

Bush and Rove began to get a sense of how the Senate worked, and after having stiffed Kennedy, the president invited him to the White House to discuss education. "The president was very familiar with education issues," said a Kennedy staffer, who went on to repeat something that has appeared in

153

numerous press reports. Bush told Kennedy that reform required "disaggregation" — reporting test scores by racial, economic, and ethnic subgroups. Kennedy was impressed by the president's familiarity with the technical language of education. (As often happens with Bush, he benefits from the lowest of expectations.) Kennedy was further encouraged by Bush's promise to make sure "the neediest children get the benefit of these reforms." The senator sensed that he and the president shared some "common ground on education."

If Kennedy was sold on Bush, Bush was sold on Kennedy. The senator won the president over early on by passing up the opportunity to take a public swipe at him after their initial White House meeting. "When they were walking out, the president told Senator Kennedy. 'There are going to be a lot of reporters out there on the lawn waiting for you to attack me on vouchers,' " said a Kennedy staff member. "When the senator refused to go down that road with reporters, and said everything was negotiable, the president decided he could work with him."

"Kennedy had two goals," said a Washington education lobbyist. "To keep vouchers [which move public tax dollars to private schools] out of the bill. And to get as much money as he could for the schools."

Kennedy won the voucher fight. There's no voucher provision in the law, but there is a mechanism that moves federal tax dollars out of public schools and into the hands of for-profit, nonprofit, and faith-based "supplemental-service providers." It's part of what Paul Houston of the American Association of School Administrators describes as one of many "twists" the federal law places on the Texas model. Principals in schools that qualify for Title I money and are classified as "in improvement" must inform parents that they are eligible for school money for private remedial services. "In improvement" means one group of students, whose scores have been disaggregated from other subgroups, failed to hit their marks on standardized tests. Title I money is federal dollars dedicated to economically disadvantaged students. If one disaggregated subgroup — African-American, Hispanic, economically disadvantaged — fails to show progress on standardized tests, the school is sanctioned and must start writing checks to parents to get outside help. The checks are drawn on the school's Title I federal funds — up to $1,500 per child.

"Follow the money" as Deep Throat told Woodward and Bernstein when they were trying to fathom the Watergate scandal. Federal tax dollars go to the school, which cuts a check to the parent, who is required by law to turn it over to a supplemental-service provider. In California 113 providers were approved at the beginning of the 2002 school year — everything from the nonprofit A Thousand Points of Learning to the very-much-for-profit Sylvan Learning Center and Voyager Expanded Learning. That smells like the beginning of vouchers, on a small scale.

Identify schools as failures, order them to improve, then take away the money that will make improvement possible, said Houston of the American Association of School Administrators. It creates the potential for a public backlash against public education.[*]

[*]This backlash is precisely what the education privatizers on the extreme Republican right are after. Consider the comments made by an ideological dim bulb in the Oregon senate when the state's schools were cutting staff and reducing the number of school days by two weeks a year for lack of funding. "I tell any parent who will listen to run — not walk — to remove their children from public

"What's going to happen in two years from now when two thirds of our schools are declared as failing?" Houston asked. (Some educators predict 85 percent.) Houston sees two possible outcomes. Parents who know their school, their teachers, and their principal are going to say that, while not perfect, the school provides their children with a good education. Other parents are going to read the "report card" declaring their child's school a failure and turn against it.

Bush's failure to fund the law at the levels he agreed to when negotiating with Kennedy make the latter more likely. It was more federal money for schools that kept Kennedy in the deal when he was working with Bush to pass his education-reform bill. A year after the senator stood at Bush's side and accepted his thanks for making education reform possible, Kennedy realized he'd been had.

The Bush budget for fiscal year 2004 (written in early 2003) provided two thirds of what Bush had promised a year earlier.

---

schools. . . . Nothing could be worse for the future of America than consigning all our youths to the public education arena," said state senator Charles Starr — chair of the Senate Education Committee.

It eliminated funding for rural education, gifted-and-talented programs, small schools, and technical education. After-school programs lost $400 million. Special education, the issue that drove Vermont senator Jim Jeffords out of the Republican Party, was funded at a rate that will get it to full funding in a mere thirty-three years from the date the No Child bill became law.

But the president's budget does include money for two experimental voucher programs that will cost $5 billion, as taxpayer money is finally used to fund private schools. Outside the confines of the bill, Bush also drastically cut "impact funds" the federal government pays on a per-student basis to districts that educate children of Army, Navy, and Air Force parents. The districts get the extra federal dollars because military kids are transient, so it costs more to educate them, and because military bases are huge chunks of real estate that are off the property-tax rolls that provide school funding.

"Kennedy got rolled," said a veteran Washington education lobbyist.

The Senate voted to restore some of the funding Bush reneged on, including $1.5 billion to special education and $5 billion in Title I funds. Moderate Senate Republicans got the message from home and joined Democrats in ignoring Bush's niggardly education budget. Kress defended Bush's budget cuts, saying there is "always a difference in what's authorized and what's ultimately appropriated." Kennedy "knew better," said Kress, "and his public position is not an honorable one." Not so, said Kennedy staffer Jim Manley. "The senator expected President Bush to live up to the funding commitments he made a year earlier."

"They're spending less money on education reform than they were offering Turkey to accept U.S. troops," said Paul Houston.

The late Paul Wellstone was one of nine lonely members of the Senate to vote against Bush's bill. When these reforms kick in, Wellstone warned, school administrators are going to be "screaming 'What have they done to us?'" Less than six months after the memorial service for Paul and Sheila Wellstone, school administrators were in fact screaming. The Department of Education's advance man in New England probably owes his life to the fact that *The New York Times* education reporter attended a hearing in Vermont, where school administrators wanted blood. Did the suits in Washington really believe 100 percent of students would pass the test?

"That remains to be seen," said federal ed's man in Montpelier, Michael Sentence. "How do you defend a law that gives the federal government unprecedent[ed] control over 'failing' schools — that tells local schools when they must fire their pupils and teachers — even though it pays a small fraction [7 percent] of public education costs?"

Obviously, not very well.

The Republican chair of Vermont's House public-ed committee demanded major changes. Vermont Democratic senator James Condos asked why a state with the most successful testing-and-assessment system in the nation was being asked "to dump our education system."

"Can the federal government be flexible?"

"Probably a lot less flexible than people were looking for," Sentence said.

From New England to the Old South, school administrators received the law with the same lack of enthusiasm. An elementary school principal in the Mississippi Delta questioned the "fire the coach" logic in the law. "If we fail to show progress, the principal can be fired. They can even dismiss the teachers and superintendent." Principals dismissed from underperforming schools can only work at another underperforming campus. "Why are we going to do better at another low-performing school?" he asked.

The principal began his school year six teachers short on a campus where the classrooms are filled with some of the most economically disadvantaged children in the nation. The state accountability system took the economic levels of students into account when it tested them. Under the new federal education law, his students are expected to compete with children from Hancock County, where a NASA facility is located. "Their educational level is always going to be higher than ours. If you have children from families in the $70,000 level, it's easier to make progress. We don't have those kids. Many of our students have never been outside of this county. They've never gone on family vacations, where kids can learn so much from travel. Even with Head Start [which the Bushies are trying to dismantle] and kindergarten, they are not ready for the first grade." The critical element for these schools is money — precisely what Bush failed to deliver in his education-reform bill.

The hallways in this Mississippi school were clean, orderly, and quiet. Every classroom this veteran principal walked into (unannounced) ten minutes after the bell rang was packed full of kids either at work at their desks, gathered around a teacher who was leading a lesson, or quietly plodding through classwork. Almost every child was African-American.

The law, the principal said, fails to take into account the realities of teaching poor kids. He also repeated a criticism that is almost universal in the nation's public schools. "This law has taken away all the creative part of teaching. We teach to the test. We'd be idiots not to. But school, real education, is not just about taking tests. Teachers know that. And so do the students. The politicians don't."

This beleaguered principal has his hands full. Ninety-six percent of his students qualify for federally assisted free lunches. Ninety-five percent of the population is African-American, as white kids flee the school to attend private "acadamies." He is struggling to increase his campus test scores. And suddenly he is told he has to test his "sped" or special education kids with standardized tests prepared for their age level, rather than the their "mental age" or IQ. And the president pushing the testing has reneged on the funds needed to help the "sped" kids through testing and assist the entire population of a school full of kids facing the academic hardships created by extreme poverty.

A year after he signed it into law, Bush's education-reform program is a tougher sell than Enron stock. The business community might love it, but school administrators aren't buying. The bill that public-ed lobbyist Paul Houston and public-interest legislator Paul Wellstone bemoan as federal intrusion is greater than its many component parts because of the extraordinary leverage it gives the federal government. It is a constant Sword of Damocles hanging over the head of the principal of every school that receives Title I aid. It uses standardized tests not for their traditional use in education — to diagnose student deficits and needs and recommend remediation — but to punish the school for the students' failure. Through it, the federal government can reshape curriculum, determine who keeps jobs and who loses jobs, which campuses are funded and which campuses are shut down. All of this is achieved with a modest federal investment that turns out to be far less than promised. The funding mechanisms in the bill, for example, provided no emergency relief for the 2002–2003 collapse of Oregon's public-school system caused by a statewide budget crisis that became too bizarre for "Doonesbury" to parody. (Actually, some Oregon legislators credit Garry Trudeau with saving the school year by embarrassing the Legislature into emergency action.) The most cynical critics of the law see it as a Trojan horse by which public education will be privatized. And if all this sounds like liberal paranoia, let's all get into group therapy with the twenty-eight school superintendents from Texas who are fighting their ex-governor's No Child law.

In the end the big losers might end up being the "neediest" children Bush told Kennedy he wanted to help. They too may well be fooled twice. Once on money and once on the quality of instruction.

Since the 1970s, poor schools have been in court fighting for equity, trying to close the spending gap between poor and rich public schools. Kids from low-income families are always more expensive to educate, because they don't show up at school "ready to learn," as the first President Bush used to say. (Poppy Bush proposed funding more preschool programs to get them ready.) Poor kids almost always attend underfunded schools. So they went to court and sued for equity. In California, Texas, Illinois, and other states they finally got there. Now, just as they've arrived, these same schools are about to see their equity money siphoned away to pay private companies to teach their children.

Some kids will escape the grim, rote-and-repetition pedagogical model. Wealthy schools that don't depend on Title I federal money will continue to provide kids with an enriched curriculum and learning experiences that make schools exciting and that attract teachers who love learning. In Highland Park, Texas, in Marin County, California, and in West Palm Beach, Florida, children will be educated. In Detroit, East St. Louis, and Newark they'll be trained. Dallas congressman Sam Johnson had it figured out in the eighties, when he was a hard-ass state rep fighting education equity. "We'll give you your money," Johnson said to African-American and Mexican-American legislators. "But you'll give us our local control." Teachers in poor schools will drill them 'til they drop; teachers in rich schools will teach.

So the answer to Dubya Bush's widely quoted question "Is our children learning?" is yes. At least some of them is. If you want your child to be part of the group that is, see to it that she is middle class, preferably white (wealthy is even better), and that she attends a school where Title I is not her principal's principal preoccupation.

Who else wins with Bush's education-reform bill?

Our testing business is positioned to provide comprehensive testing at both the state and at the school district level; as states build new accountability systems to test students in grades 3–8, we will provide full service support. We are the primary assessment provider in Indiana, Colorado, and New York, three of the first five states whose accountability systems have already received federal approval. States will continue to require support in managing many aspects of their assessment and accountability systems, including research, alignment, development, production, scoring, reporting, and most importantly, tracking. We can also provide strong support for the annual yearly progress requirement and we can do that with our new Web-based tracking system and we have the software to help disaggregate the assessment data which is all so important, making sure where some of the intervention and some of the remedial initiatives need to be focused. (McGraw-Hill Earnings Conference Call, January 28, 2003)

Our newly developed sales force has been meeting with districts to review the supplemental services opportunity that's associated with the No Child Left Behind legislation. In the fourth quarter, we experienced a surge of pre-implementation activity and consequently, we expect to begin to see large-scale programs this spring, Q2. The pipeline for supplemental-service programs is growing steadily and we expect a significant increase overall in program activity by the fall of this year, which will be Q4. We're currently approved in 23 states to supply services under the act. Operating income for education solutions was $2.3 million, which is 32 percent below last year, and was expected as we reinvested in our sales force and the development of the infrastructure to support No Child Left Behind. (Sylvan Learning Systems Earnings Conference, February 20, 2003)

The devil's in the details and the profits are in the small print. "It's a great day for education, because we now have substantial alignment among all the key constituents — the public, the education community, business and political leaders — that results matter," said an educator at Bush's January 2001 White House education summit. The educator was McGraw-Hill chairman Harold McGraw.*

*The Bushes and the McGraws go way back, with family ties *The Nation* followed to the 1930s, when Joseph and Permelia Pryor Reed turned Jupiter Island, Florida, into a haven for old money from the Northeast. At times there were so many Old Yankee blue bloods on the island it seemed as though a Louis Auchincloss novel were taking place. The Meads, the Mellons, the Paysons, the Whitneys, the Lovetts, the Harrimans — and Prescott Bush and James McGraw, Jr., vacationed together.

Their relationships on nonprofit boards are as insular and incestuous as a Sunday afternoon of croquet at the Harrimans'. Harold McGraw, Jr., is on the board of the Barbara Bush Foundation for Family Literacy and just happened to win a presidential literacy award from Poppy Bush in the early nineties. The McGraw Foundation gave education secretary Rod Paige its Educator of the Year award while he was superintendent of schools in Houston. Paige delivered the keynote speech at McGraw-Hill's "government initiatives"

Six hundred sixty-six pages of legislation Paul Houston calls the largest federal intrusion in the history of public education is about to change your kids' lives, and only the publishers are pleased.

They get their cut because the law drives demand for "product." There's just not a lot of money to put in the classroom.

After the publishers gorged themselves at the public education trough, there was a

---

conference in spring 2002. Harold McGraw III and another McGraw-Hill board member served on Dubya Bush's transition team. Barbara Bush's former chief of staff left the first Bush White House to work for McGraw-Hill and is now back on Laura Bush's staff. And McGraw-Hill's former VP for global markets is John Negroponte. The same John Negroponte who was utterly blind to death squads and torture while he was U.S. ambassador to Honduras and is now back in public service as U.S. ambassador to the United Nations.

You will not be amazed to learn that McGraw-Hill became the big corporate player shaping education policy in Austin while Dubya Bush was governor of Texas. After their consultants wrote the statement of principles for the Texas Education Agency and designed the state's reading curriculum, McGraw-Hill claimed the biggest market share in the state's huge textbook market.

light dessert for the Christian right, as the Bushies linked public piety to the money they were putting into education. In February 2003 the Department of Education sent out a warning that if schools did not allow students time for "constitutionally protected prayer," they could lose their federal aid for the poor. Now, that's sure to get reading levels up.

At about the same time, Michigan got word that if it doesn't test all recently arrived immigrants with an English-language test, it will lose $1 million in federal aid. "Is it educationally sound to give a math test and say the students don't know math when they can't read the problems?" asked Michigan education commissioner Tom Watkins in a *New York Times* story. Watkins wants the "feds to come to the heartland and listen."

"They must do away with the bad and ugly in the law," he said. "It's turning into a vehicle to bash our teachers and kids."

It's bad and ugly all over, even here in Texas. Bush's first commissioner of education, now running schools in Dallas, is making the same argument Watkins did — in kinder and gentler words. "I think that the test really needs to be reviewed," Mike Moses said. "I think it's troubling . . . there may be difficulties with the test."

Moses knows it will be bad and ugly when Dallas schoolkids take the high-stakes TAKS test next year. He is one of twenty-nine superintendents petitioning the state to back off on the standardized testing.

Maybe he'll get Odell Edwards a reprieve.

If not, and Odell passes his test and makes it out of Wheatley High, he ought to buy as much McGraw-Hill common stock as he can afford.

So he won't get fooled a third time.

· 6 ·

GREEN RABBITS AND YELLOW STREAMS

The environment is incredibly important for America in the twenty-first century.
— GEORGE BUSH, IN THE TWENTIETH CENTURY (MAY 1999)

Put yourself in this situation.

It's Saturday morning in the New Jersey town where you have lived for ten years when you're suddenly jarred out of bed by an ungodly racket. You rush downstairs to check — no kids, no cartoons blasting from the television. This is from outside.

You race out and there are two TV-news helicopters circling your house. Standing next to your children, who are dressed in shorts and T-shirts, is a man in a white space suit. A newspaper photographer is aiming his Nikon at your kids, who are watching the person sealed in his protective suit take soil samples from your yard. The same yard your kids play in every day.

172

The same earth in which you plant tomatoes, radishes, and cucumbers every year. The same dust you vacuum out of the rooms in your three-story suburban house. The same dirt that ends up in the kids' mouths when they forget to wash their hands before meals.

"I was scared to death," said Gail Horvath. "I thought I was living in another Love Canal." Horvath and her husband, Alan, are raising three children in Edison, New Jersey, in a house across the railroad tracks from one of the state's 111 Superfund sites. Make that 114. The day Gail Horvath sat in her immaculate living room and recalled men in space suits digging up her neighborhood, the local paper reported three more New Jersey sites had been added to the EPA's Superfund list.

Three generations of Gail's family live across the railroad tracks from the five acres of toxic chemicals abandoned by a hazardous-waste hustler named Arnold Livingston. The late Livingston changed corporate identities faster than Christine Whitman changed policy positions. Livingston of Chemical Insecticide Corporation (CIC) was a small-time, local waste-disposal operator who achieved a rare distinction — he left behind not one but two

Superfund sites. Even by Jersey standards, that's impressive. He also left behind a reputation more toxic than the poisonous crap he so cavalierly dumped.

The more Horvath and her neighbors learned, the more they worried. "They had my kids tested for arsenic. They've had their hair cut all these years [to test for toxic substances, primarily arsenic]. Testing. Waiting for results."

When the Horvaths bought their home in 1989 they had no idea Chemical Insecticide Corporation even existed. But there had been warnings — including one twenty years earlier. In November 1969 six Black Angus cows, bulky versions of canaries in the mine, died from drinking arsenic out of the brook in Julius Yelencsics' pasture. Edison patrolman Fred Lacik investigated the cow die-off and followed his nose. A stream of "greenish color fluid along with what looked like black oil," he reported, was draining out of the CIC plant. Under the "weapons used" question on the crime-report form, Lacik typed, "Some kind of chemicals." Livingston paid a $200 fine for the croaked cows and continued cooking, mixing, and shipping pesticides and herbicides. It would be another decade before environmental activists began to use the

174

terms "chemical trespass" and "chemical assault" to describe what Livingston was doing.

State and federal environmental agencies spent years investigating all of it. One paper trail led to the Edison municipal landfill, another to a warehouse in Maine, another to a shipping facility in Florida and at last to the garage at Arnold Livingston's house. Along the way, state regulators learned that Agent Orange, the witches' brew of 2,4-D and 2,4,5-T was mixed at CIC's Edison site.*

*Agent Orange is a defoliant, a plant killer, that was used in Vietnam. The idea was that the Vietcong wouldn't be so hard to kill if we could see them better by killing the jungle canopy that protected them. Specifically, Agent Orange was a 50:50 mixture of two phenoxy herbicides, 2,4-D (2,4-dichlorophenoxy acetic acid) and 2,4,5-T (2,4,5-trichlorophenoxy acetic acid). The dioxin that makes Agent Orange so deadly isn't even an intended part of the plant killer. Dioxin is a man-made by-product of the manufacturing process for making phenoxy herbicides like Agent Orange. Actually, when 2,4,5-T is manufactured, a "synthetic contaminant," TCDD (2,3,7,8-tetrachlorodibenzo-para-dioxin), is an unwanted by-product that cannot be removed.

Dioxin, arsenic, and lead were found at all three chemical lagoons on the site. Livingston himself recalled at least one small explosion there.

None of it seemed to concern Arnie Livingston, who stored drums and sacks of chemicals beside the family station wagon in his garage. He was not so much defensive as aggressive when questioned by authorities.

Q: Can you correlate that to any ownership of dogs and their presence at —

A: I will tell you for the record, some God damn motorcyclist killed my dog. My dog was in fine shape until somebody ran over the dog on South Maple Avenue. Cut its guts out. So it wasn't any chemicals. And the dog had lived there for twelve years.

State and local authorities weren't so comfortable with Livingston's chemicals. They spent decades gathering information about the CIC site. But no one ever warned the people buying homes near or downstream from CIC — later known as Blue Spruce, Bio-Aquatic, Tifa, and other corporate identities Livingston used. Adults hunted on the abandoned site, and children played there. In the summers the kids splashed through the brooks just downstream from the chemical dumps.

One day in 1991 an ice sculptor named John Shersick and a pastry chef named Bob Spiegel were working together at a catered banquet when Shersick made Spiegel an offer he couldn't refuse. "Do you want to go out and see some green rabbits?"

Spiegel baked elaborate cakes, taught martial arts, took care of his family, and minded his business. He had never paid much attention to the environment, which can be hard to ignore in New Jersey. But green rabbits seemed so over the top that he followed Shersick to the CIC site. "The rabbits were actually green," Spiegel reported. "The dinoseb had turned the skin and the coats of the rabbits that lived around the site a green color. If it was turning the rabbits green, what was it doing to the children?" Dinoseb, which produced this startlingly verdant shade of lapin, is one of the insecticides Arnold Livingston mixed and marketed. It's also one of those delightful "better living through chemistry" products that promised to make farmwork so much easier: an insecticide that kills insects or an herbicide that kills plants.

Shersick is an environmentalist who knows his way around central Jersey's toxic hot spots. Spiegel recalls following him onto the CIC site. "Nothing grew there. It smelled of rot and decay and pesticides and death." Spiegel saw children playing, runners jogging, and homeless people sleeping on the site. He followed the same trail of greenish yellow water Fred Lacik had found to the source of the chemicals that had killed the cows twenty-two years earlier. The same greenish yellow water — colored by dinoseb — was running out of the CIC plant into a drainage ditch that emptied into a brook. Down a slope and across a parking lot is the commercial bakery that makes hamburger buns for McDonald's restaurants in New Jersey, New York, and Pennsylvania.

Into every good story about the environment must fall one major pain in the ass. And we've got ours: Bob Spiegel, the baker-environmentalist Gail Horvath calls "my man Bob." The man who dug into Arnold Livingston's files and the chemical slop-pits he abandoned behind the Horvath house. In order to become the hero/pain in the ass of an environmental saga, it is only necessary to be obsessive, compulsive, and workaholic, to have the instincts of a trained investigator, the disposition of a bloodhound, and the skill of a research librarian. It takes a pain in the ass to get bureaucrats off their butts and moving. What makes Spiegel different from the average pain in the ass is that he has a sense of humor. "The squeaking barrel gets the attention," said Spiegel, mangling a metaphor for the cause. Spiegel (and the waste sites he adopted since he saw the green rabbits hopping across Arnie Livingston's abandoned lot) gets a lot of attention. Combining plodding research and investigation with gonzo activism, he is part Ralph Nader and part Abbie Hoffman. He damn near drove the New Jersey Department of Environmental Protection, not to mention the United States EPA, out of their bureaucratic minds. Spiegel filed innumerable Freedom of Information requests for government documents. He studied the laws and the regulations. He called and wrote both elected officials and regulators.

Proceeding through official channels is necessary but not sufficient in these cases, so Spiegel also took to holding impromptu press conferences on the CIC site. He led television-news crews to toxic hot spots. He mailed the EPA videotapes of children playing in arsenic-laced brooks and sent stuffed green bunnies to members of Congress. He "borrowed" soil samples from

Arnold Livingston's property, tested them, and publicized the results. "The soil and water samples are my secret weapons," he said. "You can call and scream that you want the EPA to fix the problem. But when you tell the EPA *and reporters* about the arsenic levels you found, they pay attention." On one occasion Spiegel walked a TV-news reporter to the front door of Arnold Livingston's office and then prudently jumped out of the way when the reporter was thrown out. Commitment has its limits.

Spiegel pored over the "hot docs" he got from the EPA, patiently piecing together all the evidence, and led investigators to a buried lagoon filled with leaking fifty-five-gallon drums. Then he found yet another lagoon missed by state and federal investigators. He brought community groups and leaders into the fight to clean up CIC. He made the fight personal: the EPA was not the EPA; it was regional Superfund director Ray Basso, assigned by Spiegel to play the heavy. "Basso is not concerned about this cleanup," Spiegel told a TV reporter. Am so, replied the harried Basso.

In 1992, seven years after CIC made the Superfund's National Priorities List, a Pittsburgh contractor installed a $2-million rubber blanket over the waste lagoon, over the buried fifty-five-gallon drums, over 2,4-D and 2,4,5-T, over arsenic, lead, dinoseb, PCBs, chlordane, malathion, sodium arsenate, DDT, benzol, lindane, rotenone, propanil, sulfuric acid, acetone, caustic soda, and the rotting hay bales that had been used to soak up all the spills. They swept it all under a rubber blanket, literally covering it up.

The cap was designed to last from three to seven years. The EPA said it would return later to remove 106,000 cubic yards of soil and to refill the 17-foot-deep pit — when a site plan was ready and when funds were available.

Bob Spiegel moved on — downstream.

He started working on two arsenic-laced streams that meander through residential neighborhoods near the CIC site. With Shersick he organized the Edison Wetlands Association. State and federal envirocrats who thought they had seen the last of Spiegel were again looking at more tapes of children playing in chemical waste, TV reporters standing with Spiegel and families who lived along the contaminated streams, and newspaper stories about soil and water stats. So the EPA changed its tactics. Operating on Lyndon Johnson's theory that it's better to have your enemies "inside the tent pissin' out than outside the tent pissin' in," the agency invited Spiegel into the tent.

The EPA responded to Spiegel and Shersick with a plan to excavate the entire streambed and dig out all the contamination. Spiegel stopped them. "My God," he said, "they were going to destroy the entire brook and make it a rock garden. There would never be any turtles or fish." The EPA actually accepted advice from the Wetlands Association and made it a partner in the cleanup. The wetlands group hired an environmental engineer and an ecological consultant. They convinced the EPA to dig out only the arsenic hot spots, lowering the health risk by 90 percent and the cost almost as dramatically.

Stepping out of a drainage culvert on a fall morning, Spiegel pointed to a section of the brook that runs behind the Edison Glen condos. The water in the stream is clear. The banks are covered with native hardwoods, shrubs, and grasses. EPA contractors and the Wetlands Association even hauled in deadwood and placed it where trees would have fallen if a storm had blown them down. Together they designed, engineered, and rebuilt a beautiful riparian area. "A model cleanup," the EPA proclaimed. Except for a few rip-rapped hot spots along the banks, the brook looks as it might have when a kid named Thomas Edison wandered around it 150 years ago.

At dusk on the same fall day when Bob Spiegel showed off the clear creek, a few hundred feet downstream Livingston's abandoned CIC site still sits, eerie. Acres of black rubber sheeting covered with disintegrating black sandbags are scattered along the seams. A rock perimeter dike is covered with thick, black cloth. Black plastic lies atop a ten-foot-deep ditch. Black fifty-five-gallon drums stand in formation. It is a giant shroud, patched and leaking, mourning the dead acres. At the end of a hot September day, the degrading rubber cap can't contain the fumes. The air is infused with a dense, sweet chemical odor that clings to your palate and wears at your airways.

From the top of a rotting observation platform you can see an EPA sign that proclaims DAYS WORKED 312 — LOST TO INJURIES 0. You can also see the second story of Gail Horvath's house and the Metroplex Bakery that makes the buns for McDonald's. Only one of the trailers backed up at the loading docks bears the golden arches logo. After news reports of yellow-green fluid oozing across the bakery's parking lot, the Ronald McDonald party wagon disappeared from the bakery, as did most of the trailers with the golden arches on their sides. In a video Spiegel delivered to local TV-news directors, even the snow in the bakery parking lot was green. On August 2, 2002, New Jersey's *Star-Ledger* reported, "Ambient air used in the bakery's production process is a potential for human exposure to contaminants."

Not good publicity for McDonald's.

In the late 1980s six bakery employees died of cancer. They lived in different neighborhoods, led separate lives. "The only thing they had in common was working at that bakery," said Ed Herman, a plaintiff's lawyer from Princeton. In 1992 he filed a lawsuit on behalf of the six widows and lost. Ten years later the loss still gnaws at him. "There were more people who wanted to sue," said Herman. "People with cancer were coming out of the woodwork." An Edison cop walked away from his home and his mortgage after being diagnosed with a rare form of leukemia. His wife later developed cancer as well.

"We would have had to do an epidemiological study," said Herman. "It would have cost our firm more than a million dollars." He consulted with big firms that had tried toxic tort cases and was told his was a long shot. "We spent a lot of money, about two hundred fifty thousand dollars, spinning our wheels to try to get these people the money they deserved for their losses. Bottom line was, without the study we couldn't prove the chemicals were linked to the cancers." (This is precisely the kind of lawsuit that is now almost impossible to file in Texas after two rounds of "tort reform" pushed by Governor George W. Bush.)

"I was convinced then and I am convinced today that the chemicals on that property had something to do with those cancers," said Herman. "It was such a high number. Too many people got too many types of cancer. The idea that the cancer wasn't caused by the chemicals is too cute for me."

"Sometimes what you don't know *can* hurt you," said Bob Spiegel.

What's in the ground under the black rubber blanket at CIC can hurt the residents of Edison — and anybody who might happen to eat a blue crab caught downstream in the Raritan River. Buried in the

EPA files is the transcript of a deposition so startling it's a wonder the court reporter didn't note in parentheses "(sound of lawyers' jaws dropping)."

In July 1983 Arnold Livingston was sitting at a table in a nondescript state office in Trenton, his attorney at his side, being questioned by the director of New Jersey's Office of Cancer and Toxic Substances Research. Late in the afternoon of a daylong session, Livingston's attorney stopped the process, warning investigators that they were "about to run afoul of National Security laws or regulations." Questioning could not continue without approval from deputy assistant secretary of the Air Force Lloyd Moseman.

When the Air Force called back to OK the questioning, Arnold Livingston related this story. While he was operating a mixing shack and four chemical slop-pits in a residential neighborhood in New Jersey, he was under contract with the United States Air Force. He had been hired to dispose of the Agent Orange that never got sprayed on the jungles in Vietnam.

He further testified that surplus Agent Orange, by then a known carcinogen, was being remixed and shipped to Brazil for use as an agricultural defoliant. Further, the Air Force was using the Rockefeller Foundation as a go-between for the military and operators like Livingston. The Air Force decided Livingston, the Rockefeller Foundation, and South America were the perfect disposal route for the defoliant associated with cancer in thousands of American servicemen and countless Vietnamese soldiers and civilians.* What didn't go to Brazil was sent to Surinam and Venezuela. "I thought it was a good idea to save the U.S. government a great deal of money and do a great amount of good for the political situation for the United States and South America," Livingston explained.

Program directors at the Rockefeller

---

*The following conditions, according to Congressman Bernie Sanders' website, are recognized for service connection for Vietnam vets exposed to Agent Orange: chloracne (a skin disorder), porphyria cutanea tarda, acute or subacute peripheral neuropathy (a nerve disorder), and numerous cancers (non-Hodgkin's lymphoma, soft-tissue sarcoma, Hodgkin's disease, multiple myeloma, prostate cancer, and respiratory cancers, including cancers of the lung, larynx, trachea, and bronchus). In addition, Vietnam veterans' children with the birth defect spina bifida are eligible for certain benefits and services.

Foundation knew Livingston because they had been helping him move his business operations to the Amazon — in the name of economic development in South America. The Air Force knew him as a producer of Agent Orange during the Vietnam War. Livingston admitted he had dumped Agent Orange waste in the Edison municipal dump. He told investigators he didn't recall warning workers who handled the product that it could cause cancer. He vented all his mixing sheds into the residential area, with no emissions protections. After telling his story, he even described himself as a victim of environmental hysteria.

The scheme was so outrageous, it is worth quoting Livingston's description in full:

In essence, the Air Force, U.S. Air Force had I think about four or five million gallons of Agent Orange at two locations. One out in Johnson Island in the Pacific and the other one was in Gulfport, Mississippi, at a naval facility. Some of the containers that they had there were leaking. Some of the containers I recall had been repackaged several times. The Air Force was looking at various alternatives to dispose of the material. They included various things and a lot of them were considered objectionable for a variety of reasons. It struck me in working on this thing that there would be a very good use for this material if it was reformulated and planned to ship the material, subject to approval of the plan, down to — it was either a refinery or a chemical plant down in northern Brazil.

A major educational program would be undertaken in the areas where brushland was to be reclaimed and good grazing land was to be made. The Rockefeller Foundation would handle all the training down there. . . . We would handle all of the chemical work, all the supplies and provide backup service in the field.

Livingston assured state investigators the Agent Orange he handled was not shipped to the CIC plant — by then called the Blue Spruce plant. Livingston had testified earlier that he mixed Agent Orange for use in Vietnam. The investigators didn't seem to buy it. The dioxin at the CIC site meant Agent Orange was either shipped, stored, or dumped there. When he was asked how dioxin got to the site, Livingston said he didn't have "the slightest idea." What didn't make it to Brazil wound up in the ground at Edison, New Jersey.

In the photo hanging behind his executive desk, a tanned, wiry, George Spadoro is dwarfed by a ruddy, pudgy Bill Clinton. Like Clinton, the Democratic mayor of Edison can be a one-question interview. Ask one, you get a disquisition. Spadoro began his career with hazardous waste. Just out of law school, he was working pro bono with a group cleaning up the infamous Kin-Buc waste dump — a regional chemical slop-pit on the banks of the Raritan River.

At ninety words a minute, Spadoro described getting Kin-Buc on the Superfund Priorities List, and the importance of the containment bulkheads that now keep PCBs out of the Raritan River, and the on-site treatment plant that pumps leachate out of clean water and back into the ground. "Kin-Buc is a Superfund success. Now we are building an esplanade there. A park on the river. It's a cleanup site that returned to its proper use."

Spadoro explained that there were "RP's" at Kin-Buc — responsible parties the feds could bill for the cleanup. Waste

Management, Inc., paid $100 million to restore that site. But Arnold Livingston is dead, and so the Edison dump is an "orphan site." Cleanup of orphan sites was paid for by the Superfund Trust, which was in turn funded by a tax on the chemical industry. New Jersey townships can't take on these huge cleanups, said Spadoro. They're even too big for the states. Only the federal government has the money and muscle for projects this size.

The Superfund tax had been in place since Jimmy Carter signed it into law in 1980. In 1995 it was was killed as part of Newt Gingrich's "Contract with America." Bill Clinton tried twice but couldn't get the Republican Congress to reinstate the tax. Even if it was expensive, the Superfund Trust is what Texans call "good bidness." The chemical industry had used the nation's wetlands as a hazardous-waste dump for decades. Then the industry was billed to clean up the mess it left behind, and for fifteen years, it worked fine. Of course, it worked slowly. Initially, the oil industry, also responsible for much of the toxic dumping, was to have been included in the tax, but big oil has so much clout it muscled its way out of the tax by threatening to kill the whole program if it was included.

In 1995, when the Republicans killed it, the Superfund Trust had $3.3 billion left in it and bills coming due. By 2002 it was down to $100 million. Superfund, in other words, is no longer a fund. Bush could have picked up some easy environmental points on this one, but both he and Christine Whitman oppose reinstating the tax.

Reporters who covered his campaign in 2000 asked the wrong questions. Bush has a chemical-dependency problem, but it's not cocaine. It's Monsanto, Dow, and Union Carbide. They wrote the checks that put him in the Texas governor's mansion. During Bush's final legislative session, his staff passed an ersatz environmental bill designed to "make Bush green." It was written by an industry lobbyist, and the green turned out to be oil-and chemical-industry money. The voluntary emissions-control bill was a spectacular failure. No one volunteered, and toxic emissions were not reduced. The Texas Legislature canned the thing in its first post-Bush session.

In 2002 Christine Whitman announced her solution for the dwindling cleanup fund. She defunded eighty-nine Superfund sites in thirteen states. One of them sits in Gail Horvath's backyard. It would cost $60 million to remove the rubber cap and dig up the contaminated soil there, more than half the money left in the trust. The United States government is not, obviously, a responsible party.

"For us, this is the second time around," said Spiegel. When Whitman was governor, she cut the state's Department of Environmental Enforcement's budget and allowed polluters to propose their own alternative if they could prove the state's cleanup plan was too expensive. She ended unannounced inspections of polluters and suppressed state-agency reports that warned of high pollution levels. Perfect woman for the job at Bush's EPA. It's not just the orphan sites that are being abandoned here. Under the Superfund law, polluters are ordered to clean up their waste sites. If they fail, the EPA does the job — and then bills the company triple damages. That's a dandy incentive, but it disappears when there's no money for the feds to do the cleanup. "It's a hollow threat," says Spiegel. So Superfund-site cleanup is likely to stop not just at orphan sites but even where there are responsible parties.

"The cleanup at orphan sites has effectively been stopped," said Spadoro. "The industries were paying a relatively small fee to clean up a problem they had created."

The mayor has been playing the game long enough to know that Bush's promise to pay for Superfund cleanup out of general appropriations means nothing. The deficits, the recession, the tax cuts, and the wars have dried up the funds. Every year, he said, cities will be fighting for general-appropriations money to clean up their own sites. Spadoro may sue the EPA; the city's legal department is looking into it. But even if Edison wins, that means some other site in New Jersey — the state with the highest number of Superfund sites and the nation's highest cancer rate — loses.

Gail Horvath understands that. "I saw a woman on TV the other night," she said. "She said she wanted her site cleaned up. I see her and I want to get greedy. I want my site cleaned up. But why am I against her? I don't want to see someone else's site not cleaned up because my site is."

Spadoro, the pol, sees it as a straight payback. The chemical and waste-disposal industry guys, who helped pick up the tab for Bush's campaign and convention, are getting what they paid for. Jersey is a state where watching patronage and political payoffs is a spectator sport, but Spadoro thinks payback politics should stop when lives are at stake. "I recognize that political payoffs happen. But there's got to be some morality, some integrity. There's got to be some decency in these things."

Said Horvath, "You see this neighborhood? This is not sitting in President Bush's backyard. It's not in his yard. This is not happening in Christie Whitman's house. If they had to live in my house, maybe they would make a different decision. Come live in my house, come live with my children. Then say there is not enough money to clean up the Superfund site behind my house."

Political causes come into vogue and then pass from fashion. People are dying nowadays from fresh horrors — terrorism, anthrax, SARS, deranged kidnappers. Hey, toxic-waste dumps — that's so ten minutes ago. The media and the public's attention have moved on. No one has even considered putting toxic waste under Homeland Security laws. And you must admit, cancer is not a spectacular death. It could be decades before children who grew up around Arnie Livingston's chemical dump get cancer. If they would just turn bright green in the meantime . . .

•7•

Kill the Messenger

*The solution is not to eliminate the
federal role in protecting the environment.
The solution is reform — reform that
sets high standards.*
— Governor George Bush,
August 2000

*He fired the best and most decent
man that ever worked at the EPA.*
— Marie Flickinger, April 2002

"I had run out of hope."

That's how Marie Flickinger felt in 1992 after she learned that an EPA contractor was fixing to incinerate toxic sludge on the site of the abandoned Brio Refinery, right in the heart of her neighborhood. Flickinger, who had studied the cleanup plan up one side and down the other, was desperately worried about the threat to the elementary school, the hospital, and the junior-college campus nearby. The toxic sludge in the neighborhood was bad enough, she thought; how the hell could the EPA think about making it worse?

Flickinger had researched the birth defects, the miscarriages, and the spontaneous abortions that seemed like an epidemic in the residential subdivision near Brio. She had watched Little Leaguers walk off the baseball diamond near the site with their cleats covered with a chemical tar. She had smelled the malodorous black substance seeping from driveways.

The EPA was prepared to incinerate 245,000 tons of toxic sludge left by Monsanto, Atlantic Richfield, and other corporate citizens in the soil of a fifty-eight-acre site, twenty miles south of downtown Houston.

Flickinger is the maverick publisher of a community weekly newspaper. She never quite got it that the function of a small-town paper is to sell ads. Once the ads are sold, the paper is supposed to recap the city council meetings, write about high school sports, and keep the community informed of important birthdays, weddings, and funerals. Instead, Flickinger used the *South Belt–Ellington Leader* to report on the problems with the EPA's plan. The agency, she argued, hadn't done a proper site characterization. They didn't know what was in the soils and sludge they were preparing to burn. They didn't know where the sludge pits were. They hadn't tested for metals. And they hadn't looked carefully at the birth defects and miscarriages in the neighborhoods near the abandoned refinery.

According to the EPA, the site was used for "by-product recycling, copper catalyst regeneration, and petrochemical recovery." Sediment was cleaned out of industrial and refinery tank bottoms; anything that was reusable was extracted. Styrene and vinyl-chloride tars were stored in open, unlined ponds waiting for processing. All this was done in one of the state's environmental hot zones, where the Great State's Bermuda Triangle of Superfund sites overlaps Houston's Bubba Belt. As they put it in Southeast Texas, "A lot of dangerous chemical shit was boiled, baked, buried, and slopped across about fifty-eight acres of black gumbo swamp on the edge of Mud Gully. Then the bakers and sloppers upped and hauled ass." Five thousand families lived very close to the site they left behind.

The experts at the EPA had figured out the problem, said Flickinger, but their solution was all wrong. Their plan to dig up the sludge and burn it was a greater public-health threat than leaving it all in the ground. At the Brio site, you didn't need a weatherman to know which way the wind blows. You just followed your nose. The earth regularly belched to relieve itself of the chemicals brewing together under the ground. Toxic air emissions drifted through residential neighborhoods, the playgrounds, the school yards, and the junior-college campus. Common sense — but not the EPA report on the site — indicated that digging up the pits would increase the problem, and that burning the sludge on-site would in turn create another round of deadly emissions.

"The EPA wouldn't listen to us," Flickinger said. "They treated us like hysterical housewives." By 1992, all Flickinger had to show for her five-year fight over the Brio Superfund site were warnings from local advertisers that the *South Belt–Ellington Leader* was the problem. It was causing "bad publicity" for the South Houston community.

"Bad publicity!" Flickinger said. "The EPA was getting ready to burn toxic material in a residential neighborhood, and they didn't even know what they were burning."

When a botched EPA cleanup plan threatens your life and the lives of your neighbors, who you gonna call?

Flickinger called EPA national ombudsman Bob Martin.

She said she was beyond "out of hope" when she made the call to the ombudsman's Washington office. She had already tried this route, when Martin's predecessor, Robert Knox, was in charge, and she had gotten nowhere. She had tossed Knox's number in the trash. The regional EPA office continued to ignore her and her neighbors.

Then providence took a little role. One morning Flickinger dragged herself to work, feeling beaten down by the EPA and resigned to a plume of toxic smoke drifting through her neighborhood. On the ground in front of the *Leader*'s office Dumpster was the crumpled business card of Robert Knox. She had nowhere else to turn, and the scrap of paper beckoned her to call. She decided to give it one more try.

This time Bob Martin answered the phone.

A Makah Indian from Washington State, Martin spent the eighties directing an association of Indian tribes that own mineral-rich lands. He represented Indians in environmental fights in court and before administrative agencies. He ran his own environmental cleanup company. Working as an environmental lawyer for Native Americans, Martin learned a good deal not only about environmental advocacy but also about the nature of the federal bureaucracy. When Robert Knox left the ombudsman job, Bob Martin applied and was hired at the end of George H. W. Bush's presidency.

By the time Flickinger called, Martin already had some sense of how the agency worked. After two weeks on the job he had gone to Pennsylvania to look into complaints about an EPA cleanup. He went to meetings. He listened to the concerns of the people living near a Superfund site and was appalled by the agency's contempt for the community. "I used to think that the government mistreated only Indians," he said at one public meeting. "I now know they mistreat all Americans." That quote made the newspapers. The next day an EPA administrator walked into Martin's office and handed him a letter of retraction to sign. "I told him that was exactly what I said. I can't retract it," Martin said. His refusal to sign the letter was a small gesture, but it affirmed the independence of the office established by Congress precisely to be independent.

The office wasn't much. Martin had a staff of four, an annual budget of $100,000, and a toll-free phone line. Yet the ombudsman fielded over four thousand complaints a year. His is — or was — an office whose sole authority lay in issuing reports in response to complaints from people who believe the EPA is not responding; or is responding on the cheap and not properly cleaning up a site; or is responding with a cleanup that puts a community at risk. By the time George W. Bush took the oath of office, Martin had more than one hundred active cases.

Martin said the unusual office was created as a result of an unusual circumstance: "Provision 113 of the Superfund Act states that once the bureaucracy makes a decision on remediation of a Superfund site, no court in the land can hear any challenge to the case until the remediation is complete. There is no judicial review. So if the agency makes a mistake, the only recourse the public has, the only recourse members of Congress responding to constituent complaints have, is the office of the ombudsman." The power of that office derives from its independence from EPA interference.

Over lunch in late April 2002 Martin talked in a quiet voice in a restaurant full of loud Washington suits. "Precluding judicial review is very rare in America. If you are going to have 113-H, you need to have a balancing factor that provides due process for the American people. That factor in the EPA's administrative process is the national ombudsman's office. That process *was* the office of the ombudsman."

The process worked for Marie Flickinger.

For years everyone at the EPA had treated her "like a bloomin' idiot," she reported. She had a hard time imagining that anyone at the agency would treat her differently. "I called Bob Knox and got Bob Martin. I figured he thought I was some kind of nut, raising hell with the agency. I thought he was going to patronize me.

"I told him we had court documents," Flickinger said. The court records Flickinger found suggested that the EPA task force members had altered their documents. Flickinger had read transcripts and depositions of private lawsuits filed against companies whose waste was processed at Brio. She had looked at state-agency records and talked to the men who had worked on the site characterization. She had even

203

climbed into a school-district Dumpster and learned the school-district newsletter was written by an attorney working for one of the companies responsible for the waste at the Brio site. To avoid a public panic, the school district was refusing to allow students to transfer away from the school near the Brio site. She concluded that the site map was incorrect because a man who had bored sample holes told her he was working thirteen inches from a backyard, not seventy-eight, as the EPA claimed. Ultimately, she proved that the waste extended under the houses.

She told Martin about the thirteen neighborhood pregnancies that had ended in horrible birth defects, about children born with genitalia that were neither male nor female. She told him the EPA's Brio report didn't mention mercury, but she had found a Monsanto document that asked what had happened to the mercury.

Martin surprised her. He told her he was coming down to have a look at the site. When he called back to tell her the EPA wouldn't pay for a plane ticket, Flickinger offered to buy him one. Martin suggested instead that they meet at an EPA conference in Dallas. Flickinger showed up in Dallas with a book of documents that convinced Martin the agency had failed.

"I own a newspaper, so I had an advantage few people have," Flickinger said. But the *Leader*'s twelve-thousand-reader circulation and a small coalition of local activists were no match for the EPA. Without Martin there was no way to stop the agency's plan to burn vinyl chloride, dioxins, PCBs, and a host of other toxins catalogued as "tentatively identified compounds." The agency also didn't know there was mercury in the Brio pits until Flickinger put Martin onto a Monsanto paper trail that led to a mercury-waste stream. "You can't burn mercury," Flickinger said. "You change it to a gas, but you don't destroy it.

"They were going to do this in the middle of a community of seventy thousand people, near a hospital, near schools," Flickinger said. "We were going to have to close the college [San Jacinto Junior College] down. Waste Management had built an incinerator. When Bob issued his report, that sucker was ten days from starting to burn waste. And they didn't even know what was in the waste they were going to burn. The incinerator was torn down. It never burned a teaspoonful."

Today the Brio site is sealed off behind a fifty-foot-deep concrete wall, covered with a gas containment layer and studded with air-monitoring devices and vents that capture toxic-gas eruptions. Standing water and groundwater is pumped and treated, which has lowered the level of toxins in the bodies of fish caught in Clear Creek. The creek had the highest trace amounts of volatile substances ever detected in fish tested in the United States. (We believe the greatest geographical misnomers in Texas are Clear Lake and Fort Bliss.) An elementary school and 677 homes that were also contaminated have been abandoned.

Brio was Martin's first big case, and he used it to expand and define the powers of an office that was almost an experiment when he drew his first paycheck.

By the time George W. Bush appointed New Jersey governor Christine Todd Whitman EPA administrator, Martin had worked with EPA directors appointed by the elder George Bush and Bill Clinton. He had been at odds with all of them — most recently with Democrat Carol Browner over a controversial incinerator in East Liverpool, Ohio. It was all part of the job. As the Bush administration began to take shape, it was obvious that Whitman wasn't a real player. Early on, she was so often blown away at cabinet meetings that secretary of state Colin Powell began to call her "the wind dummy."* Eleven months after Whitman was appointed, she finally got her feet on the ground and made a decision.

She got rid of Bob Martin.

In November 2001 she ordered her deputy administrator to inform Martin that she was moving the ombudsman's office inside the agency, where it would be under the control of the inspector general. A Government Accounting Office report issued months earlier had recommended greater independence for the office. The report was ignored.

Martin took Whitman to court. And won. At least, he got to win for a while. Federal judge Richard Roberts handed down a temporary restraining order barring Whitman from closing the independent ombudsman's office and moving it into the agency's Office of Inspector General. The inspector general, it should

*A wind dummy, according to Secretary of State (and former general) Powell, is an inflatable dummy combat pilots toss from an open hatch to gauge wind direction and velocity over landing zones.

be noted, answers to the director of the EPA.

The restraining order was shorter than the leash Whitman wanted to put on Martin. In April 2002, Judge Richard Roberts concluded that Martin had not exhausted his administrative remedies. Until he did, the federal courts were not the appropriate forum to hear his case. Martin would have to appeal first to the Merit Review Board, then return to court. Whitman was in no mood to wait. Martin was out of town on EPA business when Whitman seized not only the moment but also 140 file boxes from Martin's office containing information about cases Martin was working on.

"They came in like storm troopers," said Hugh Kaufman, the chief investigator in the ombudsman's office. Along with the case files, agents from the inspector general's office removed all computers and telephones. In order to make sure Martin couldn't soldier on with only his cell phone and a laptop, the raiders changed the locks on the ombudsman's office door.

Who says Christine Todd Whitman wasn't capable of decisive action in the two and a half years she spent at EPA?

After the raid, Martin was ordered to

report to work in the inspector general's office. He could have continued to draw his $118,000 salary by answering a hot line, but he chose to resign. Under the inspector general, the ombudsman no longer has any independence, or control of budget or staff. He would be working for the agency he was supposed to be watchdogging. Martin said he could not surrender the ombudsman's independence. In fact, he was slightly emphatic: "Never, never, never, never."

During our interview at a restaurant overlooking a turning basin off the Potomac, Bob Martin looked like an unmade bed. He had spent the previous night and early morning poring over the legal papers his attorneys had drafted in response to Whitman's raid on his office. Martin is a bear of a man with long hair that frames a strong face. In a sport coat with no tie, he looked like anything but a high-level Beltway bureaucrat. He had been fired while he was on the road and returned home to find his office sacked and his lawyers waiting to meet him. He spoke of all this with a calm, quiet authority that must have been useful during the years he spent fighting bureaucrats. "I would not accede to [working in the inspector general's office]," he said. "I would never destroy the office we worked to build. So they had to resort to a bold power move."

Martin claimed Whitman wanted his job because he had gone to the press about her husband's conflict of interest concerning the Shattuck Superfund site in south Denver. Citigroup owns the Shattuck site. Until recently, Whitman's husband, John, worked for Citigroup. He had received a substantial bonus from Citigroup the previous year. At the time of this writing he is working for a venture-capital group that was a spin-off from Citigroup Capital. While Bob Martin was meeting with Shattuck community groups in Denver, John Whitman owned $250,000 in Citi stock.

In Denver's Overland Park neighborhoods, Martin had found that Shattuck was one of a dozen Denver Superfund sites where radioactive metals had been processed. The sealed pit in the working-class neighborhood was the only site where the EPA left the radioactive waste in the ground. Shattuck's residential neighbors claimed the buried waste was the source of radioactive water in the North Platte River and in the groundwater surrounding the site. They wanted the material excavated and hauled away.

Martin was pushed out before he could finish what he had started at Shattuck. He didn't cash in on his years of experience at the EPA. He's now directing a nonprofit environmental-advocacy group in Florida. "I've even picked up some of the clients I had when I was at the EPA," he said.

The neighborhood groups Bob Martin worked with in Denver prevailed. A year after he left Washington, the radioactive waste that was leaching into the water was being hauled away. Citigroup was picking up only $7 million of the estimated $35 million cost to remove soil contaminated by a half century of processing radium and by making chemicals that contained uranium, molybdenum, and rhenium. Call Bob Martin in Tallahassee, and he'll tell you the cost of the Shattuck cleanup will be much higher than $35 million. In his lawsuit, he alleges the cleanup agreement approved by the EPA will save Citigroup between $30 and $100 million.

Citi's gain will be the taxpayers' loss.

Citigroup is a huge company that seems to own part of everything, and there was nothing to suggest that John Whitman was involved in decisions regarding Shattuck. Christine and John Whitman have both denied any impropriety. Still, the close ties between Christine and John Whitman, Citigroup, and the Shattuck dump wouldn't pass the smell test even in Texas, where we're used to bidness and politics sleeping in the same bed and feeding at the same public trough. In the end, the EPA's inspector general issued a report clearing Whitman of all conflict charges. (The inspector general did, of course, work for her.)

But that's another story. It's easy to lose sight of the permanent damage being done. Busting the ombudsman was a small part of a big plan that began with Ronald Reagan, continued with Newt Gingrich, and now is in the hands of Bush & Cheney. The dirty secret is that the Superfund isn't super anymore. What was once a $3.8 billion trust bottomed out $28 million in 2003 — not even enough to cover one of the hundreds of abandoned sites in the country. The money's gone. In 1995 Newt Gingrich killed the special tax on chemical companies that had provided money for the Superfund since 1980. Bill Clinton couldn't persuade a Republican Congress to reinstate it. And they'll be serving beer in Lubbock (which has been dry since Prohibition) before Dubya Bush proposes a tax on chemical companies.

Superfund cleanups are now paid for by general revenue — that is, by you and me rather than the chemical and oil companies who made the mess. Martin was sent packing because an independent ombudsman could force the EPA to work on sites it is required by law to clean up, and to find the money to do so. It's tough to cut taxes when people believe the money might be better spent cleaning up the radiation waste across the street from where they live.

So who, other than Christine Whitman, might have wanted Bob Martin out of the picture, and wanted the ombudsman's office neutered? Near the end of Martin's lawsuit, Judge Roberts asked the lawyer representing the EPA for his consent to extend the temporary restraining order for a week. It was a request so routine that most lawyers answer with a nod. "I don't have the authority to make that decision," said the lawyer defending the agency against Martin's suit. The lawyer who lacked the authority to make a pro forma decision wasn't the EPA in-house counsel you would expect in an employee-sues-boss case. It was assistant attorney general Robert McCollum, who answers to John Ashcroft and two elected officials: Dick

Cheney and George W. Bush.

Every crime has its motive, and there is an explanation for the crime the Bushies perpetrated against the American people by destroying the ombudsman's office.

Ten years earlier, when Marie Flickinger finally had the EPA on the run, she got word from a local lawyer that EPA administrator William Reilly would be in town and would like to meet with her. The lawyer told her someone from Baker Botts had talked the EPA chief into coming down to Brio. Flickinger didn't graduate from Yale Law; she graduated from high school in Council Bluffs, Iowa, but there's no slack in her rope. She knew that the law firm that had arranged for the EPA director to come to Houston was the same firm that represented many of the industries that dumped their waste at Brio. "Baker Botts!" she said. "They represent the polluters." Flickinger was on vacation when the EPA chief came to Houston. She saw no reason to change her plans.

The political spectrum in America isn't from left to right. It's from top to bottom. Marie Flickinger knows up from down as well as Baker Botts and Bush & Cheney. The EPA ombudsman worked for the people on the bottom. Dubya Bush's administration —

like his daddy's — works for the people on top. Therein lies the motive for the killing of the ombudsman.

"There are things you can do when you have power," said Hugh Kaufman, who has been at the EPA since Richard Nixon created the agency in 1970. "But you don't do them — because of the harm they can cause a year, two years, or five years down the line." Kaufman helped write the Superfund law, and when Ronald Reagan tried to undermine the Superfund program, Kaufman's whistleblowing sent one EPA official into retirement and another to jail. (Reagan's EPA administrator, Anne Gorsuch, resigned and the Superfund program administrator, Rita Lavelle, did six months in jail and five years' community service after Kaufman revealed they were diverting Superfund money to Republican Party supporters.) Whitman's dismantling of the ombudsman's office is precisely the sort of thing a public official with power can do — but shouldn't.

"This is such a loss," says Flickinger. "Without Bob that office is going to be a joke." She's right, unless the new ombudsman, Peggy Boyer, was joking when she said, "The ombudsman's job is not to monitor, and when people have questions,

215

provide answers." Boyer was responding to the whining neighborhood environmentalists living around Denver's Shattuck Superfund site.

"I don't even know where to call," said Deb Sánchez. With her husband and two children, she lives three hundred feet from Shattuck's radioactive pit. She has years invested in a fight to get the waste out of her neighborhood.

Every Superfund site has a Deb Sánchez, or a Bob Spiegel, or a Marie Flickinger pushing the government to do the right thing in their neighborhoods. But this administration has disconnected the last-hope number you used to be able to call.

• 8 •

READY TO EAT?

*Did I keep last year's resolution to
eat less cheeseburgers? The answer
is, yes, to the extent that I'm now
comfortable in having a
cheeseburger today.*
— GEORGE W. BUSH AT
THE COFFEE STATION, CRAWFORD,
TEXAS, DECEMBER 31, 2002

Rittenhouse Square, six blocks southwest of
Philadelphia's City Hall, looks like some elegant sliver of Manhattan. Art students
sketch the Romanesque façade of Holy
Trinity Church. Old chess players share
wooden benches with young lovers. Strollers
cross the diagonal walkways in one of the
five squares set aside by William Penn for his
Greene Country Towne. The statue of "Billy
Penn" himself is perched safely atop City
Hall, and had he been placed facing a
slightly different direction, the great Quaker

217

would have been able to gaze down on Dr. Frank Niemtzow taking his daily walk around the square with his wife, Rosalie. The doctor lived in the elegant Dorchester, two buildings west of Holy Trinity. In 2002 he was ninety-eight years old and still completely with-it; if a ninety-eight-year-old can be said to be spry, Dr. Niemtzow was. He graduated from medical school in 1928, served in World War II, and invested most of his life's energy in a medical practice in Freehold, New Jersey. There, in 1949, he delivered and then attended to the sore throats and earaches of a child named Bruce Springsteen, just as he had delivered and attended to hundreds of other children born in that small corner of the USA. After sixty years of practice in Jersey, Frank and Rosalie retired to the Rittenhouse Square high-rise. In winters they closed up the Philadelphia condo and opened their house on Longboat Key in Florida. Rosalie died in 1996, but six years later the doorman of the Dorchester was still watching over the doctor as he crossed Eighteenth Street so he could walk in the park or soak up the sun while sitting on one of the wooden benches engraved with the names of Philadelphia's Jewish and Gentile aristocracy. Frank Niemtzow missed his wife, but his children, and their children, lived nearby.

It was a wonderful life.

In August 2002 Dr. Niemtzow was admitted to Presbyterian Hospital at the University of Pennsylvania with a liver infection. For a man two years this side of one hundred, he was remarkably resilient. "Eat lots of protein," his doctor told him as he was being sent home to recover. This was sound advice, but it plunged Dr. Niemtzow into a medical nightmare as bad as anything he had ever confronted in his small family practice.

Listeria is a common bacterium. So common it is found in the soil under the Rittenhouse Square gardens, carried by the dogs that walk through the park and the cats that graze the trash barrels behind the upscale restaurants just off the square. For the most part, *listeria* is as harmless as it is commonplace. But *Listeria monocytogenes* is a nasty bug — the strain you want to avoid. It is psychrophilic; it thrives in cold. In your refrigerator *Listeria* is as robust as the green-black mold growing on that chunk of parmigiano you bought two years ago. Once you eat it, it's like a time bomb; it can take up to two months in your body before it makes you sick. If your immune system is suppressed, if you are pregnant, if you are very old or very young, just a small amount of it can kill you.

Frank Niemtzow was careful about what he ate. He was Jewish and avoided pork, and he did not eat the fatty foods that have turned us into a high-cholesterol nation. When the doctor at Presbyterian told him to eat lots of protein in order to rebuild the strength the liver infection had cost him, the old family practitioner doubled up on prepared, ready-to-eat deli turkey. What could be safer? Soon he was back in the hospital. When a doctor specializing in infectious diseases told him he had listeriosis, Niemtzow, who knew a good deal about public health, was shocked. He couldn't imagine how he had been exposed to the bacteria. When he learned he had contracted the disease by eating "ready-to-eat" turkey from one of two regional meat-processing plants infested with *Listeria*, he thought it a piece of bad luck.

It was much worse than that.

The industry doesn't want you to know it, but "ready-to-eat" meat is not ready to eat. A USDA website warns that ready-to-eat meats — cold cuts — if not thoroughly cooked, are a risk to pregnant women, the young, the old, cancer patients, anyone whose immune system is suppressed. The industry has successfully fought to keep that warning off packaging labels and grocery-market coolers. Do you know anyone who cooks ready-to-eat deli meats? Almost all of it is perfectly safe, but every now and then a *Listeria*-tainted batch of luncheon meat or hot dogs makes it into supermarkets and restaurants. Some of the people who eat it die: five hundred a year in the United States.

Late in his second term Bill Clinton responded to a deadly outbreak of listeriosis in the Midwest by starting the slow process of writing rules to require USDA testing in all plants that process ready-to-eat deli meats. He faced the usual opposition from the industry, but by that time, Clinton had turned the USDA and its Food Safety Inspection Service into something that was beginning to look like a public-health agency. Clinton's *Listeria* regs were ready to be printed in the *Federal Register* — which is to say, put on the books — when George Bush moved into the White House in January 2001. The *Listeria* regs were immediately put on hold by Bush's chief of staff, Andrew Card.

They were on hold when Frank Niemtzow ate his ready-to-eat deli turkey.

They were on hold when he checked out of Presbyterian Hospital for the second time, terribly weakened by his devastating bout with listeriosis.

And they were on hold when the Niemtzow family was sitting shiva to mourn the death of their father and grandfather.

Frank Niemtzow was a very old man. He would have died of something before long, even if he hadn't gotten listeriosis. But Clinton's USDA rules were written to catch the very food-borne bacteria that led to Dr. Niemtzow's death — to protect the very old and the very young.

Unfortunately for Dr. Niemtzow — and for the six others who died in the same outbreak and for forty-six other people who were sickened and for the three women who miscarried — the Republican Party is the party of unregulated meat and poultry. That is not a partisan charge; it is a statement of fact. The Republicans win elections in the "red states" in the center of the country, where cattle and chickens are produced and slaughtered. Democrats win their elections in the "blue states" on the coasts. Republicans use the USDA to pay off their contributors from the red states. The result of that crude electoral calculus is laissez-faire food-safety policy whenever a Republican is in the White

House. (If you must eat while the R's control the White House, both houses of Congress, and the judiciary, you might want to consider becoming a vegetarian about now.) In the 2000 election, the corporate food-production combines donated $59 million in both hard and soft money, 73 percent of it to Republicans. Forget hanging chads. It was the hanging sides of beef in IBP's hamburger factories that made George Bush president.

We're not suggesting that Republicans have a monopoly on bad food policy. As governor of Arkansas, Bill Clinton carried *beaucoup de* water for Little Rock chicken magnate Frank Tyson. (If that water came out of Arkansas' rivers, it was increasingly polluted by Tyson Industries.) But after two years in Washington, Clinton saw that his cozy relationship with Tyson Foods wasn't polling well and so distanced himself from Tyson. No courageous stand for the people was involved; Bill Clinton couldn't take the heat, so he got out of the chicken.

Bush, like Clinton, was a Southern governor whose career had been promoted by the CEO of a large poultry processor. The chief of Pilgrim's Pride Corporation is Lonnie "Bo" Pilgrim, Bush's chicken guy.

He's a charming old Texcentric who appears in his own ads and loves to tell people that he marches "to the beat of a different drumstick." Bo is one of Bush's top ten donors, and he bankrolled other Republican candidates who backed Bush. He also hosted a big Bush fund-raising bash in his home in Pittsburg, Texas — a baronial estate locals refer to as "Cluckingham Palace."

Lonnie Bo was making public policy long before George W. got elected governor. Bo's something of a legend in the Great State — where elected officials can't be bought but can be rented if the price is right. In the late eighties the price was right at $10K. During the legislative session, Lonnie Bo walked onto the floor of the Texas Senate and started handing out checks to senators — the "payee" line was left blank. The senators were about to vote on a workers' compensation bill that would have saved Pilgrim's Pride millions in payments to workers who had lost fingers or who were crippled by repetitive-motion injuries. ("It was such a poultry sum I wouldn't have accepted it," said one senator who missed the handout.) To everyone's amazement, it turned out to be quite legal to hand out checks on the floor of the

Texas Senate. The law was later changed to cover that odd contingency. Money can no longer be stuffed into the pockets of legislators during the four months the Lege is in session every two years.

So Bush came to Washington with a pre-existing condition in favor of lax regulation on bad food. Not only was he elected president as the candidate of the party of tainted meat and foul poultry, he'd been elected both governor and president with the help of one of the biggest chicken kingpins in the South. It's no surprise Bush killed off his predecessor's *Listeria* regulations. He was just doing what God and the party of poultry intended him to do.

It was a deadly policy decision.

Neither Bush, his chief of staff, Andrew Card, his political strategist, Karl Rove, nor ag secretary Ann Veneman can plead ignorance. They were warned. Former agriculture undersecretary Carol Tucker Foreman was utterly dismayed that the *Listeria* regs she had lobbied Clinton to enact weren't safely on the books before the Bushies moved into the West Wing. She started to work the Bush cabinet even before it met. Tucker-Foreman knew that food-poisoning victims planned a protest on the day Veneman was scheduled to take the oath of office. She got word to Veneman that the *Listeria* regs could save lives and suggested the protesters might stay home if the regulations were pulled off Bush's kill list. No agriculture secretary wants to begin her term surrounded by mothers holding unseemly, poster-size photos of children killed by *Listeria monocytogenes* and *E. coli* O157:H7. It makes a special event so much less fun. The back-channel negotiations worked. Veneman got the White House to remove the *Listeria* rules from a long list of Clinton policies the Bushies were killing. So the food-safety protestors stayed home.

Then the *Listeria* rules disappeared.

They certainly disappeared as a news story. Food-safety advocates — including Foreman, now with the Consumer Federation of America, and members of Safe Tables Our Priority (STOP) — kept the pressure on George Dubya's aggies. (They are literally Aggies. Our food policy is shaped by political appointees and civil servants from the nation's land-grant colleges, and Texas Agricultural and Mechanical University leads the pack. Land-grant colleges are for the most part focused on animal husbandry — a phrase that has inspired hundreds of bad ovine-Aggie jokes. In other words, what these universities focus on is production rather than food safety.)

From his office at Texas A & M — and for a time from the office he was appointed to at the USDA — Dr. Russell Cross has influenced what you might call the supply-siders who raise and slaughter cattle and poultry. Cross is no longer at the USDA, but Bush appointed one of his disciples, Texas A & M professor Elsa Murano, as the agency's undersecretary for food safety. Murano spent her first year in office explaining why the microbial testing the Clinton administration almost got on the books would not keep contaminated meat out of stores and restaurants. Food-safety advocates knew the testing requirement wasn't a guarantee, but, they argued, if companies were required to test their production lines and products once they found deadly bacteria, our food would be safer. But the Bushies came into office determined to undo much of what Bill Clinton had done.

Just because you didn't read about this food fight in your daily newspaper doesn't mean it wasn't an epic battle. While the media were obsessed with a "child-kidnapping epidemic" that did not exist, food-safety advocates and the industry were fighting over regulations that can literally cost or save your child's life. One confrontation at a May 2002 conference brought the life-and-death nature of the debate into focus. Rosemary Mucklow of the National Meat Association stood up and said the Centers for Disease Control's statistics on deaths by food-borne pathogens were way too high. "I want to know where the bodies are buried," she demanded. When Nancy Donley stood up to respond, it was as though all the oxygen had been sucked out of the room. "I can tell you where one body is buried," said Donley. Donley's six-year-old son died an agonizing death in 1993 after eating a hamburger tainted with *E. coli* O157:H7. Even as Donley grieved for him, she also took action by organizing a food-safety lobbying group, STOP.

In panels, symposia, and hearings, food-safety advocates pushing the Bush administration toward aggressive meat inspection were confronted by Bush appointees like Murano, who are inclined to accommodate the industry. The fight over the *Listeria* rules was often the most intense because the problem had been identified and the solution proposed.

The story remained below the media's radar screen until a Pennsylvania company had to recall twenty-seven million pounds of lunch meat because of *Listeria* contamination. Unfortunately, they — or another company processing ready-to-eat meat in the region — missed the deli turkey that led to Dr. Niemtzow's death. (A twenty-seven-million-pound recall is exactly what it sounds like — a recall and not the recovery of twenty-seven million pounds of meat. Most of the meat had already been eaten, much of it by children who were served it through the National School Lunch Program — a fact kept very quiet by the USDA.)

The Wampler processing plant in Franconia, Pennsylvania, is a squat building that sits close to a state highway about thirty miles northwest of Philadelphia. The large industrial building that houses the main plant has an odd two-story brick office affixed to the front of it that separates management from labor. A plastic banner announces the number of hours worked without injury. Tall vent pipes atop the building fill the air with the scent of roast turkey and smoked chicken. Trucks and forklifts move in and out of the parking lot. At the side entrance, workers wearing standard-issue hair nets gather at a doorway to talk on cell phones, smoke, drink coffee, and joke (in Spanish) about their bosses. Management let us know, in English, that reporters are not welcome.

No chickens are slaughtered here. Two-thousand-pound bins of raw turkey and chicken meat arrive daily from the South in refrigerated trucks. The meat is ground, seasoned, tumbled, injected, emulsified, smoked, heated, cooled, and pressed into large turkey roasts. It is squeezed into casings to make turkey franks, which are then vacuum-wrapped and shipped all over the country. Despite the old saw about the two things you never want to watch being made, this particular form of sausage making is more repulsive than a legislature at work because it's done in an environment that encourages the growth of *Listeria monocytogenes* — something you can't find even on the floor of the Texas Senate.

No sign on the outside of the building suggests that Wampler is a Pilgrim's Pride company, owned by our old outlaw from Texas, whose company is always at the top of the fines-and-enforcement list at our state's environmental agency. No company logo, no silhouette of the company founder, no life-size reproductions of Lonnie Bo in a pilgrim hat, cradling a white fryer in his arms, appears on the sides or backs of the trucks that transport his chicken. It's enough to make a Texan homesick. But Wampler is indeed a Pilgrim's Pride property, acquired in 2001.

There are thirteen hundred slaughterhouses and processing plants and only seventy-six hundred USDA inspectors watching over what goes on there. Because of the concentration and mechanization of the meat and poultry industry, the risk of poisoning by a food-borne pathogen is increasing. One mistake by a worker ripping the entrails from six cows a minute, and a feces-smeared carcass is ground and mixed with a herd of clean cows hanging from the production chain. Inspectors can see the fecal smears, but bacteria can be found only by microbial testing. The inspectors, who work under enormous pressure, are the last line of defense between invisible, microscopic foodborne pathogens and your family's dinner table. When they fail, or when the system dominated by the meat industry fails, the results can be fatal. The death of Nancy Donley's son is described in Eric Schlosser's remarkable book *Fast Food Nation*:

Her six-year-old son, Alex, was infected with the bug in July of 1993 after eating a tainted hamburger. His illness began with abdominal cramps that seemed as severe as labor pains. It progressed to diarrhea that filled a hospital toilet with blood. Doctors frantically tried to save Alex's life, drilling holes in his skull to relieve pressure, inserting tubes in his chest to keep him breathing. . . . Toward the end, Alex suffered hallucinations and dementia, no longer recognizing his mother or father. Portions of his brain had been liquefied. "The sheer brutality of his death was horrifying," Donley says.

For almost two years Vincent Erthal was the USDA inspector on the second shift at Wampler's Franconia plant. Erthal describes the plant as one of the dirtiest he had seen in his twenty years with the USDA. Leaked internal documents obtained from another source support his claims. They describe meat residue from the previous day stuck on equipment; old meat on the tines of forks used to mix meat products; liquid filled with "unknown black foreign particles (possibly from the overhead cooling units)" dripping through a hole in plastic covering six hundred pounds of meat; water splashing from the floor onto food products; workers washing their boots and allowing water to splash onto food and food-preparation surfaces; condensation on ducts and pipes above the food-processing area. One hundred sixteen pages of USDA inspectors' reports obtained under the Freedom of Information Act include many similar violations during the year before the recall. In the reports, Erthal repeatedly warns of condensate that was contaminating food and food-processing equipment.

The documents covering a period before Wampler's October 2002 recall refer to dozens of earlier violations of USDA guidelines. Water from the floor splashing onto the food products was a red flag. Erthal said he worried about the backed-up drains and standing water in the plant. When the USDA finally got around to taking samples for *Listeria,* the strain of bacteria that cost Frank Niemtzow his life was found in the drains. It was a little late. Tons of ready-to-eat chicken and turkey had already been processed and shipped, and most of it had already been eaten.

It didn't have to happen. The rules the Bush administration killed during its first week in office would have required regular testing for *Listeria* — and quick action if it was detected.

When Inspector Erthal finally went

public with his claims in November 2002, Elsa Murano's response was to chill, if not kill, the messenger. Murano said the inspector was making "serious allegations."

"I need to know, frankly, if what he's saying is right, is true, is accurate, then we need to correct that and make sure it doesn't happen again," Murano said. She added that instead of going public, instead of contacting California congressman Henry Waxman and instead of asking for help from the nonprofit Government Accountability Project, Erthal should have gone to the USDA's Office of Inspector General. "All of our employees have available to them the Office of Inspector General, and Mr. Erthal didn't do that," Murano said.

Wrong.

Erthal spent two frustrating years filing reports that were ignored. Exactly one year before the recall, he pleaded with the agency to file an enforcement notice. Once the notice is filed, USDA inspectors can be pulled from the plant and that shuts the plant down. Initially Erthal was rebuffed by his colleague on the day shift and by day-shift managers from Wampler. He had a stack of critical reports hand-delivered to the district office in Philadelphia, but they were intercepted. Finally, he showed the reports to a circuit manager who e-mailed the district office requesting an enforcement order that would give Wampler three days to clean up its plant or be temporarily shut down. A month later the USDA finally took a look at Wampler. "We found pretty extensive *Listeria* throughout the facility," said USDA spokesman Steve Cohen. *Listeria monocytogenes.*

You might think Murano would give the whistle-blower a commendation and urge other inspectors to come forward when they find problems.

There was no commendation.

"I'm a peon inspector," Erthal told us. "They're a little bit above the law. They don't have to pay attention to a peon inspector. You know who Bo Pilgrim is? Bo Pilgrim is personal friends with George Bush. He helped finance his presidential campaign. He gave him millions of dollars." (Actually it was hundreds of thousands.)

The federal bureaucracy is huge and has a complex management hierarchy. But bureaucrats know who the CEO is. Vince Erthal may overestimate Bo Pilgrim's influence, but he knows about his relationship with the Boss. That's the way cash-and-carry government works.

Erthal and other inspectors also knew the institutional culture changed when George and Laura moved into the White House.*

Bush's top food-safety appointee at the USDA doesn't even believe in testing, and she's not shy about saying so. Before Elsa Murano took a swipe at Erthal in the press, she was making speeches about the failures of testing. "Testing," she said, "failed to prevent the outbreak of listeriosis in the Northeastern United States, and it failed

*An internal USDA memo (November 2002) to inspectors in Kansas obtained by the Government Accountability Project (GAP) suggests how the culture was changing. It warns inspectors that they bear a large responsibility when they stop the company's production line to check for contaminated meat. Their supervisors will only support inspectors' decisions if there is visible evidence of gross contamination on sides of eviscerated beef moving by them on the production line. "Identifiable and verifiable ingesta or feces is as follows: material of a yellow, green, brown or dark color that has a fibrous nature. Milk is cream colored to white fluid, not clear." One problem with the standard established by the memo, according to Carol Tucker Foreman, a former USDA food-safety undersecretary, is the fact that a smear of feces that is not

to catch the contaminated product linked to the outbreak until after an exhaustive investigation in partnership with the Centers for Disease Control and Prevention. . . . My view is that we cannot test our way out of this problem. We cannot test enough product or plant environments to find all the *Listeria monocytogenes* that is out there threatening food safety."

She's wrong.

The outbreak was not limited to the Northeast, as she suggested. Meat loaded into a refrigerated cooler one morning in New Jersey can be unloaded in Texas two days later — which is where some of Wampler's chicken and turkey ended up. School cafeterias in Wharton, Texas — just down the Brazos River from A & M, where Murano taught — received some of the Wampler products that were later recalled,

---

fibrous yet can still cause deadly *E. coli* food poisoning. In large processing plants, ground beef is mixed together and one contaminated flank can contaminate tons of ground beef. "Remember, YOU are accountable for this very serious responsibility of stopping the company's production for the benefit of food safety" reads a warning no inspector could consider encouragement to use all legal means available to protect public health.

as did Houston area schools. If you didn't see the headline POTENTIALLY LETHAL TURKEY DELIVERED TO LOCAL SCHOOLS, that's because the USDA decided to keep it quiet. Agency bureaucrats know Wampler's products are distributed through the national school lunch program, but the public didn't know until former USDA veterinarian Lester Friedlander found out that tainted meat had been served in the school his grandchildren attend. Friedlander tipped off food-safety activists in Washington, who confronted the USDA.

Murano was also wrong about testing failing to stop the product from being distributed. Wampler had tested and found *Listeria* in its New Jersey plant and said it made the tests available to the USDA inspectors. "Made available" was later defined as having left the test reports in an unlocked drawer. The inspectors working for Murano didn't conduct any testing. Under a new system put in place while Clinton was in office, the company writes a sanitation plan that identifies critical control points where inspectors watch over the process. Testing for *Listeria* was not in Wampler's plan, Erthal said. Wampler takes samples and tests them in their quality-assurance lab, but that information was never made available to the USDA inspectors. Testing by the USDA didn't fail; it wasn't done. And testing by the company didn't fail. The company's tests found *Listeria;* the results just weren't reported.

Murano's solution to this perfect catch-22 was a risk-assessment study of the *Listeria* problem — something both the USDA and the FDA had already done before writing the Clinton rules. Until the study was done and a permanent solution proposed, Murano urged companies to share their test results, since they have more information about contamination in their plants than the USDA could ever gather. "People are dying," said Donna Rosenbaum, a microbial biologist who helped found STOP. "There is a deadly pathogen out there. People are getting sick right now. We were pressing them hard to put the Clinton rules on the books. No, they were going to do a risk assessment." The regs Bush killed would have required much more extensive testing any time the company testing turned up harmful bacteria.

Until the risks are thoroughly assessed by yet another study, the lunch meat you buy may be a biohazard. You might want to cook that ready-to-eat smoked turkey before you make that sandwich for your kids. And do thoroughly scrub the counter or anything else that has come into contact with the meat.

Those of us who eat meat are getting some help from a "blue state" Democrat in Congress. California congressman Henry Waxman, who seems to be pretty much right on every issue he takes up, wrote to Murano's boss, ag secretary Ann Veneman, asking the same questions Frank Niemtzow's surviving family members are asking. Why wasn't this tragedy prevented? "First, we understand that USDA knew about sanitation violations at the Wampler Foods plant in Franconia before it initiated the investigation that ultimately led to the recall," wrote Waxman. "Second, we have learned that Wampler Foods was conducting its own environmental tests for *Listeria* at its plant but failed to disclose this information to USDA inspectors at the time of the testing. . . . As a matter of responsible corporate conduct, Wampler Foods should have shared results of its *Listeria* testing with the USDA." (In a separate nine-page letter to Veneman, Waxman laid out the concerns raised by Vincent Erthal, whom he had interviewed. He also urged Veneman to ensure that Erthal is not subjected to any "retaliatory action.")

Waxman wasn't entirely alone. Long before the public learned Wampler's Franconia plant was contaminated with *Listeria*, Iowa Democratic senator Tom Harkin was trying to shovel some of the bacteria out of the USDA's Augean Stables. Harkin is a red-stater with a good record on food safety. He is also the ranking Democrat on the Senate ag committee and has been pushing two bills that would allow the USDA to conduct microbial inspections of meat and poultry plants and to allow for mandatory recalls. The government can recall infant cribs, toys, cars, and insecticides but not tainted beef, said a member of Harkin's staff. That authority was removed by a court decision in Texas. Dallas-based Supreme Beef Processors won a suit against the USDA and stopped government testing of beef for *Salmonella*. (Someday the other forty-nine states are going to wise up and secede.) The decision was upheld by the Fifth Circuit Court — one of the most conservative appeals benches in the country, which Bush has set out to move even farther to the right with his appointments of Charles Pickering and Priscilla Owen.

Harkin proposes measures that would give the USDA a mandate to test for microbes;

to provide for mandatory recall of tainted meat; and to institute fines on irresponsible slaughterhouse operators. His legislation also requires plant supervisors to inform the secretary of agriculture if a plant is shipping products that don't meet safety standards. The Bush administration opposed all of these proposals. The Bushies also quietly dropped the Clintonites' appeal to the Supreme Court of the Supreme Beef decision that has stopped the USDA's microbial testing of meat products.

Harkin scheduled oversight hearings for January 2003 to take a close look at the USDA's food-safety practices. The hearings would have allowed him to ask other questions, such as why almost all of the professional staff at the USDA's Office of Public Health and Science have left their jobs, and how Secretary Veneman and Undersecretary Murano intend to use the office.

We often lament the lack of real differences between Democrats and Republicans, but we must acknowledge that food safety is one place where the differences are large and evident. Clinton shook up the USDA. He made radical (considering the history of the department and the power of the meat and poultry industry) changes. He separated the marketing and inspection departments, noting that there is a self-evident conflict of interest between people whose job it is to promote meat products and others whose job it is to keep that product safe. He created an Office of Public Health and Science, staffed with physicians and epidemiologists. The agency had always been as partial to veterinarians who specialize in what makes cows sick as it was hostile to physicians who specialize in what makes people sick. The Clintonites embraced the radical notion that someone ought to be looking at the pork, chicken, and beef to make sure it isn't contaminated.

Harkin held on to his seat in Iowa in the 2002 midterm elections, but his party lost its slim majority in the Senate. The new Agriculture Committee chair, Mississippi Republican Thad Cochran, has argued against Harkin's meat-and-poultry safety proposals. Don't bet your paycheck on Senate hearings looking into USDA food safety.

As ranking minority of the ag committee, Harkin kept pushing for increased food safety. With so much bad press regarding the Wampler recall, the USDA had to do something. Two years and six months after the Bush staff killed Bill Clinton's *Listeria* rules, they finally did. They wrote their own.

It was a year too late for Dr. Niemtzow.

It was also what the resident public intellectuals at the Coffee Station in Crawford, Texas, call a chickenshit deal. To use a slaughterhouse metaphor, Bush's political appointees at USDA gutted the Clinton rules. They dropped the key requirement: that companies test meat products at the end of the process anytime testing turns up two positive incidents of *Listeria* contamination in the plant environment or on food-contact surfaces.

Niemtzow's son Stuart is realistic. His father, at ninety-eight, didn't have many more years to live. But he was living independently, full of life, with a sense of adventure lacking in many younger people. Three months before he died, he was visiting his son and grandsons when they decided to go out to eat. Stuart mentioned Big George's Stop-n-Dine — a West Philly soul-food restaurant Bill Clinton likes. "That sounds interesting," the old doctor said to his reluctant grandsons. They were the only white people in a restaurant full of African-Americans, and the family patriarch urged his grandsons to be a little more adventuresome in what they ate. "This is really pretty good," he said, urging the two white kids from the suburbs to try something different.

When Dr. Niemtzow died, he still had a plane ticket for Florida. The doctor may not belong on a listeriosis poster. He was old, but the appointed hour of his death should not have been determined by the failure of a government regulatory agency to do its job.

"It was a national crisis, and they were not providing the information needed to solve it," said Stuart Niemtzow in mid-December. "We didn't have any idea. When we first heard listeriosis, when he got sick, we started asking ourselves all these questions. Did this happen at a Mexican restaurant where we went to eat? Did I give him soft cheese, and did that make him sick?"

Stuart Niemtzow now wonders: where was the USDA?

He first heard of an "outbreak" while driving and listening to the local all-news radio station. He wonders why the government agencies that were aware of the outbreak didn't warn the public.

Even though the USDA had the information, no one had called the hospital. No one informed the Philadelphia Health

Department. No one provided the doctors at Presbyterian Hospital the information that might have saved Frank Niemtzow's life.

Stuart Niemtzow came to a simple conclusion about what had happened to his father. "The government regulatory agencies failed to protect the people. Under the Bush administration, the regulatory agencies are the wolf guarding the chicken's nest. My father, oddly enough, was a fan of Bush."

When he realized his government had failed to protect his father and offered him no remedy, Stuart Niemtzow did what many people do. He called a lawyer. He had read about a class-action lawsuit filed by Chicago trial lawyer Kenneth Moll. Both Stuart Niemtzow and his father, weakened though he was before his death, were angry because it looked as though there had been a cover-up. "My father felt as though he had nothing to lose. He didn't want this to happen to other people. He would have been happy to have the money, but it was not something he cared about. He kept saying, 'I've been wronged. This should not happen to anyone else.'"

Dr. Niemtzow had the small satisfaction of seeing the lawsuit filed in a Philadelphia court before he died. "At his age, he needed all the help he could get to re-cover," his son said. "And the government agency responsible for food safety never let us know."

• GUT REACTION •

WHERE'S THE BEEF?

Would you like some shit to go with your quarter pounder?

They don't ask that question at McDonald's. But a leaked USDA memo shows there is more than red meat in the ground beef that ends up in the nation's fast-food chains, school cafeterias, and home kitchens. The memo was released to the press by the Government Accountability Project, a nonprofit, public-interest group that works with whistle-blowers. It was originally distributed in November 2002 to USDA inspectors working in Kansas, where 20 percent of the nation's meat is slaughtered and processed. GAP warns that the memo means the USDA is backing away from its "zero tolerance" position on fecal contamination of meat. Food-safety critics and federal inspectors see the memo as another indicator of change in the institutional culture of the

Bush USDA, which has already presided over the two largest ground-beef recalls in the agency's history.

The memo was leaked the same week the USDA announced its plans to include irradiated meat in the food it purchases for the National School Lunch Program. Irradiation uses gamma rays, X rays, or accelerated electrons that alter the molecular structure of food in an attempt to kill pathogens and insects.

Elsa Murano, Bush's USDA undersecretary for food safety, was a regular radiation ranger when she taught at Texas A & M University. Critics of Murano's nomination complained that she had compared irradiating food to cooking it in a microwave oven, in order to make irradiation sound less ominous. They also said she is too close to the industry. A week after she made the claim about irradiation being like cooking in a microwave, A & M received a $10 million research-and-development grant from the Titan Corporation, a leading food-irradiation company.

"They are increasing the speed of production lines in slaughterhouses," said Carol Tucker Foreman, the director of Consumer Federation of America's Food Policy Institute. "That results in more contamination of the meat. You can kill the bacteria by irradiating the fecal material on the meat. But irradiated feces in your meat is still — still," she hesitated. "Well, it's still . . ."

It's shit, Carol.

Before you answer yes to the question at the top of this story, you might want to ask if the fecal material in the hamburger is "cold pasteurized" — the irradiation proponents' cool new euphemism for zapping meat with gamma rays. The process does kill the bacteria in the shit.

It doesn't make it easier to swallow.

For appetizing reading, peruse the USDA's Kansas memo:

GENERAL INFORMATION AND CONDUCT

You must understand the responsibility you accept when you stop the company's production process by stopping the line. If a product that is going into the food supply has been directly contaminated and you can justify the production loss that will prevent its entrance into the food supply, then you will be supported because that is your scope of work. There must be verifiable reason and justifiable action for supervision to support your work.

Stopping the line for "possible" cross contamination from split saws and trachea removal is unjustifiable unless you can verify that there is direct product contamination. Verification is OBSERVATION of gross contaminate not SUSPECTED contaminate. This is the only criteria for stopping production.

(On page 1, above, the memo assures the consumer-safety inspectors (CSIs) that two final rail inspectors provide a fail-safe system at the end of the production line. On page 4, below, it warns rail inspectors about stopping the line.)

RAIL INSPECTION

Be sure your rail inspection decisions are verifiable and your actions are justifiable . . .

There is a ZERO TOLERANCE for contamination from ingesta, feces, and milk on the carcass at final presentation at the rail. We will allow the company a chance to trim it off on the moving line unless it is so excessive, that it must be corrected with the line off. You are responsible for time the line is off. Turning off the line must be justifiable and verifiable if we are to support your action. Remember, YOU are accountable for this very serious responsibility of stopping the company's production for the benefit of food safety. Be sure that supervisors can support your decision. Identifiable and verifiable ingesta or feces is as follows: material of a yellow, green, brown or dark color that has a fibrous nature. Milk is cream colored to white fluid, not clear.

Paul Johnson is acting chairman of the National Joint Council of Food Inspection Locals. Johnson sees the USDA's Kansas memo as a threat to public health. "By not taking immediate action when you suspect there is a problem," he said, "you increase the odds that one contaminated piece of meat can contaminate machinery, employees, and other products. Further, inspectors know that a small smear of feces can have deadly consequences just as easily as an amount large enough to have 'a fibrous nature' — yet the USDA prohibits us from taking action that could protect consumers."

Felicia Nestor of the Government Accountability Project warns that "feces is feces whether it's fibrous or not. . . . The USDA is abandoning the zero-tolerance standard for any fecal contamination on beef and replacing it with a new standard: 'wholesome unless there is gross contamination.' It's impossible for this standard to coexist with the agency's claim that it makes decisions based on science. 'Gross' is an inherently subjective standard."

• BUSH v. THE TRIAL LAWYERS •

WHO YOU GONNA CALL?

Reading Peter Perl's *Washington Post Magazine* story about the last big listeriosis outbreak in 2000 is chilling.

The Bil Mar Foods case attracted little public attention in 1998, partly because the news media were riveted on Bill Clinton's impeachment trial and the U.S. bombing of Iraq, while the public was additionally preoccupied with the holiday season. But it was also because the Agriculture Department — in contradiction of its own policies — failed to issue a press release informing the public of the danger, even though the CDC had reported four deaths.

The listeriosis in Bil Mar's Michigan meat-processing plant killed twenty-one people and sickened more than one hundred.

Four years later, in the fall of 2002, no one was impeaching the president, but the public was so preoccupied with Iraq and the holiday season that when fifty-four fell ill and eight died, they received little notice. The cause was listeriosis.

We can even apply a line from Perl's reporting on the earlier public-health tragedy to the one reported in this chapter two years later.

"No action was taken by the USDA — until it was too late."

Too late for Lois Wagner,* of Union County, New Jersey. A neighbor called Wagner's daughter and son-in-law when she noticed newspapers in Wagner's yard and mail in the mailbox. The son-in-law arrived to find Lois lying crosswise on the bed. "She was conscious," he said, "but I thought she must have had a stroke."

Her daughter said, "I spoke to her, but what came out of her mouth was not un-derstandable."

Lois Wagner didn't feel old despite her seventy-seven years. She lived alone and cooked for herself. She mowed her own lawn and raked her leaves. She drove to the store or to Pennsylvania to visit relatives and walked four miles every day.

Lois Wagner was still in intensive care when doctors from the hospital's infectious diseases staff told her family she had

*Name changed at the subject's request.

listeriosis. After two weeks in the hospital, she was still in intensive care and unable to communicate, although if pressed she could come up with a person's name. The family was told to expect a very slow recovery. The woman who walked four miles a day could take only tentative steps on the sidewalk in front of her house.

The *Listeria* had caused meningitis, so the extent of the damage was revealed only gradually. Wagner's brain had been traumatized by the swelling. "They told us it's going to take time."

After the Union County Department of Health called Lois's daughter and asked her to write down everything Lois had eaten over the past several months, the daughter realized the impossible situation she and her mother were in. Her mother couldn't begin to recall what and where she had eaten.

She was faced with either full-time assisted care at home or life in a nursing home. By the time Lois Wagner got home, she was coherent enough to know that she needed assistance — and a lawyer.

Her son-in-law tracked down Kenneth Moll, a Chicago trial lawyer who tried the Bil Mar case in 2000 and had filed a class-action suit against Wampler Foods in a

Philadelphia court in 2002. "I got online and typed in *listeriosis* and *lawyers*. I didn't want someone taking the case unless they had experience with this type of litigation. And we needed a law firm with the resources to handle the case. I knew there was a lot of work to be done."

In an interview Moll said he was disturbed by how little the USDA had learned since the Bil Mar suit two years earlier. "I talked to employees when I was working on that case," he said. "They told me the USDA was basically working for the company.

"You have got to give USDA more power to force a recall. I went to Washington, D.C., to a public meeting. I was very much on the side of USDA. I said they need power to recall. The power to shut down a plant. They need to be able to fine companies. They need stiff fines that will affect them. They don't have any of those powers right now."

Nor is it likely that the USDA will get those powers under the Bush administration. The Bushies believe government's role "is to get out of the way and let business and entrepreneurs do their work," as the president often says. If Bush and his political adviser Karl Rove have their way, much of the power Ken Moll has in a courtroom will be eliminated as well.

Tort reform — limiting the access people like Lois Wagner have to the courts — is one of Rove's passions. "In my opinion there are too many lawsuits . . . and the legal system is jury-rigged. And it's rigged in a certain way."

Bush fixed that lawsuit problem down here in Texas.

He's committed to fixing it in the other forty-nine states.

• 9 •

Dick, Dubya, and Wyoming Methane

I've run an oil company.
— President George W. Bush

I've run an oil-service company.
— Vice President Dick Cheney

Reporters describe deputy interior secretary J. Steven Griles as having had a "checkered career." We're as ready as the next journalist to throw down a cliché, but this one seems to miss badly. In fact, Griles' career has been singularly consistent, a monochrome in the primary color of American business — *Wall Street Journal* gray. Like most of the gray suits doing time in "public service" in the Bush administration, J. Steven Griles is all business.

It's not unusual for presidents to hand over the management of federal departments to corporate executives or corporate lawyers — though most draw the line at actual lobbyists. Bill Clinton appointed a Wall Street insider, Robert Rubin, to run Treasury, although when it came to public lands, he appointed Bruce Babbitt, a Westerner with genuine understanding of the fragility of arid country. Clinton also appointed former Texas land commissioner Bob Armstrong to help ride herd on the federal ranges. Both Babbitt and Armstrong had spent their lives in government, and both were deadly earnest about being stewards of the public trust. They even tried to increase the bargain-basement fees Western ranchers pay to graze their cattle on public land, a sure political loser.

Griles had also put in time in government before Bush II; he's a Department of Interior recidivist. He left his first gig at Interior when the Reagans moved back to Santa Barbara, although he hung on to that job long enough to try to get rid of the man regulating the coal company that was offering Griles a big private-sector pay-check. Hey, we're used to the revolving door, but you're supposed to wait until you get to the outside before you start working for the corporate world. This embarrassing little story resurfaced in *The Washington Post* twelve years later when John Mintz and Eric Pianin took a critical look at the man George W. appointed to the number-two position at Interior. Here was career public servant Carl Close, one of the last no-nonsense officials remaining at the Office of Surface Mining after the Reagan years, trying to get United (coal) Company to comply with federal law. And there was Reagan political appointee Steve Griles, headed out the door for a job at said United in 1989, quietly trying to oust Close from OSM. The *Post*, which loves a Washington-insider story like few other papers, had covered Griles in the eighties, when he presided over budget cuts, staff reductions, and a decline in enforcement actions at the Office of Surface Mining. "We tore this agency to hell," Griles said in 1982. "Now we have to build it back up." He never did get around to the rebuilding.

Griles is a native of Virginia, but his interest in hydrocarbons is as big as the American West. While working for Reagan interior secretary James Watt, he endeared himself to the minerals-extraction industry by backing the giveaway of eighty-two thousand acres of federal oil-shale leases at the cut-rate price of $2.50 an acre. ("A fire sale with no fire," observed the late congressman Mo Udall.) Coal companies loved Griles laid-back attitude toward enforcement at OSM. Oil companies were charmed by his zeal for offshore drilling. He was so enthusiastic about drilling off the California coast that he bullied the U.S. Fish and Wildlife Service into rewriting a report that warned of dire environmental consequences if drilling were permitted. Angry members of the state's congressional delegation, led by Leon Panetta and Mel Levine, raised so much hell the drilling program was put on hold.

Panetta, who became Bill Clinton's chief of staff, turned up the unsanitized version of the Fish and Wildlife report Griles had forced the agency to rewrite. Levine found the Griles memo bullying the Fish and Wildlife folks. "Steve Griles might as well have been speaking for industry as he was for the Department of the Interior," Levine said as he waved the memo in front of reporters' noses. "The positions were indistinguishable," said Panetta. Griles' memo was the "smoking gun of an industry whitewash." He may have mixed his metaphors, but he got the facts right. Threats of lawsuits and bad press followed. It was too much for George Bush I to manage so soon after taking office. Poppy Bush "went wobbly," as Margaret Thatcher once said she feared he might in the Persian Gulf.

He backed away from Reagan's big drilling program, and for thirteen years the California coast was clear. Griles' attempt to hide the environmental costs of drilling for oil stopped Reagan's plan to turn the California coast into the kind of offshore oil field that gives the Texas coast its special, ah, charm.

Griles drill-at-all-costs memo was both an embarrassment and additional proof that he was industry's sweetheart. His résumé was so hot that when he left United to open up his own K Street lobbying firm, coal, oil, and gas companies beat a path to his door. By the time the Supreme Court declared George Bush winner of the 2000 presidential election, Steve Griles was the perfect industry candidate to manage mineral rights on public land.

Newsweek's Howard Fineman and Michael Isikoff followed Griles to the American Petroleum Institute's Washington headquarters nine days before Bush and Cheney took the oath of office. Griles, still a lobbyist, was working with the Bush transition team to both sell and shape the new administration's program. At the Petroleum Palace on L Street, the tone of the meeting was "OK, what do you guys want? You're going to have the ear of this White

House." The gathering quickly became a feeding frenzy. Oil and gas execs and lobbyists anticipated a feast that would include looser rules for drilling on federal land, more exploration for oil and gas in the Gulf of Mexico and Alaska, and lower royalty payments for offshore mineral rights. The party got so crazy, the guy from the wildcatter's association began to shout about repealing the Endangered Species Act.

It was a prelude to the industry socials in Dick Cheney's office four months later, where the same greenhouse gang would rewrite the nation's energy policy. While industry insiders at the Petroleum Institute ran down their wish lists in January, the president of National Environmental Strategies took notes. NES is a lobbying firm that represents oil, coal, and energy companies. Its president and principal owner was Steve Griles. By the time Vice President Cheney's National Energy Policy was released to the public, Griles was the number-two man at Interior. From his office in Washington, he was looking west, kicking ass, and taking names.

Men like Ed Swartz are the heroes of the modern Republican Party's creation mythology. He is the man Ronald Reagan

264

pretended to be when he rode his horse around Rancho del Cielo at Santa Barbara. Swartz is a Western rancher who pays his own way. He believes in property rights, an individual's constitutional right to own a gun, and a work ethic that can turn twenty sections of semiarid range land into a productive cattle ranch. He brands his own cattle, mends his own fences, and waters his own pastures. He was chairman of the Campbell County Republican Party and is a member of the National Rifle Association. He even smokes Marlboros — with an evident pleasure that seems almost sinful.

Swartz has lived for years with the open-pit coal mines that were regulated by the agency Griles tore to hell back in 1982. He uses the mines as points of reference — Eagle Butte Mine, Caballo Mine, Buckskin Mine — when he gives directions to his five-thousand-acre ranch north of Gillette, Wyoming. The state he lives in produces one fourth of the nation's coal, and the county he lives in produces 97 percent of the state's coal. The Swartz ranch sits in the middle of Campbell County, so Swartz understands full well what fuels the economy on the northern border of Dick Cheney's home state. He doesn't have a problem with exploitation of the region's mineral wealth.

Like other ranchers in northern Wyoming and southern Montana, Swartz is caught up in the biggest minerals-extraction boom ever to hit a state that lives by the boom-and-bust cycle. There's nothing like a minerals-extraction boom to bring out the worst in the people doing the extracting.

It's not coal that has Swartz suing his own government and returning to a regional environmental group he helped found thirty years ago. It's coal-bed methane, locally called CBM. Methane is a clean-burning natural gas that can be found in most coal formations. In the 1980s a simple technology was developed to release the gas. Wells are drilled into coal seams, and sections of casing pipe are strung together and inserted into the coal formation. When the water is pulled out of the formation by a submersible pump, the gas flows up the pipe. CBM wells cost only about $50,000 to drill and can be completed in two or three days.

There is an estimated 12.5 trillion cubic feet of methane trapped in coal "cleats" or seams in northern Wyoming — enough to supply the nation with natural gas for about a year. Cheap, quick access to it started a CBM gold rush in Wyoming's

Powder River Basin. Landmen show up unannounced, lay contracts on kitchen tables, and tell ranchers "I'm going to make you a rich man." One northern Wyoming landman drove a huge SUV with a plastic dorsal fin attached to the top and signs on the doors that read LAND SHARK. Others persuaded owners of private mineral rights to sign $4-an-acre leases, then flipped the contract within days for $6, $8, $10, or $20 an acre. (For a point of reference, some federal leases sold for $400 an acre.) Millions of dollars were made before anyone even drilled a well. "Their standard line was, 'This deal won't be here tomorrow,'" said a rancher who had yet to sign away her mineral rights. Small drilling companies cut roads, drill wells, and lay pipelines, only to be gobbled up by big players like Marathon Oil, now the number-one CBM producer in northern Wyoming. Eighteen thousand wells were drilled. Five thousand miles of new roads were carved out of Wyoming ranch land, and a web of pipelines was buried in the ground to move the gas to high-pressure arterial lines that carry it out of the region. Production goals in the National Energy Policy, released by Vice President Cheney in May 2001, are fueling a second boom. Its size and scope make the first one look like a small increase in production.

Sitting at the kitchen table of his modest frame house, Swartz slowly drew on a Marlboro and used the index finger of his free hand to trace the Wildcat Creek drainage basin. "If it wasn't for cigarettes, coffee, and nervous energy, I couldn't keep working," he said, in what came close to an apology for the smoke-filled kitchen. The Bureau of Land Management map is two years old, but much of the land in the watershed above Swartz' ranch is covered with dots marking existing CBM wells. "Damned arthritis," Swartz said as he reached across the table to point to a yellow shaded area that indicates federal ownership of mineral rights.

Swartz is a striking man with Paul Newman–blue eyes and an aquiline nose. Dressed in a plaid Western shirt, jeans, and boots, he looked like a cowboy from central casting, but he's the real deal. He wrests a living out of a ranch situated on coal-burnout land that requires forty acres to graze one cow — in wet years. "My grandpa homesteaded this place in nineteen-four," Swartz said. "He came out here as a cattle foreman for one of those English barons who had enough money to take advantage of all this land being given away. When the Englishman gave up, Grandpa bought out his brand and cattle and took a homestead. Then my grandma took a homestead. Later, my dad and his two sisters took homesteads. My dad helped some World War I veterans set up a homestead. He proved them up and helped them build their cabins. When they left, he bought them out."

Ranchers who homesteaded the rugged hills and breaks of northern Wyoming had large tracts of land but little water. Annual rainfall averages eleven inches. But it's been a while since rainfall has been average. For five years the region has been in the grip of a drought that has ranchers caught between cloudless skies and the cattle market. All over the region, ranchers are selling off cattle in an effort to survive the drought. By the time Ed and his son, Tony, finished branding and castrating calves and "selling off dries" in May 2001, they had reduced their Black Angus herd of 360 to 220. The drought-ravaged land can't provide for much more than that. "You've got to be a good manager," Swartz said. "This isn't farm country. This is grazing country. Look at those hills out there. The only thing those hills are good for is to graze ruminant animals." To water his livestock, Swartz has built tanks he fills with well water. He's buried miles of pipe below the freeze line and uses gravity to move the water from the tanks to his pastures. He didn't ask the government to do it. "Instead of pissin' and moanin' about water, I did it myself. It's my outfit. I want to have something for my son, and if I do it right, it'll be here."

But Swartz depends on natural irrigation of the rich alluvial creek beds on his ranch to provide grazing and hay for his cattle. He and his father built thirteen "spreader dikes" — staggered berms that extend two thirds of the way across the streams at right angles, reaching out like fingers from alternating sides of the bank. They force the snowmelt or rainwater to meander from bank to bank rather than flowing down the channel. By the time the creek dries up in summer, grasses in its bed are thoroughly watered. Two irrigation dams allow Swartz to flood hay meadows beyond the creek bed, then return the water to the stream. "For years, if there was a flood come down that crick, hell, we'd just kick it out onto the meadows. All these years, we've never killed any vegetation. My father never soured a meadow. I never soured a meadow. The cricks are the heart of this ranch. Kill the cricks, and we can't make a living here."

Coal-bed methane wells produce far more water than gas. To release the million cubic metric feet of gas produced when a handful of wells were drilled in 1991, three million barrels of water were pumped out of the ground. By 2001, the 250 million metric cubic feet of gas produced in Wyoming produced 513 million barrels of water. Hitting the coal-bed methane targets the Bush energy planners set for the Powder River Basin will require enough pumping to cover the state of Rhode Island with one foot of water.

Since 1999 some of that water has been flowing down Wildcat Creek and through Ed Swartz' ranch. It was pumped out of wells drilled upstream from the Swartz ranch and impounded by Redstone Resources. When the drilling company's in-stream reservoirs are filled, the water flows down the Wildcat. Swartz calls it "killer water." It's so high in saline content that when it interacts with soils, it kills most plant life. "The grass along this creek was belly high," said Swartz. "Look at it. It's all dead."

Swartz had gone to court years earlier to defend his water rights and prevailed —

winning on appeal in the Wyoming Supreme Court. "I thought I'd cut a fat hog on the ass when we won that lawsuit," he said. And he probably had. That was before the CBM boom. The fight he's in now reminds us of another porcine metaphor. When Jim Hightower was Texas agriculture commissioner he was fond of saying, "Before you can clean up the water, you've got to get the hogs out of the creek." Hightower wasn't referring to the four-legged variety. He is an outspoken critic of two-legged corporate hogs who place short-term financial gain ahead of public interest. (As a fellow Texan, he joined us in trying to get the word out about Enron back when they spent $525,000 to buy an equity position in a Texas governor by the name of George W. Bush.) The corporate porkers Hightower worried about are essential to the ecosystem of every market economy. But — as we have learned from Enron, Global Crossing, etc. — they work only when regulatory agencies serve as swineherds. The creek that waters Ed Swartz' ranch is full of hogs. What's missing is a government agency looking out for Ed's, and the public's, interest.

"We get no help from the state of Wyoming," Swartz said. "They love the money too much." The limited CBM program that started while Bill Clinton was president, mostly on land where mineral rights were in private hands, helped turn a $700 million state deficit into a small surplus, and everyone from the governor to the county commissioners in Gillette is promoting its unrestricted development. "We love gas," Governor Jim Geringer gushed on one occasion in 2001. The local county commissioners are such avid CBM boosters that they rejected the report of an industry Ph.D. they hired to look at the effects of development. It contained "too many negative comments," one commissioner said.

Wyoming ranchers banded together under the banner of the Powder River Basin Resource Council and looked to Washington, hoping the EPA would at least require some environmental safeguards.

At the Bush-Cheney Interior Department, Swartz had to plead his case before a man who had worked as a lobbyist for the very company Swartz claims is destroying grazing along Wildcat Creek. Redstone Resources was one of Steve Griles' clients. In addition to Redstone, Griles lobbied for five other big companies drilling coal-bed methane wells in northern Wyoming. He organized the Coal Bed Methane Ad Hoc

Committee, an industry group working to sweep away restrictions to CBM production. On Capitol Hill he lobbied for Western Gas Resources, which describes itself as the largest acreage holder, gatherer, transporter, and producer of CBM gas in the Powder River Basin.

"Hell, he's one of them," Swartz said.

At the Bush-Cheney Interior Department, they're all "one of them." If Deputy Secretary Griles steps aside because of his conflicts of interest (which he has yet to do), Swartz will be kicked along to Rebecca Watson, the Montana lawyer Bush appointed as assistant Interior secretary for land and minerals management. Watson has a CBM history of her own. She was legal counsel for Fidelity Energy, another big methane operator working in Wyoming, and was also a staff attorney for the Mountain States Legal Foundation. The Denver-based nonprofit law firm, founded by James Watt in 1976, is the most notorious anti-environmental operation in the west. Watt laid out Mountain States' agenda in brief when he said: "We will mine more, drill more, cut more timber."

The whole CBM bunch is so inbred it might have walked right out of a Faulkner novel. Mountain States Legal Foundation board member Karen Kennedy runs a pro-methane "grassroots" group in Swartz' hometown. Her husband, John, is a methane operator who once got mighty close to Fist City with Swartz when he called him a liar during a fact-finding bus tour with the governors of Wyoming and Montana. ("Ed made a smart move when he didn't knock the little son of a bitch on his can," said another rancher of the encounter.) Back in Washington, the president is a former oil-field landman. When Dick Cheney was still CEO of Halliburton, its oil-service division was already tapping into the new revenue stream in Wyoming's methane beds. And secretary of the interior Gale Norton is an alumna of the same Mountain States Legal Foundation founded by Watt.

Ed Swartz, as they say in Midland, is shit outta luck.

When no one at Redstone answered Swartz' letters and phone calls, and after state environmental regulators assured him the water in his creek was just fine, he hired a lawyer. He's suing two state regulators and Redstone Resources. His suit presents the dizzying possibility that Griles and Watson will have to appear as witnesses for both Redstone Resources *and* the Department of the Interior. If the case is argued in winter, they can all ride snowmobiles to the federal courthouse in Cheyenne. Becky Watson was lead attorney for the Montana Snowmobile Association, and Griles is a snowmobile enthusiast.

A month after Swartz filed suit in spring of 2002, he estimated he had spent $45,000. "I'm paying for lawyers on both ends of this lawsuit," Swartz said. "As a taxpayer, I'm paying the salaries of the lawyers at the state agencies. Now, I've got to pay my own lawyers to sue them. I'm getting shit full of it. If I don't win this lawsuit and get the state of Wyoming to restore my resources, I don't know what I'll do." (While Swartz was paying lawyers, Griles continued to be paid $248,000 a year from his former lobby firm, National Environmental Strategies. Apparently it's all legal. Griles no longer works for the company. Nor owns any interest in it. But he's getting four annual payments of $248,000 from his former firm because, the Associated Press reports, "he brought in so many clients while he worked there.")

Swartz will need more than a win in court to clean up the crick. He points to yellow sections of the Bureau of Land

Management map that covers his kitchen table. They represent federal ownership of mineral rights and account for two thirds of the land in the Wildcat Creek drainage basin above the Swartz ranch. Each section is virgin yellow, without a single dot representing a CBM well.

When Swartz filed his lawsuit in the spring of 2002, there were fewer than fifteen thousand CBM wells in the Powder River Basin. All were on land where mineral rights are privately owned. If the Bushies at Interior have their way, in ten years the yellow sections on Swartz' map will look like a Seurat pointillist landscape.

It's all in the plan. After the Senate in 2002 blocked Bush and Cheney's plan to drill in the Alaska National Wildlife Refuge in the first ANWR showdown, Norton, Griles, and Watson pushed Interior into every energy reserve in the West. The outlines of the Cheney energy plan are sketched out in "National Energy Policy: Report of the National Energy Group."*

*You won't be allowed to see who met with Cheney to make your energy policy, because the vice president refuses to release any list of lobbyists who met with the task force. The Government Accounting Office sued the vice president, something the

The "CBM play" in Wyoming is the largest natural-gas drilling project ever pursued by the federal government. It might even save us from terrorists. At a Denver coal-bed methane conference in April 2002, Becky Watson said that after the terrorist attacks of September 11, increased national gas production is essential to "our way of life, our economy and our national security."

If we don't drill, bin Laden wins.

To do their part to defeat Osama bin, ranchers in the Powder River Basin will have to accept:

- 51,444 new coal-bed methane wells;
- 17,000 miles of new roads (enough to drive from Los Angeles to New York six times);

---

oversight office had never before done in its eighty-one-year history. After losing in federal district court, the GAO abandoned its appeal when the Republicans took control of both houses and threatened the GAO with a substantial reduction in funding if it pursued its appeal. It is known that Enron CEO Ken Lay met with the energy task force, as did several other Enronites. It's a safe bet that the names of several of Steve Griles' clients are on the list. Ed Swartz didn't make the cut.

- 20,000 miles of new pipeline and 5,300 miles of above-ground power lines;
- 278,000 acres of topsoil and vegetation destroyed;
- disposal of 1.4 trillion acre-feet of water, enough to provide water for sixteen million people, all of Wyoming's current population, for thirty years.

Swartz doesn't oppose CBM development. "It's not a bad program, if it's done right. But these people are all blow and go, and to hell with everybody else." Swartz has no faith in the Interior Department. "The U.S. EPA is the only friend I've got in government," Swartz said. He's probably right.

Six days after the Senate shut off access to the Alaskan National Wildlife Refuge, a lame-duck regional EPA director in Denver delivered a nine-hundred-page environmental-impact statement that declared the Powder River drilling scheme an environmental disaster. Region 8 EPA administrator Jack McGraw ruled that the plan to drill fifty-one thousand new wells on eight million acres of ranch land in Wyoming could not proceed. McGraw graded the project EU-3: the lowest possible environmentally unsatisfactory rating. He warned that

- the plan did not deal with the increased salinity in groundwater;
- groundwater will be produced in volumes exceeding federal law;
- insufficient attention is paid to air pollution the drilling will create;
- the coal-bed methane water will so increase the salinity of the Belle Fourche and Tongue Rivers that they will no longer be usable for irrigation (they account for 98 percent of surface water on the Wyoming side of the Powder River Basin);[*]
- soils that come in contact with the CBM water could be permanently damaged.

The anti-government evangelists on the right of the Republican Party have taught the public to loathe the words "career bureaucrat," but many of the nation's nameless, shirtsleeved, not-very-well-paid functionaries

_____

[*]It seems McGraw was right on target. A year after he filed his report, *The New York Times* sent a reporter to Gillette, where he found methane bubbling out of the Belle Fourche.

try to serve their assigned mission rather than an individual administration. This story should have ended with the EPA living up to the mandate spelled out in the first two words of its name by forcing the Interior Department to obey the law.

If you need a happy ending, try a romance novel.

As he had done in 1988 when he savaged U.S. Fish and Wildlife for pointing out the environmental risks of drilling off the California coast, Steve Griles assaulted a public servant. Under his "United States Department of the Interior — THE DEPUTY SECRETARY" letterhead, Griles attacked EPA assistant administrator Linda Fisher. "I learned yesterday that your Region 8 Acting Director is proposing to send a letter indicating the above draft Environmental Impact Statements are deficient from a water quality analysis. The Acting Director is taking this significant action despite the fact that the Regional Administrator for Region 8 starts on Monday, April 15, 2002."

Not a subtle message. THE DEPUTY SECRETARY of an executive department, a man four pay grades below THE PRESIDENT, was leaning on a bureaucrat of lesser stature at another federal agency.

The letter implies that with the new regional administrator, the fix was in and on the way. Griles even argued that the EPA letter and report should not be sent. It would "create, at best, misimpressions and possibly impede the ability to move forward in a constructive manner." In other words, an environmental-impact study conducted by experts in the field that took one year and one million dollars to complete — and concluded that two of the nation's rivers could be destroyed — was a "misimpression." Griles had no environmental or engineering study supporting his conclusion. He didn't need facts; he had raw political power.

There is another parallel between Griles' 1988 letter to Fish and Wildlife and his 2002 letter to the EPA: both disappeared from the files of their author. When Leon Panetta filed a Freedom of Information Act request with Interior in the 1988 case, he was told the letter Griles wrote didn't exist. He obtained it through a FOIA request at Fish and Wildlife, the recipient of the letter. When we filed a Freedom of Information request with Interior in April 2002, we were told the letter Griles wrote didn't exist. We obtained it through a FOIA request at the EPA, the recipient of the letter. Every federal agency has an ocean of documents; perhaps this is a mere coincidence.

Griles' behavior may have been predictable, but this time around it proved more of a problem. Confronted by Oregon senator Ron Wyden, who was offended by Bush's appointment of a minerals-extraction lobbyist to a high position at Interior, Griles feared his nomination was in jeopardy. So he promised to recuse himself from any decisions involving his clients or former clients — not permanently but for one year.

Such clever accommodations are always amusing. The Senate (and the public) has to buy the argument that after a year Griles will forget that Redstone Resources paid his firm $40,000 in 2000, that Devon Energy paid the company $80,000, that Dominion Resources retained his services for $20,000, and that each of his former clients were drilling for methane in Wyoming while the Senate was voting on his nomination. And that he was still, in 2003, being paid $248,000 a year from National Environmental Strategies.

To keep his promise, Griles would have to recuse himself from all issues involving coal-bed methane in Wyoming. On April

8, 2002, he sent his second letter of recusal to Interior secretary Gale Norton. Four days later he wrote to the EPA, attempting to block the draft environmental-impact statement on CBM in the Powder River Basin.

Griles should have bided his time. A regional director more friendly to oil and gas exploration has taken over at the EPA in Denver. The deck was stacked in Griles' favor, and Ed Swartz was left with one fewer friend in the federal bureaucracy.

In late spring the fifty-mile drive south from Swartz' ranch in Gillette to Patricia Clark's ranch at Pumpkin Buttes is so beautiful it makes your heart hurt. The sky is a brilliant blue. The hills are deep green. There are so many pronghorn antelope among the cattle and horses that a journalist from another state is tempted to ask the ridiculous question: "Are those antelope domestic?" (The answer is a bemused "no.")

Clark is a short, stout woman with a freckled complexion and light brown hair pulled back in a simple ponytail. She and her teenage daughter and son live in one of three modest houses surrounded by out-buildings and corrals. With her sister and brother-in-law, Clark runs a fifty-thousand-acre ranch. They raise Hereford/Salis/Red Angus cross cattle, handsome red animals with a lot of body mass. Six of them graze in the dry bed of a creek on the Clark ranch. ("They're not as gentle as they look," Clark said. "You ought to see what one of them did to my sister's arm when they were branding yesterday.") Compared with the sleek pronghorns grazing alongside them, the cattle look like minivans.

Outside the oldest of three houses on the ranch is a tower of deer antlers that stands six or seven feet tall. "A hundred years of deer," Clark said. The ranch was started by Clark's great-grandfather 106 years ago. Clark runs the business side of the ranch and is more likely to be found at the keyboard of a computer than on horseback. She has an air of quiet confidence as she pads around the kitchen in her stocking feet. She also has the ability to instantly retrieve from a low bank of file cabinets in her office any photo, map, or contract she needs. What she pulls from her files are not photos of prize cattle for sale at auction, or maps of pastures. They are topographical maps covered with small dots that chart the progress of fifty years of drilling and mining. And photos of grass damaged by coal-bed methane water.

"This is our third boom," Clark said. "We went through the uranium strikes in the fifties. It happened again with the oil boom of the seventies. Now we've got methane." She pointed to section 36 on the map, which is covered by dots. "I don't know how many," she said. "Maybe five thousand holes on the ranch. There are holes all over the uranium beds." Section 36 is "a pincushion." In situ uranium mining is discreet. A well is drilled, and ammonium hydroxide is pumped into the shaft. When the chemical dissolves the yellowcake, it's pumped to the surface. No uranium has been produced on the ranch because the price is so low that U.S. miners can't compete with the Canadians.

Some of the wells remain uncapped, but Clark said she recalls no problems from the uranium miners on her ranch. She had few problems with oil-drilling companies, although one operator tore up her roads. "They had no conscience about tearing up our roads and leaving them in a condition that made it impossible to pull our horse trailers on them. You've got to have a good surface agreement to make them work with you."

Wyoming ranchers pay attention to surface agreements, because the surface of their land is all most of them own. Seventy percent of the rights to minerals under the Clark ranch are owned by the federal government; 10 percent are owned by the state, and the remaining 20 percent are owned by the Clarks. These "split estates" create problems. The party who owns the minerals has a right to the land — the right to build roads, put in pipelines, and run power lines.

If uranium and oil were manageable under these split arrangements, CBM is not. "Methane has already caused a lot of problems," Clark said. Four or five wells are often drilled at each well pad, and eight well pads are allowed on each section (260 acres) of land. Huge, roaring screw compressors pressure the gas into transmission lines. Methane is sometimes "vented" into the atmosphere. "Then there is the water," Clark said.

Like Ed Swartz, Clark has lost some of her grass to methane water produced by one of Steve Griles' former clients. Some water spilled out of a reservoir and ran down the creek near the ranch houses, killing several cottonwoods in a region where trees are rare and precious. When the vegetation began to return, the cattle wouldn't go near it.

The problem, Clark noted, is the high SAR (sodium-absorption ratio). "An SAR up to eight is OK," Clark said. "When you get to twelve, it's considered a problem. Over twelve is dangerous. Well, the SAR on the water coming out of those wells was eighteen to nineteen. And there was a fifty- to two-hundred-fold change in the soil composition wherever there was methane water." (You have to be a soil scientist to ranch in this part of the country.)

Clark has overcome a fear of speaking in public. She religiously follows the first rule of participatory democracy: "I go to meetings. Meetings with the BLM. Meetings with methane companies. Meetings with ranchers. Meetings with government. Every time I ask for help with a problem, I'm told the same thing. 'That's a civil matter.' That means 'I'm sympathetic, but that's not my problem.' When you hear that in town council meetings, at the county commission, in the state offices, and from federal officials, that's when you turn to your local environmental group." Clark is also a member of the Powder River Basin Resource Council.

By sheer persistence — and attending meetings — Clark got the director of the industry-friendly Wyoming Department of

Environmental Quality to visit her ranch. She explained to him that the drilling company had produced 45 acre-feet of water in thirty days. She had him do the numbers: based on fourteen wells, the companies would produce 781 acre-feet of water. "That's more than they can store in every one of these reservoirs they have planned here. So, you see, it's a *real* big problem." She persuaded the state agency to suspend the drilling on her ranch until the companies figure out what they're going to do with the water.

Standing by a small reservoir on her ranch, the snowcapped Bighorn Mountains clear and sharp a hundred miles at her back, Clark pointed to the damage done by the methane water. It's a clearly defined swath of brown, like a hole cut out of the native grasses. Farther down, on Willow Creek, it's worse. "There is not a blade of palliative grass in there. One half of that crick is a waste to us. It used to be grass. And this is a ranch where we have to fight for every blade of grass."

From an altitude of one thousand feet, Wyoming's future looks even more disturbing. As he climbed out of the tiny Sheridan, Wyoming, airport in his single-engine Cessna, Reg Goodwin turned north

289

toward the Montana state line. Sitting in the front seat was Jill Morrison, a rancher and full-time employee of the Powder River Basin Resource Council. Goodwin donates his Cessna and services to LightHawk — a kind of nonprofit volunteer environmental air force. In the backseat, freelance photographer Ann Fuller, also working pro bono, was still loading her cameras when the plane reached the first location Morrison wanted to shoot.

"Look at that," Goodwin said. "It's everywhere. Everywhere! I had no idea." Goodwin banked the plane, opened the front window. Fuller leaned forward to stick her head out and shoot as the plane circled. Below, a stretch of low hills and river bottom known as Lower Prairie Dog looked like a Brueghel the Elder painting. But in the place of dancing and ice-skating peasants were hundreds of machines. Bulldozers kicking up clouds of dust as they dug "perc ponds" to hold methane water. Backhoes digging pipeline easements. Drilling wells working on several locations. Large float trucks carrying heavy equipment. Banks of 1,250-horsepower screw compressors, each the size of a Texas double-wide, pressurizing gas lines. Small spreader trucks broadcasting snow-white gypsum that oil operators hope will neutralize the damage they have done to the soil. There were old pits filled with a green-brown water near flowing wells and new pits, shiny black with plastic sheeting to retain water that is yet in the ground. Less than a year earlier, this entire landscape was a pastoral stretch of rolling hills above the tiny, meandering Tongue River.

Goodwin banked the plane to the right and headed south, following the interstate down to Gillette. Along the way, the contrast between the undeveloped federal mineral rights and the "fee land" in full-blown development could not be more stark. Verdant hills covered with native grasses bumped up against what looked like industrial parks. South of the rugged Powder River Breaks, Morrison pointed to the left and the plane slowly descended toward a huge CBM water pit sitting a few hundred feet from the Powder River. Goodwin followed the river for a while, then headed dead south for Gillette, where he was to pick up a rancher who would photograph his ranch before drilling began.

Hours later and back on the ground, Gillian Malone, a Powder River Basin

Resource Council organizer and researcher, stood on the banks of Spotted Horse Creek. Bathed in a white moonlight, a half dozen dead cottonwoods behind her looked like ghost trees. What remained of two dozen more dead cottonwoods was stacked in five pyres. From a mile upstream, the loud, low hum of a screw compressor was audible. Bill West, the owner of the ranch and the downed cottonwoods, couldn't make it, nor could his wife, Marge, who called to say, "Mr. West is real sorry he couldn't be there." West had problems more immediate than his downed cottonwoods. Three days earlier while loading cattle he was caught between a gate and a panicked steer, and he had just gotten out of intensive care. Malone had surveyed the damage before, but she seemed stunned. "It looks worse at night," she said. The Wests are Powder River Basin Resource Council members, pushed into environmentalism by the CBM drilling on their land. "They're the very best kind of people," Malone said. "Modest, hardworking ranchers. This shouldn't be happening to them."

The two great misconceptions about the American West are that it is an almost endless open space and that the land is extremely rugged. In fact, the West is both finite and fragile. From the earliest paintings by Albert Bierstadt, which were immensely popular in the East, to the great Western films of John Ford (and those of lesser mortals), the notion has been planted in the national psyche that the West is a tough, wild, indestructible place of vast spaces in need of "taming." It's damned hard to get rid of those notions; that's why we keep using the West as our national dumping ground for everything from bombing ranges to atomic weapons to nuclear waste (and congratulations to Nevada on its selection as the site of the national nuclear dump).

The land is not only destructible, it is painfully frail — there are still scars left in the earth from the wooden wagon wheels along the Oregon Trail. Because the land is arid, it cannot heal itself — once it's screwed up, it stays that way; it doesn't come back from overgrazing, clear-cut timber, or anything else. As Walter Prescott Webb argued in *The Great Plains*, one of the great ecological tragedies in America is that anyone ever put a plough in the earth west of the ninety-eighth parallel.

Economically, the West has always been

treated like a colony, its natural resources exploited, usually by Eastern corporations that then move on, leaving ruin behind. The West is dotted with more ruins than Italy. It is necessary to live lightly on that land. The most precious and scarce of all the West's resources is water. To poison water in the West is to commit an act of such shortsighted folly that it is a wonder even greed can blind people to the monumental stupidity of it.

Ranchers here fear what's coming in the northeast corner of a state as fragile as any in the American West. Drilling companies are buying and "holding" leases. Waiting on the final word from Washington. Waiting for the BLM to decide. "The BLM is very aware of what's gone on out here," Clark said. "There's no reason they can't do this right. And if they don't do it right, they can ruin us."

WARM IN THE WHITE HOUSE

First and first and foremost, we've got to make sure we fully fund LIHEAP, which is a way to help low-income folks, particularly here in the East, pay their high fuel bills.
— GEORGE W. BUSH, PRESIDENTIAL DEBATE, BOSTON, OCTOBER 2000

Let's begin by demonstrating our grasp of the obvious: George W. Bush has never faced the choices Luz Cruz wakes up to every day. He doesn't know much about cold houses. Maybe that's why he refused to release the $300 million in federal funds that would have helped Cruz keep her house warm in the winter of 2003. This remarkable example of compassionate conservatism is enough to make you wonder if the country has completely lost its gag reflex. While the president was cutting the heating subsidy for people in Luz Cruz' desperate circumstances, he was also pushing a $337 billion cut in dividend taxes that benefits only the very rich. Bloomberg News Service applied Bush's proposed tax cuts to Bush's own 2002 tax returns and to those of Vice President Cheney. The resulting savings would be $44,500 for Bush and $326,555 for Cheney.

If you think Bush later changed his mind and released $200 million in the Low Income Home Energy Assistance Program (LIHEAP) funds in January 2003, you have been misinformed. The story was just complex enough so that it was reported wrong. More on that later.

On a Saturday morning in late January 2003 Luz Cruz sat at the kitchen table in her North Philadelphia home. Her three children sprawled on the floor watching cartoons. Piles of bills were scattered across the kitchen table waiting for Cruz to puzzle her way through them. It was 15 degrees F. outside and the house was almost warm, but the bills had Cruz sweating. The eastern seaboard was in the grip of a cold spell that brought snow to the Carolinas' Outer Banks and single-digit temperatures to Philadelphia. Cruz owed the gas company $992.45 and had no idea how she was going to pay it. In a rich Puerto-

Rican–flavored Spanish sprinkled with English, she told the story of how she got into this fix.

"*Mi mamá era mi* backup," she said. Unfortunately, *mamá* the backup died a year ago. Luz' husband divorced her and went back to Puerto Rico. She has yet to see her first child-support check. Her eleven-year-old daughter, Jennifer, a child with large, expressive eyes who is timid in two languages, has chronic asthma. At times Jennifer requires treatment every four hours with a nebulizer, a portable appliance that allows her to breathe a med-icated mist. When she goes into respiratory distress, she checks into a nearby hospital. After her mother's death, Cruz left her job as a hairdresser in order to take care of Jennifer. The family lives on the $248.50 the Pennsylvania Department of Public Welfare provides every two weeks. Like taxation, welfare is redistribution of wealth. Based on her current income, it would take Cruz fifty-four years to get the $326,555 redistributed to Dick Cheney under Bush's 2003 tax plan.

Cruz' North Philly neighborhood doesn't have a lot of curb appeal. Some of the row houses are tagged with condemned signs. Some have already been demolished, and the lots between the standing homes give the effect of missing teeth. Some are occupied by squatters. But the Cruz house is well kept and painted a tropical blue and yellow that looks like better times in Puerto Rico. The mortgage payment is $341.

Cruz said she is lucky the gas company didn't cut her off in the fall when she was trying to negotiate a payment plan. The city doesn't allow cutoffs in winter. She was trying to cut costs and deal with her bills so she wouldn't get cut off in spring or summer and face the following winter with no heat. That had already happened to ten thousand Philadelphia households.

In order to save $10 a week, her son rides the *"wawa"* to school in the morning but walks home when it's warmer in the afternoon. (When Cruz talks about the *wawa*, you realize you can take the girl out of Puerto Rico, but you can't take the Puerto Rico out of the girl. A *wawa* in Puerto Rico is an *autobus* in most Latin American countries.) Joshua's walk home from the local high school is only a couple of miles. No big deal, he said. He's a tall, healthy kid who wants to be a chef. The $40 he saves each month will help pay the gas bill down enough so maybe the gas won't be shut off in the spring.

Cruz washes clothes at the Laundromat because it's cheaper than using her own water and electricity. She keeps the thermostat as low as she can without risking the children's health. She has no car so there are no car expenses. She tries to cut costs at the grocery store, *"pero es muy difícil,"* she said. She would like to go back to work but doesn't see a way out.

The last thing Luz Cruz needs is for George Bush to make her life harder. When Bush cut $300 million from the annual budget of LIHEAP — the heating-oil and gas subsidy program designed to help people in Luz Cruz' situation — her assistance was put on hold. She has gotten LIHEAP assistance in the past but is having a hard time in 2003. Even if she does get it, the $250 annual stipend from the federally funded program will not cover her delinquent bill. In fact, it won't even cover the current bills, which run about a hundred dollars a month. "It would help," she said. "Sometimes I think I'll let them have the house and go back to Puerto Rico. I can find work in a beauty salon there, and it's never cold."

It was probably not a bad time for Cruz to leave. The Delaware hadn't seen this much ice since George Washington crossed it. There were ice-skaters on the Schuylkill. Household energy prices this winter were up 19 percent for natural gas, 45 percent for heating oil, and 22 percent for propane. Two rounds of Bush tax cuts for the wealthy made the federal budget harder to balance. By moving just 500,000 low-income families off LIHEAP — in the direction of energy independence — the president saved $300 million, *one thousandth of his dividend tax cut.* Too easy for him to pass up.

The Low Income Home Energy Assistance Program has been in place since 1974. By 2001 it was helping 4.6 million low-income families, half with children under eighteen, keep their homes warm in winter. Bush didn't intend to wipe out the subsidy for all of them, just for half a million. His numbers-crunchers even came up with a plan to get two bangs for their buck. A warm winter in 2001 had left LIHEAP $500 million in surplus funds, which could be rolled back into general revenue if not spent. The president's 2003 budget provided $1.4 billion instead of the $1.7 appropriated the previous year. Add the $500 million surplus from 2002 to the $300 million cut from the budget in 2003, and you have practically a billion dollars to apply to tax cuts. All you have to do is cut off heat for people who rarely turn out to vote and never make political contributions.

If there are cold hearts in the White House, at least there are heroes in one of the country's most durable community organizations. In her quirky mix of Spanish and English, Cruz said she was hanging her hopes on a grassroots group known by its odd arboreal acronym. "ACORN *tuve* an action," Cruz said. The leaders and members of the Association of Community Organizations for Reform Now are perennial trench fighters for economic justice in the nation's cities. The "action" Cruz referred to was a protest in Philadelphia. But ACORN's work extended beyond Philadelphia. During the big freeze of 2003, ACORN members and organizers seemed to be everywhere, or at least everywhere the poor were caught between the harsh realities of an arctic cold spell and George Bush's budget. Among its more creative efforts were takeovers of Republican Party headquarters.

In Chicago, for example, fifty ACORN families moved into the party offices, over the objection of the party's employees.

They found their way to the databases and faxed and phoned Washington. They advised the White House switchboard that ACORN had taken over the Republican Party of Illinois and would give it back when President Bush released the emergency LIHEAP funds. Their timing was driven by more than cold weather. They moved into the offices the night before the president was to arrive in Chicago to lay out his budget: the budget that cut $300 million in LIHEAP funding. And to make the case for eliminating the taxes investors pay on stock dividends.

As Dubya Bush's advance team checked into their hotel, ACORN squatters were checking into the Republican Party office. "This place is warmer than most people's homes," said a man sitting on the floor. WGN-TV put the claim to the test, dispatching reporter Juan Carlos Fanjul to the living room of eighty-one-year-old Doris Rodgers, one of the people occupying Republican Party headquarters. The temperature on Fanjul's digital thermometer read 32 degrees F. The cops decided to arrest two elderly women. Eighty-one-year-old Mahaley Somerville and sixty-nine-year-old Gwendolyn Stewart were "cuffed and stuffed" into a patrol car in front of the party offices. "It's warm in jail," said Somerville as they hauled her away. "It's cold in my house."

TV news is done by formula. Every newscast began with a variation on "When President Bush arrives in Chicago tomorrow, he'll find that for some people it's just as cold inside their homes as it is on the city's streets . . ." Most stories went on to describe conditions facing fourteen thousand households without heat. WGN even sent a reporter into the Cook County Jail to ask Somerville what she would like to say to the president.

ACORN was equally imaginative in Rhode Island, where forty-five poor, urban protestors confronted Republican state party chair Bradford Gorham in the law offices of Gorham & Gorham. (Why do these folks always have names that sound like the *Mayflower* passenger manifest?) "I still don't know why they were here," Gorham told a reporter from *The Providence Journal*. "I kept asking the chief fellow, and he kept saying, 'I'm cold, it's warm in here.'

"It disrupted the place. . . . I mean people were shouting at the top of their lungs. They filled the whole downstairs of the office building. They were leaning against the fax machine, leaning against the printers and the computers. After that, one guy got very insulting. I said, 'Would you please leave,' and he just stood there looking stupid."

Gorham said the demonstrators had "sleeping bags and things like that. They were ready to camp out there on the floor. I said, 'Oh, Lord, I've got a sit-in demonstration.' And after the police came, they left."

When a reporter asked Gorham if the protesters had a point about Bush's budget cuts, Gorham said he wasn't sure. Then he wavered: "Nobody wants to see people cold or hungry or anything. I don't want to see that happen."

There were also a few heroes in Congress. Even before ACORN raided the Rhode Island Republican chairman's office, the state's Democratic senator had drafted an amendment to the appropriations bill. Jack Reed's amendment took all discretionary LIHEAP funding away from the president and restored it to mandatory "formula" funding that Bush cannot control. The amendment increased LIHEAP funding from the $1.4 billion proposed by Bush to $2 billion. The amendment won on an 88–4 vote.

Then Reed and Maine Republican Susan Collins fired off a letter to the president, urging him to immediately release the emergency contingency money, since it was no longer under his discretion. They demanded he use the power of the executive branch to get the money to the people who needed it. The senators' language was diplomatic, but one of Reed's staffers said the amendment intentionally took all discretionary funds from the president. Bush could either wait to see the money spent in the following fiscal year or release it immediately. He could no longer deny it to people who couldn't afford heating oil and gas.

Fort Worth writer Sam Hudson tells young reporters that "trousers are the most manly ass-covering, though some men try to cover their asses with paper." In a response to the 88–4 Senate vote and the letter from the two senators, George Bush covered his with paper. Two sheets, to be precise. One was an executive order releasing $200 million from the discretionary funds over which he was losing his discretion. The other a press release in which the president announced the release of funds. This adroit move allowed him to save his face and cover his ass at the same time. By releasing $200 million of the $300 million in the fund, he maintained the illusion that he had a choice. The $100 million he didn't order spent will be included in the mandatory funding for LIHEAP in the year to come.

The president's press release provided the angle for most news reporters writing about LIHEAP. Some news stories went so far as to describe the Senate vote and make it clear that the president had no choice, but most people concluded that President Bush had done right by millions of Americans in need of help with their heating.

It was too late for many. The money, released in late January, could not ensure that the ten thousand households without heat in Philadelphia would have their heat turned on. Or the fourteen thousand freezing homes in Chicago. But it did help tens of thousands of people across the country, where states responded to increased fuel costs and increased demands for help by reducing the size of LIHEAP grants, cutting staff, and reducing the number of months covered.

If you don't believe the help is desperately needed, get into your car. In any city in the country you are a short drive from the people Michael Harrington described fifty years ago in *The Other America.*

In Philadelphia there are entire neighborhoods where a reporter can find "heat-or-eat" horror stories by knocking on doors and asking a few questions. If you're aiming for diversity, within four miles of Philly's Center City hotels, where dinner for two means a $200 tab, there's a heap of multicultural LIHEAP stories. Luz Cruz lives four miles north of Center City, in the shadow of Temple University. Four miles west, near the University of Pennsylvania, Frances Hassell lives in an eighty-year-old row house that seems to be collapsing from the front porch inward. "Look for the torn blue tarp on my roof," Hassell said. "That's how I tell people to find my house." She is a tall, fair-skinned woman with red hair, struggling to make it on a $570 monthly SSI check. Her husband, a World War II veteran who was almost twenty years her senior, died a few years ago. She's disabled and on her own. Last year her $250 LIHEAP grant helped. "It hasn't come through yet this year," she said. She has been unable to complete the application process because when she calls all she gets is a recording. Her gas bill is averaged over twelve months. "I'm supposed to pay sixty-four dollars and some change. This month they sent me a bill for one hundred sixty-four dollars. How am I going to pay one hundred sixty-four dollars?"

Four miles northwest of City Hall Alma Brown keeps her thermostat set well below seventy. Brown, a seventy-year-old African-American woman living on Social Security, is also disabled. "I get only Social Security, but I been managing pretty good," she said. For years she sewed uniforms at the Army Quartermaster Building in South Philadelphia. LIHEAP has helped in the past, but with temperatures in the low teens in January, she was still waiting for a response to her 2003 application. "I'll get it," she said. "But it's not going to be as much as last year. They cut everybody back." Brown was just starting to do the numbers. She had been managing pretty good, but a lower LIHEAP grant, fuel bills up by 45 percent, and a fixed income make it much harder.

Funds get cut and people "fall through the cracks." *The Philadelphia Inquirer* reported in late January that Delia Brown, seventy, Betty Clark, sixty-six, and Bobby Rivers, seventy-seven, had fallen through the cracks. Big-time. On the weekend most Americans were watching the Super Bowl, they died in their homes. Their heat had been cut off. The cause of their deaths was a combination of heart disease and hypothermia. They froze to death. The County Assistance Office would not say whether they had applied for LIHEAP assistance. The Philadelphia Gas Works does not discuss customer accounts.

• 11 •

THE UNITED STATES OF ENRON

He was a supporter of Ann Richards in my run in 1994. And she did name him the head of the Governor's Business Council. And I decided to leave him in place just for the sake of continuity. And that's when I first got to know Ken . . .
— GEORGE W. BUSH ON KEN LAY

I strongly supported him when he ran for governor of Texas — both times. I supported his father back before that. Indeed, I believe in both his character and integrity. As well as the policies he's proposing.
— KEN LAY ON GEORGE W. BUSH

"Do you think there were dinners?"

Kathryn Widme was sitting in the Ol' PasTime Tavern in Rainier, Oregon, trying to make some sense out of the last three years of her life. "You know. Dinners. Ken

Lay. In the White House with Bush. Were there dinners?" Widme is a tall, striking blonde in her early fifties. She is one of thousands of people whose lives were destroyed by Ken Lay, Jeffrey Skilling, and Andy Fastow, the smart guys from Houston who converted other people's money and lives into derivatives. Widme wanted to know if Lay is the casual acquaintance George Bush now says he is, or if he was tight enough with Dubya and Laura to make the A-list of White House dinner guests.

Rainier is the bluest of blue-collar towns: a jumble of wharves, piers, sheds, and bars strung along the Columbia River. Wood-frame houses and double-wides cling to the green hills of the gorge, and most of the town sits in the shadow of the spectacular Lewis & Clark Bridge that connects Rainier to Longview, Washington.

Lay, dubbed "Kenny Boy" by George W. Bush, never made it to the Ol' PasTime, or to the Riverview Restaurant next-door, where Widme worked evening shifts after putting in forty hours a week for Lay at Portland General Electric. He did drop in for a couple of visits at PGE's Trojan nuclear-power plant, fifteen miles south of Rainier. "His helicopter would land," Widme said. "He would come to all-hands meetings at

Trojan. He told us we were doing a great job. Everybody was doing a great job decommissioning the plant. . . . We always saw that smiling face of Ken Lay. Did you ever see him when he didn't have a shitty smile on his face?"

Lay's message was always the same. The company is fine. The stock is fine. Finances are fine. The future's so bright I gotta wear shades. Everyone was on-message, including PGE's president, Peggy Fowler. Everything was going to be fine. "When the stock would drop, there was always a reason," Widme said. "They could explain it. They were merging with Dynergy. There was always some good explanation."

So Widme kept all her 401(k) retirement funds in Enron stock, even though a Paine Webber accounts manager had warned her to diversify. "But there was Ken Lay with his shitty-ass grin."

Widme doesn't blame Lay for her lost 401(k). Like many Enron employees, she blames herself. "What a fool I was," she said. "What fools we all were."

Widme has an unusual habit of stopping as she talks. Not pausing, as if she's weighing her words, but stopping, gathering the strength to say them. She stopped a lot while talking about what happened after

Enron acquired the company she worked for. "Ken Lay and Skilling inflated the value of the stock. Ken Lay told us what a great company this was. The papers were full of stories about this great company. And we believed them. They walked away with millions of our money, and we believed them.

"Portland General Electric. Who would think that while you were working at this company that is one hundred years old this would happen to you?"

Kate Widme is a single parent. She patched together jobs and the child support she got from her ex-husband to raise a son who is now a pilot on the Columbia. In 1987 she landed a good-pay temporary position at the Trojan nuclear-power plant. When Trojan was shut down by Oregon's voters, she moved on to another temporary gig. Then she got lucky. In 1997 she got a permanent job with PGE. She began working "four tens" for Portland General Electric, followed by night shifts and weekends at the Riverview.

The work at PGE's recycling warehouse in Portland was dirty and physically demanding: lifting rolls of cable, porcelain insulators, and wooden cross-arms. It was also fifty miles from home. "We had to get up at three-thirty to make it to Portland by six," she said. But permanent employees got 401(k) accounts with matching company contributions. Widme moonlighted as a waitress so she could make the maximum monthly contribution to her retirement account and still have enough money to live on. "It was a real drain. Working a ten-hour day and driving to your night job. . . . But for me, it was a great deal. I would be set for life. That 401(k) was my retirement. My future." When two slots on the Trojan plant's decommissioning team opened up, Widme and her friend Diane Tillotson ended their daily grind commuting to Portland and signed on as rad-waste handlers. The work was still dirty and physically demanding, but it was close to home.

At Trojan it was all Enron all the time. "One guy always had the stock ticker running on a computer screen," Widme said. "He would shout out stock quotes two, three, four, five times a day, and everyone would cheer. A guy named Ollie had eight hundred thousand dollars in his 401(k). He would push people. He was telling everyone, 'This stock is going crazy!'"

Then shares valued at almost $100 fell to $80, then $60, then $40. Enron man-

agement locked employees out of their accounts. Those who held only Enron stock
were wiped out. "I was destroyed," Widme
said. "I had migraines. I had ulcers. I was a
mess." No one she knows went to a single
session with the grief counselors PGE provided. "No one wanted anything to do
with the company," she said. "I found my
own shrink."

Kathryn Widme admits she doesn't have
the greatest Enron horror story: "I didn't
lose the house on the hill." She lost only
$75,000. But it was all the retirement she
had. It was $5,000 annual bonuses, $1,000
special bonuses, and tips earned during
night shifts at the Riverview — all depos-
ited in her 401(k). It was doing the numbers and calculating when her account
would hit $500,000.

Until the bottom fell out.

*It was so silly. Why didn't he just say
Ken Lay was a strong supporter and gave
him a half-million dollars and is a good
friend, and he's really sorry Ken's in
these terrible circumstances?*
— ANN RICHARDS
ON GEORGE BUSH AND KEN LAY

There were dinners for Lay at the White

House during the first few weeks after Dubya Bush took the oath of office. And lunch at the White House the day after the inauguration.

There had to be. Governor George W. Bush was a creation of Enron.

It was more than money. The blessing of Ken Lay and Joe B. Allen — the political *patrón* at Enron's hometown law firm — put Texas candidates on the gold standard. Lay could also destroy political careers — as a prince of a congressman by the name of Craig Washington found out after casting one anti-Lay vote. Washington had represented his district in both the Texas House and Senate before he was elected to Congress. He was strikingly handsome and charismatic and an eloquent and impassioned speaker. He voted his constituents' interest. Washington was defeated in the Democratic primary by a candidate recruited by Lay: city council member Sheila Jackson Lee.

A corporate fat cat from River Oaks took out an incumbent African-American candidate beloved by voters in a minority district carved out of Houston's black community for the late Barbara Jordan. That's real identity politics.

"Silly," as Ann Richards described it, is a

kind description of what Bush said about his Kenny Boy. The president lied. Anyone with free time and a cheap calculator can walk into the offices of the Texas Ethics Commission and get the numbers from Bush's campaign filings. When he ran for governor in 1994, Enron gave Bush $146,500; he got $47,500 in direct contributions from Ken and Linda Lay. Lay gave Ann Richards $12,500. By 1998, when Bush rolled over an underfunded Democrat named Garry Mauro, Lay, the company PAC, and Enron execs had more than a half million dollars in Bush's two campaigns.

The $1,000 cap on federal contributions made it harder for Ken and Linda to show their love for George W. when he ran for president, but no campaign-finance law ever stood between a creative contributor and his candidate. Lay became a Bush Pioneer, raising $100,000 in $1K contributions. Both major parties used clever mechanisms to get around the toothless campaign-finance laws then on the books. Bush's "Pioneers" corps was one of those mechanisms, and Ken Lay was a pioneering Pioneer.

Lay individually contributed more than $275,000 to the Republican National Committee, and Enron provided $250,000 for the Bush coronation at the Republican National Convention in Philadelphia. Ken and Linda also contributed $10,000 to the Florida recount fund. During the recount, while Al Gore was stuck on the ground wondering who to sue, Enron's corporate air force flew Bush-campaign operatives anywhere they needed to go. Bush family lawyer James Baker III shuttled back and forth on corporate jets owned by Reliant Energy, the Houston utility where he serves on the board. Halliburton's aircraft were also pressed into service. The grand total of Enron contributions to Bush 2000 was $700,000.

Ken Lay was part of the political patrimony Poppy Bush handed down to his son. Years before Lay dined at the White House with George W. and Laura, he was an overnight White House guest of George and Barbara Bush. He earned his stay, raising money for the elder Bush's 1988 presidential campaign by cohosting a $1,000-a-plate fund-raiser in Houston and by encouraging Enron employees to contribute to the Bush presidential campaign. None of this had anything to do with influence and access, not a thing. By the time Lay was giving his time and money to the Bush Pioneers in 1999, he was tired of the cynicism of those who criticized this splendid system. At a 1999 company meeting in Houston, Lay stood, smiling, before thousands of Enron employees and said: "They don't think an individual can make a contribution because they believe in the candidate. They're always doing this to get some benefit."

By that time Lay had already gotten "some benefit" from the Bushes. Rodolfo Terragno was the Argentine minister of public works under President Raúl Alfonsín. In 1988, Terragno said, he got a cold call from an Enron salesman. "He told me he had recently returned from a campaign tour with his father" and that awarding a huge gas-pipeline contract to Enron "would be very favorable to the United States." Terragno said the caller was George W. Bush. Bush denied making the call and faxed a list of written questions back to the reporter who broke the story — answering "no and none" to each question. To prove he hadn't made the call, Bush even faxed his daily calendars to *The Nation*'s David Corn, arguing that this should be the end of the story. Bush's "proof" was the absence of any mention of Terragno in his daily calendars. (Bush strategist Karl Rove went ballistic when the story appeared in *The Texas Observer*, where it first ran, calling and shouting at the editor, "You've destroyed the integrity of the publication!")

Rodolfo Terragno could teach Rove a thing or two about integrity. Eleven years after he blew the whistle on Bush and Enron, Terragno was back in government, as cabinet chief for Argentine president-elect Fernando de la Rua, and George W. Bush was poised to win the U.S. presidential election. Again Terragno refused to budge from his story. The former journalist had been forced to live in exile for ten years, until the military dictatorship ended with the election of Alfonsín. Terragno had stood up to death squads and looked into the eyes of his country's military dictators. He wasn't going to change his story to accommodate the Bushes. He still says George W. Bush had called him to pressure him to award a multimillion-dollar pipeline contract to Enron. He did allow that it was a very remote possibility that it might have been another son of George Herbert Walker Bush on the other end of the phone line, but as Terragno had called it earlier and as he recalled it later, the son on the phone was George W.

Terragno said Enron had no real presence in Argentina and no capital. They showed up at the last minute with what he described as a laughable outline of a proposal, after other companies had been working for more than a year to win the huge *gasoducto* project. Enron tried to lock in natural-gas futures at a price far below the market value — which would have allowed them to sell it at a higher market rate, kind of like they did with electricity in California in 2001.

Bush-family lobbying for Enron didn't stop with a phone call. In 1990 Poppy became the first American president since Eisenhower to visit Argentina. A few days after the visit, his ambassador in Buenos Aires, Terrence Todman, sent a stern letter to Argentina's minister of finance. If Argentina didn't stop giving preference to its domestic industries, eight big American corporations would take their money and go home. Enron was at the top of the list of companies Bush's ambassador was forcing on the people of Argentina. The ambassador even set a deadline, weeks before the new government of the spectacularly corrupt President Carlos Menem would decide which company got the *gasoducto*. Todman's letter was marked "urgent" and "confidential."

Menem — a golf buddy of Poppy and Bush junior — did the deal for Enron and even allowed the Houston company to take advantage of a tax waiver available to Argentine companies working on projects in the national interest. Neil Bush showed up to play tennis with Menem the day after he won his election; Carlos and Poppy still play golf together.

After Poppy Bush left the White House, he could no longer use the diplomatic corps as Enron capos, so he resorted to a more direct approach. In April 1993 the emir of Kuwait sent a Kuwait Airlines plane to pick up Bush and his entourage. The elder Bush wasn't quite three months into retirement. He was traveling to Kuwait to accept that nation's highest award for his role in liberating the Kuwaitis from Saddam Hussein. James Baker III and retired lieutenant general Thomas Kelly tagged along on an Enron sales junket that could earn them hundreds of thousands of dollars — and hundreds of millions for Enron.

The disgraceful account of Baker and Kelly turning a quick buck on the blood of American soldiers who died in the Gulf War was laid out by Seymour Hersh in *The New Yorker*. Baker III was cavalier in his response to Hersh's questions. His spokesperson said her boss was doing business on behalf of America. Kelly was more blunt. "This is a full-time job. I've worked my ass off learning all I could about it. . . . The fact I was in the [Gulf] War doesn't cut any slack at all." He added that he and Baker were "meticulous in not meeting with anybody until Bush left."

Lay saw nothing wrong with the former president advancing his sales force. "Is it bad taste for American companies to do business with Kuwait? . . . What's wrong with hiring former American officials to encourage investments anywhere in the world? Jim Baker has given me some very helpful advice to be more competitive in the world. I ask you, what in the hell is wrong with that?" Almost makes you wonder if Enron could have been saved had it survived long enough to take advantage of the markets President Dubya Bush opened up in Iraq.

Neil and Marvin Bush also made the Kuwait trip with Poppy. Marvin was selling electric security fences. Neil came home with his parents but returned a few weeks later, hoping to persuade Kuwait's Ministry of Electricity to cut him in on any management fees Enron would earn running Kuwait's reconstructed power plants. Lay was the chair of the Host Committee at the 1992 Houston Republican National Convention. His guy lost to Bill Clinton, but eight years later Lay was again "getting serviced," as they say around the barnyard, by the Bush administration.

The Bushes' servicing of Ken Lay and Co. continued until Enron collapsed and Dubya Bush started to act as if Ken Lay were part of the Axis of Evil. Until that happened, Lay knew he could count on the Bushes. In 1997, at Lay's request, Governor Bush went to bat for Enron, calling then-Pennsylvania governor Tom Ridge to push for the deregulation policies Lay wanted in place in Pennsylvania.

Before he became the poster boy for corporate corruption, Lay managed to get Federal Energy Regulatory Commission chairman Curtis Hebert fired and replaced him with Enron's handpicked candidate. The new FERC member, Pat Wood, had worked on the same utility-deregulation bill in Texas that Enron wanted to impose on the nation. Hebert was a Bill Clinton appointee, named to the commission in January 2001. He's not exactly a pro-consumer radical. A Republican who served in the Mississippi Legislature, Hebert was a close ally of the most powerful Republican in the Senate, Trent Lott. (This was before Strom Thurmond's one-hundredth birthday party.) Lay called Hebert to tell him that unless he changed his position on retail competition in the energy business, he'd be sent home to Mississippi.

Lay did tell Hebert that the final decision on his job "was going to be the president's, certainly not ours." That's what the president would call a "nuanced message."

It was a revealing episode. One of the president's corporate sponsors was threatening to fire the chair of the commission that regulated that contributor's business. Lay did it. Three months after the phone call from Lay, Hebert was out and Pat Wood was in.

Taking out a sitting U.S. congressman in your home state is no small feat. Busting a sitting presidential appointee who had the support of the Senate's leading Republican indicates some awesome clout, and Ken Lay hardly broke a sweat when he sent Hebert packing.

Lay's scheme to consolidate the states' electricity grids into four giant regional transition organizations was more than a states'-rights son of the South like Hebert could swallow. Lay had another grudge against Hebert. In May 2001 Hebert had ordered FERC investigators to look into the complex derivative-financing schemes Enron and other electricity traders were using to "game the market."

Dinners?

With the election of G. W. Bush, Lay had enough stroke at the White House to get more than the occasional free meal. He was writing policy and making appointments. Before his Ponzi scheme collapsed, Lay managed to make two FERC appointments. He had to work harder for the second one, calling Bush political strategist (and Enron shareholder) Karl Rove to make the case for Nora Mead Brownell, a Pennsylvania utilities regulator best known for her anti-regulatory zeal.

Call it the Lay Legacy. His company is in ruins. He's struggling for liquidity and reduced to a modest $9.5 million worth of residential real estate in Houston. His wife is selling off their household goods at her used-furniture boutique, Jus' Stuff. And the president he helped elect has disowned him. But his appointees to the Federal Energy Regulatory Commission are still with us. Kenny Boy Lay, the little guy with the University of Houston economics Ph.D. and the thousand-megawatt smile made sure you and I get FERCed every time we flip a light switch.

At last everyone in the country knows what it's like to live in the Great State of Texas.

"Write it so the boys in Lubbock can understand it," Bush said of his September 2002 national-security document. The boys in Lubbock might observe that Bush and Co. are "slicker than greased owl shit." Consider the widely held belief that despite all the money Enron gave them, the Bushies gave nothing back. You won't find much reporting in your daily newspaper or on Fox News that contradicts this. But we live in a time when some of the best reporting is being done by journalists working outside the corporate mainstream — like investigative reporter Sam Parry at the online site *consortiumnews.com*.

Parry has documented and published a long bill of particulars describing what Bush did to keep Enron afloat. In fairness to the mainstream press, some of Parry's work was gleaned from newspapers, but the constraints of "objective" journalism work to stop reporters from thinking on the page and from putting news in context. Put into context, the Bush effort to save

Enron is what the boys in Lubbock would describe as a "BFD."

If you were paying an electric bill in California, you probably remember 2001 as the year your bill increased by 800 percent. It's what Bush didn't do about that mind-boggling rip-off that smells like a dead skunk in the middle of the road. Bush and Cheney used the bully pulpit of the White House to stop FERC from imposing even temporary caps on electricity rates in California.

As early as August 2000 a Southern California Edison employee warned FERC regulators that Enron and other companies were gaming the market by withholding electricity and creating phony congestion. But there was no chance Lay's regulators would step in and stop the gouging without enormous pressure from the White House and the Congress. An April 7, 2001, memo from Ken Lay to Dick Cheney became Bush and Cheney's no-caps mantra: "The administration should reject any attempt to re-regulate wholesale power markets by adopting price caps or returning to archaic methods of determining the cost-base of wholesale power," Lay wrote. Even temporary price restrictions "will be detrimental to power markets and will discourage private investment." In California almost a year later Bush said, "Price caps do nothing to reduce demand, and they do nothing to increase supply."

California senator Dianne Feinstein repeatedly requested a private meeting with Cheney to discuss California's energy crisis but was turned down — once in a letter with her name misspelled. She did get into two group meetings, but Cheney seemed distracted. "When someone is looking at their watch it gives you a pretty good idea that they want to get out of the room," Feinstein told *The New York Times.*

In the end the Bushies had to give in. It was not Feinstein who convinced them. Republicans in Congress warned Bush that the administration's opposition to caps could cost the party control of the House. Wood, Brownell, and their fellow FERCers on the five-member commission voted to cap electricity prices in California.

After Lay's fall from power, Pat Wood said of his former patron, "I never sat down and had a beer with him." Maybe Indian prime minister Atal Bihari Vajpayee should have invited Wood out for a beer and asked him how to deal with the corporate heavies from Houston. It turns out the energy from a gas-fired utility plant Enron built in

Dabhol, India, cost several times what other generators were charging Indian consumers. So Enron decided the Indian government needed to pay some $250 million in unpaid bills or buy the plant. It is not unusual for the U.S. government to go to bat for U.S. companies trying to make good on foreign contracts. Clinton's Commerce Department had, in fact, tried leaning on India to meet Enron's demands. But the Bushes collect foreign debts with a zeal we haven't seen since secretary of state Philander Knox ordered the Marines to seize the customs houses in Nicaragua.

Just as Poppy had done in Argentina, Dubya turned the State Department over to Enron. He had a senior State Department official deliver a démarche, an official warning, to the Indians. Cheney leaned on Indian opposition leader Sonia Ghandi. "Good news is that the VEEP mentioned Enron in his meeting with Sonia Gandhi," reads a National Security Council e-mail. It's the NSC and the VEEP that illustrate the Bush administration's slavish devotion to Enron. While it's unseemly for the Commerce Department to serve as a private bill collector for a U.S. company, well, at least it's commerce. The NSC is supposed to be in another line of work.

When doing the bidding of their corporate sponsors the Bushes are industrious. In India, Overseas Private Investment Corporation chairman Peter Watson was almost as unsubtle as Terrence Todman had been in doing Poppy's bidding in Argentina. In an e-mail to Prime Minister Vajpayee's national security adviser, Watson warned that India had better deliver on Enron's Dabhol plant. "The acute lack of progress in this matter has forced Dabhol to rise to the highest levels of the United States government . . . and could have a negative effect regarding other U.S. agencies and their ability to function in India."

Dubya Bush was prepared to lean on Vajpayee during a White House visit on November 8, 2002 — the very day the SEC finally got around to delivering subpoenas to Enron and announcing that the company was the target of a federal investigation. An internal White House memo sent at 2:33 p.m. stopped him: "President Bush cannot talk about Dabhol," warned the memo.

Not a great moment in American foreign policy. Condi Rice brought together the State Department, the Treasury Department, the Office of U.S. Trade Representative, and the Overseas Private Investment Corporation and still failed to collect on Enron's debt. (The whole sordid tale is told in Robert Bryce's *Pipe Dreams*.)

There is more on the domestic front.

Ken Lay could get private face-time with Vice President Cheney, but Senator Feinstein couldn't — even while Lay's electricity hustlers were plundering the state Feinstein represents. Lay had at least one meeting (that we know of) with Cheney while the vice president was looking for direction in how to shape the nation's energy policy. Lay also joined Cheney on an American Petroleum Institute panel in Colorado in June 2001 — while Enron was squeezing record-high electricity bills out of Californians. Others from Enron met repeatedly with Cheney.

As Parry and *The Washington Post* reported, after the Enron meeting with the vice president and his energy-policy group, Cheney's energy task force changed a proposal to include a provision to boost oil and natural-gas production in India. The amendment was so narrow it was obvious it was designed to help bail out Enron's bad investment in India. It wasn't the only pro-Enron energy policy; California congressman Henry Waxman found seventeen proposals that had been requested by

Enron — all in the draft of the vice president's energy plan.

Even as Enron was collapsing, undersecretary for domestic finance Peter Fisher called Enron president Greg Whalley "six to eight times." Commerce secretary Don Evans was in touch with Enron executives, and Bush was getting ready to muscle the Indian prime minister even as SEC investigators were kicking in Enron's doors.

We're not arguing that the Bush administration could have saved Enron (for its investors and from itself), nor do we hold them responsible for what happened at WorldCom, Tyco, Adelphia, Global Crossing, and dozens of other "isolated bad apples" engaged in corporate plunder. Maybe they couldn't have foreseen what was coming. And maybe that's because they were too busy dismantling the federal agency that was supposed to do the foreseeing and the overseeing.

On the Sunday after Bush's hollow sermon on Wall Street in the summer of 2002, Tim Russert interviewed Securities and Exchange chairman Harvey Pitt about Bush's attempt to gut the SEC. As Russert read from an Associated Press clip, poor Pitt — to borrow a phrase from LBJ — looked "like a jackrabbit in a hailstorm.

Hunkered down and takin' it."

"It says," Russert read: "President Bush's 2002 budget proposes staff reductions in securities fraud investigations and enforcement even as the Securities and Exchange Commission acknowledges that the jumpy stock market brings more opportunities for abuse. . . . The SEC budget proposal, the first since Bush took office, also includes staff reductions in inspections of mutual funds, now owned by 49 percent of all U.S. households."

Pitt sputtered and protested that when he asked Bush for an additional $15 million, the president had said, "No, here's twenty million." Russert moved on to an article from *Fortune*, a magazine not known for its advocacy of peasant land reform:

> The SEC's enforcement staff is stretched so thin that many in the investigation are likely to fall by the wayside. How many lawyers, you ask, does the SEC have to study the disclosure documents of 17,000 public companies? About 100, says Laura Unger, the commission's former acting chairwoman. The number of senior forensic accountants in the enforcement division — the kind of experts who decipher

Enron's balance sheets — is far fewer than that. If that isn't bad enough, staffers are leaving in droves. The reason is a familiar one: money. The SEC's attorneys and examiners are paid 25 to 40 percent less than those of comparable federal agencies. Employee turnover is now at 30 percent, double the rate for the rest of the government. Which means that in three years or so, virtually the whole staff could be replaced.

The SEC budget Russert ripped apart was drafted before Enron's collapse made the news. Six months after Enron filed bankruptcy, an SEC spokesman was trying to explain the agency's slow response to stock market fraud. The SEC was "stretched to the max." Its one hundred lawyers reviewed the annual reports of seventeen thousand companies. The agency's $459 million annual budget had been frozen for ten years, and Bush was even then proposing only a 20 percent increase, a little more than $100 million. Former SEC chairs, like Unger, a Republican, were making the news-chat circuit pleading for more funding, begging Bush to double the budget just to allow the agency to handle the current caseload.

It wasn't until January 2003, when most

of the damage to the equities market had been done, SEC chair Harvey Pitt had become a household face, and investor groups were screaming for relief, that the president decided to push for an SEC budget increase. He proposed $842 million, 92 percent more than Congress had appropriated the previous year.

The Bushies had another serious second chance to get on the right side of the corporate-crime issue, by backing Maryland senator Paul Sarbanes' accounting-standards bill. The Sarbanes bill set out to prevent accounting firms like Arthur Andersen from cooking books for companies like Enron. Of course the accounting industry opposed it. The White House also opposed it and backed an accounting-industry bill written by Ohio Republican Michael Oxley. It wasn't until Republican congressmen began defecting like CEOs stepping forward to restate their company earnings that the White House got religion. The House passed the Sarbanes bill unanimously. A president who is slicker than bus-station chili signed the Sarbanes bill and took credit for it.

It's a long way from Washington, D.C., to Longview, Washington — the city that sits across the Columbia River from Rainier. "Why doesn't the government just seize their assets?" Diane Tillotson asked. "They have so much. And pay us back the money they took from us. Why isn't that happening?"

The question is usually answered in Washington with platitudinous blather about the complexity of the transactions, the number of competing interests, and the dangers of overreacting and bringing on unintended consequences.

The truth is that the Bush administration can't seize the assets of "they" who have so much because "they" is "the government." Dubya Bush might have been a perfectly suitable president to preside over the bubble economy of the 1990s. But now we've got ourselves saddled with a guy who can't clean up the mess after the bubble burst, because his corporate sponsors made it all happen.

Diane and her husband, Ed, are more than a half million dollars poorer for what Enron did to Portland General Electric. Diane, like her friend Kate Widme, was a short-timer. Ed has worked at Portland's Trojan nuclear plant since 1982. The two of them are middle-aged, recently married, and so much in love they practically lit up a dark Italian restaurant in Longview where we met.

Ed also wonders how this could have happened to him. "We're a good company. We're a power-generating company. We make something of value. We also own Electricos Brazileros."

In March 2000 Ed had $500,000 in his PGE/Enron 401(k). He managed to hold on to $45,000 because he moved some of his money out of Enron stock. "Want to know what I'm buying?" he said. "Telayfonos day Mayheeco," he said, in painful gringo Spanish. Teléfonos de México, the privatized company that took the place of Mexico's nonfunctioning public utility, has split its stock once in the three months since Ed bought it. "Doubled my value and it pays dividends," he said.

We live in interesting times. George Bush and Ken Lay have driven a middle-aged American union man to flogging a Mexican stock.

Diane didn't do so well. Her retirement was tied up in Enron stock, and her 401(k) account is almost worthless. She does have a stock-option certificate Enron sent its employees to celebrate an earnings milestone. "They gave us an option to buy fifty shares of stock," she said. "Thirteen each year." The company made a big deal of it, Diane said, mailing out a fancy option certificate. By the time she could exercise her option it was too late. Enron's stock was in the tank. "It's not all bad," Diane said. "The certificate is worth two hundred fifty dollars on eBay." That's about $225 more than the Enron stock in her retirement account is worth.

Diane and Kate Widme printed up T-shirts that read: IF THIS IS THE U.S.A., WHERE IS MY 401(K)? The back of the shirt was marked with Enron's tilted-E logo and the lines WE SELL: STOCKS — SHARES — TEE-SHIRTS. The two women sold the red, white, and blue shirts at an Enron party at the Riverview. The bartender at the Ol' PasTime Tavern bought two. "To support my friends," she said. "I sleep in one of them." If Diane and Kate (there is a certain Thelma and Louise quality about them) had just used Enron's mark-to-market accounting, they could have declared tens of thousands in T-shirt profits. As it turned out, they covered the expense of buying and printing the shirts.

"Ken Lay. Linda Lay. They say they are broke," Diane said. "They don't know what broke is. Broke is looking for change in your car seat for money for food for your kids. I've done that, and that's broke. I don't think they understand what they did to us."

At least the Tillotsons have each other.

And a plan.

"Market America," said a beaming Ed Tillotson. "It's a home franchise business. You can buy anything from them. I'm going to focus on health and nutrition." The Tillotsons' enthusiastic discussion of Market America quickly turns to a recruiting rally. Anyone who can sell vitamins, health-care products, nutritional supplements — and the Market America program, earning profits from each associate signed up — can start planning retirement.

Diane has a friend in Market America. "Her husband is an attorney and he's doing less attorney work," Diane said. "Kind of getting out of that because they're making so much money."

Ed prompts Diane, reminding her of "a real booboo story." Diane started and quit Market America. If she had stuck with the program, she'd be set today — like friends who kept building their home franchise businesses. "They and their husbands are now retired and traveling across the country. Like we would be doing except for Enron."

"This is a real job," Diane said. "And it has helped so many people. Lots of people."

Despite their evident mutual affection and enthusiasm, there is a sadness in the Tillotsons' description of their new business enterprise. Ed and Diane are rock-solid America and were earning good wages providing something as necessary as electricity. When Oregon residents voted to shut down the nuclear-power plant, they went to work dismantling the plant, Ed as a metal worker, Diane a rad-waste handler. Then thieves and speculators turned the stock market and their company into a Ponzi scheme. Defrauded by the biggest corporate crime in modern American history, Ed and Diane Tillotson are working their own small pyramid scheme at the rocky bottom of the country's retail sales economy.

You gotta hope they pull it off.

"It gives me hope," Diane said. "Hope. When Trojan is done, we will have our own business. We will have a job. And we will have control. No one will steal your money from you."

They are signed on to a class-action shareholders suit. That's the only other small hope they have. Diane and Ed also say they have given up on the notion of Washington doing anything for them.

Asked if this means he's lost faith in his government, Ed Tillotson answered in a heartbeat. "Yeah. But this is the second time. I was in Vietnam."

• 12 •

ARMY SURPLUS: TWO VETERANS AT ENRON

The California crunch really is the result of not enough power-generating plants and then not enough power to power the power of generating plants.
— GEORGE BUSH TO *THE NEW YORK TIMES*, JANUARY 14, 2001

This was like The Perfect Storm. *First our traders were able to buy power for $250 in California, sell it to Arizona for $1,200, then resell it to California for five times that amount.*
— FORMER ENRON TRADER STEVE BARTH

I can categorically say that it was not ever in the interest of Enron Energy Systems to see wholesale energy prices escalate.
— ARMY SECRETARY AND EX-ENRON EXEC THOMAS WHITE

Tim Ramsey is one of those invisible Americans we depend on when we're alone in the dark. If you live in Beaverton, Tigard, Lake Oswego, or one of a half dozen other suburbs south of Portland, Oregon, you owe him. When a winter storm roars in off the Pacific and knocks your lights out, Ramsey's the guy who climbs the power pole to turn your lights back on. His job at Portland General Electric is just the second one he's ever had. He showed up at IBEW Local 125 thirty-five years ago with his Army discharge papers in hand. The Oregon electric utility hired him as "a grunt." He's been running cable, climbing poles, and testing power circuits ever since.

Because a coworker once swung a boom too close to a transmission line stretched across I-5 south of Portland, Ramsey has the no-eyebrows look of Congressman Dick Gephardt. The boom on the repair truck hit a high-voltage cable, and "the most beautiful blue arc of electricity" Ramsey ever saw found its way to the ground through his boot. "They never grew back," Ramsey said of the absent eyebrows. It could have been worse, he added. "Damn near killed me."

Even without much in the way of eyebrows, Ramsey is a striking man. Broad shoulders, handsome, weathered face, intense blue eyes, iron gray hair. At one time he was a millionaire. He earns top union scale — about $60,000 a year — and lives on eight acres in a quaint Willamette Valley town at risk of being turned into a giant Pinot Noir vineyard. With Tim's PGE check and the money his wife, Donna, earned as a waitress, the Ramseys sent their two daughters to college and made the mortgage payments. They were comfortable. The girls are out of college and working. The couple had $360,000 in their retirement account, but neither of them ever expected to be worth a million.

Then PGE was bought out by a high-flying Texas energy-trading company. The $360,000 in Ramsey's 401(k) was rolled over into Enron stock. Three years later Tim and Donna Ramsey were millionaires, with a little to spare. Tim's Enron/PGE retirement account was worth $1.1 million. In October 2001 the bottom fell out of Enron's stock. Now the account is worth nothing.

Ramsey blames himself.

Sitting in a booth in a freeway chain restaurant that serves the same club sandwich in Portland, Oregon, as it does in Portland, Maine, Ramsey spoke with confidence but chose his words carefully as he took the fall for a crime he didn't commit. He used his forefinger or his fully extended hand in a slow slicing gesture to make a point. He looked you in the eye and spoke with the quiet authority common to men who have mastered their craft. You sense he would be no less confident if George W. Bush were sitting across the Formica table. But when Ramsey described being robbed by Enron, he changed. Everything changed. A visible sadness spread across his face. His eyes narrowed. Everything seemed to slow down.

"Number one: it's my fault that I lost all that money," Ramsey said. "I was locked out. But it wasn't that bad. We were warned."

There's no number two.

On October 17, 2001, Enron locked workers out of their 401(k) plans while a new investment firm took over management of retirement accounts. Executives and directors were not locked out. They saw the company collapsing and dumped $1.1 billion in shares. By the time workers could get to their 401(k) accounts, the Enron stock they had counted on for retirement was worthless. One coincidence sure to be mentioned in shareholders' suits is the fact that employee 401(k) losses were $1.2 billion — just $100 million shy of what Enron's insiders walked away with. After all that, Ramsey is still willing to give Enron the benefit of the doubt. He said workers were warned about the lockout; he could have moved his stock. By the time he was locked out, his 401(k) had lost more than half its value and was down to about $500,000. But Enron had been delivering the American Dream into the accounts of its workers. The stock had fallen, but it would come back. That's what the analysts said. That's what Enron CEO Ken Lay said. That's what Portland General Electric CEO Peggy Fowler said. "We were led astray," Ramsey said.[*]

Ramsey gives himself some credit, for what it's worth. A friend who knew the

[*]By spring 2003, as Oregon was limping through a deficit crisis unlike anything the state had experienced since World War II, it began to appear that Enron had led state and local governments astray too. A number cruncher for the city of Portland was poring over Enron's Securities Commission filings and discovered Enron's taxes weren't paid. Enron-owned PGE had collected more than $35 million in taxes from Portland ratepayers over a three-year period. But the taxes never made it to the Oregon Treasury.

stock market warned him to diversify. He intended to. Then his brother ended up in the hospital in Phoenix. "I was going to pull my money out, but I had to go," Ramsey said. "At least I was thinking in the right direction." He was watching TV in a Phoenix hospital room when the Enron-bankruptcy story broke. "I knew right then I'd lost everything," he said.

Ramsey showed up when his government called him into the Army in 1974. Now he wonders where his government was while Enron executives were cashing out and leaving workers holding worthless stock. "Weren't there government agencies watching them? Look at that Andersen outfit. Look at all those analysts telling us the company would never go broke. Our government wouldn't let these people rob us." Ramsey doesn't have much faith in the government's will to prosecute Enron's executives and board members. "If you or I walked into a store and stole something," he said, "we'd be going to jail." Ramsey assumes but has a hard time accepting that many of the plunderers at Enron are above the law. If he can't have justice, he'd settle for equity. "They're not going to lock them up. But they could at least freeze their accounts and monitor their travel." The money, as Tim Ramsey sees it, belongs to the workers and shareholders it was stolen from.

"When this first happened, it didn't hit," he said. "Two to three months later, I started to get really pissed off." Ramsey thought about filing for bankruptcy, but then he would lose his house. "If I was in Florida like O.J., I'd be in better shape," he said. "You can file bankruptcy and keep your house there." Ramsey owes $100,000 on his home, and the equity he has in it is about all he now owns. Donna can't go back to waitressing because of health problems. Ramsey soberly said he has a plan. "I'll work 'til I drop," he said with a grim humor.

He finished his lunch and walked out to his PGE work truck, on his way south to test some cables in Lake Oswego.

Secretary of the Army Thomas White could tell Tim Ramsey that building a house in Florida isn't all that easy. The former chief of Enron Energy Systems has had his share of problems with the waterfront mansion he is constructing in Naples, Florida. The city's building code prohibits walls higher than three feet. Gates and gateposts are limited to six feet. White wanted to build a six-foot-nine-inch wall with a ten-foot gate, but the city council reacted as if he were going to string a chain-link fence around his 15,145-square-foot mansion.

Council members complained about White's "fortress mentality" — as if this were not the beach home of the secretary of the Army. They also told the architect hired by White to lobby the council that most houses in Old Naples have no gates, and nobody in the city has a fence as tall as the one White planned to build. How humiliating. Here the secretary of the Army is building a $5 million residence, only to be treated as an arriviste, lacking the aesthetic sensibility shared by residents of the elegant island city.

It got worse. Weeks later the secretary was subject to the most disrespectful questioning from a *Los Angeles Times* reporter, who insinuated White was building a house in Florida because the state's bankruptcy laws will protect him from shareholders who would take him to court with claims against the millions he earned during his eleven years at Enron. "That is one cockamamie theory," the angry secretary said. "I mean, really, people ought to get a life."

White's beachfront house in Naples wasn't the only real estate deal that created problems for him in 2002. In March he ordered the pilot of the Defense Department jet on which he was traveling to stop in Aspen, Colorado, where Enron stars Ken Lay and Rebecca Mark have winter getaways. The purpose of the layover was to allow the secretary and his wife to sign the papers on a $6.5 million, three-story house they were buying there. Secretary and Mrs. White — and their son and daughter — also planned to squeeze in ten days on the ski slopes. After eleven years living with all the comfort an Enron executive is accustomed to, you could hardly expect Mr. and Mrs. White and the kids to scramble for open seating on a Southwest Airlines flight. Nor does the Army secretary spend all his time at tony vacation spots. The Vietnam veteran and West Point graduate actually works in Washington. Despite his fondness for slumming with the troops on run-down Army posts across the United States, he's not exactly living in MOQ — married officers quarters. In June 2001 Secretary White purchased a $5.2 million Washington penthouse, just a place to hang his helmet when he's in town.

Good thing Secretary White is not

buying a home in California or Oregon, or he could find himself signing legal documents that have nothing to do with real estate. The attorneys general for both states are looking into the role he played in Enron schemes that caused rolling blackouts during the summer of 2001 and resulted in residents of California paying the highest electric bills in the state's history. The schemes created an electricity shortage but not a money shortage. The money flowed like high-voltage electric current from the pockets of small-business owners and consumers to the bank accounts of Enron and its executives.

There were some "unintended consequences" of Enron's "gaming" the California electricity market. Ask eighty-four-year-old Nate Annas, who had to stock up on battery-operated lamps and canisters of oxygen so he could continue breathing. The rolling blackouts shut off power to the ventilator in his room at the Sommerville Senior Living Center in San Jose. Annas has emphysema, and by May 2001 he had already been through one rolling blackout, with no lights, air-conditioning, or bedside ventilator. Annas can get by without air-conditioning, but if a blackout shuts off his breathing device at the wrong time, he could die.

Enron energy traders didn't intend to put Annas in a bind when they cooked up electricity-piracy schemes with clever names like "Get Shorty" or "Fat Boy." They were having too much fun and making too much money. To make the money, they did have to inflict some pain on the California market. "As the [electric utilities] credit exposure gets too high, we will limit the amount of power we deliver into California," said Enron executive Jeffrey Skilling in late 2000. Skilling assumed that if electricity were kept off the market, the state would step forward and provide money for the utilities to pay what Enron wanted to charge for each kilowatt-hour, and that is exactly what happened.

No one would suggest that Secretary White face reckless-endangerment charges for what happened to Nate Annas and others like him. Or that he intended to harm the hundreds of small businesspeople who saw their electricity bills climb like Enron's stock value. Still, two years into the Bush presidency, Jeff Skilling was pacing the floors of his nine-thousand-square-foot faux Mediterranean villa in Houston, waiting to be indicted. So why was Tom White still secretary of the Army? White ran Enron Energy Systems while the rolling blackouts cruised across California; surely he knew more about Enron's plunder in California than Skilling did. "Thomas White told us the California electricity crisis was our chance to turn EES into a profitable unit of Enron," former Enron exec Steve Barth said. "He said the energy crisis in California would put EES on the map."

Nate Annas must have been too low on the energy chain to concern Tom White.

Democratic senators on the Commerce, Science and Transportation Committee wondered if White was aware that his company had put Nate Annas and the states of California and Oregon in a real bind. "I admire the fact that you were in the Army for twenty-three years, a graduate of West Point in 1967, a Vietnam veteran, selected by General Colin Powell, when he was chairman of the Joint Chiefs of Staff, as his executive assistant, and first in your West Point class to make general," said North Dakota senator Byron Dorgan at a committee hearing. "That is an awesome record, exemplifying duty, honor, country." That was as good as it got for White. After Dorgan's little encomium, the testimony and the story turned to Enron. Democrats on the committee wanted to know what

White knew and when he knew it.

They asked about White's Enron shares and about his eighty-four phone calls or meetings with Enron executives while White was in government and Enron was collapsing. They wanted information about the $13 million in cash from the company for "phantom stock" and the $12 million White earned selling his stock after he was sworn in as secretary. They wanted to know what White's conversations with Enron employees had to do with his stock sales. "Phone calls that occurred after 9/11, you know, after we were attacked," said California senator Barbara Boxer. "After we — actually you — had personnel in Afghanistan working twenty-four/seven. And these escalating phone calls and sales of stock."

Proving criminal intent — or what President Bush calls "malfeeance" — in complicated, private stock trades is dicey. Enron's "gaming" the California market is easier to grasp. The senators tearing into White in July 2002 had enough information to understand what Enron inflicted on residents of California and Oregon.

"The skyrocketing power prices then enabled Enron Energy Services to go out and sign the contracts with businesses that feared they'd be hit again with expensive electricity bills," Dorgan said.

Senator Boxer arrived at the hearing with a letter from a former Enron trader named David Fabian. "There is a single connection between northern and southern California power grids," Fabian wrote. "I heard that Enron traders purposely overbooked that line, then caused others to need it, which allowed Enron to price-gouge at will." In internal documents Enron called the practice "phantom congestion."

Like Annas, Enron traders had to prepare for hot weather.

"What we did was overbook the line we had the rights on during a shortage or in a heat wave," a former Enron trader told Jason Leopold, who is writing a book on the energy crisis in California. "We did this in June 2000, when the Bay Area was going through a heat wave and the ISO [the state's grid operator] couldn't send power to the north. The ISO has to pay Enron to free up the line in order to send power to San Francisco to keep the lights on. By the time they agreed to pay us, rolling blackouts had already hit California and the price for electricity went through the roof."

Fabian wasn't the only Enron ex to go public with his story. Dorgan confronted White with the public admissions of former Enron exec Steve Barth who said, "This was like *The Perfect Storm*. First our traders were able to buy power for $250 in California, sell it to Arizona for $1,200, then resell it to California for five times that amount." Dorgan then said to White, "EES — the organization you ran — were able to go in to large companies and say, 'You sign a ten-year contract with us, and we'll save you millions.'"

Were these guys smart, or what?

When he was appointed, White must have looked like the perfect candidate for W. Bush's cabinet. A former general, out there with a shoeshine and a smile, selling kilowatts and conservation to California and privatized utilities services to the Army. When he filled out the financial-disclosure form required of cabinet officials, White owned between $25 and $50 million in Enron shares, $25 to $50 million in stock options, and $5 to $25 million in phantom stock awards — a promise to pay a future bonus in appreciated stock or its cash equivalent. Not bad for the vice chair of the Enron division that lost $500 million while billions were being extracted from California.

You'll be happy to learn White made out like a bandit on his Florida mansion, too. He agreed to lower his gate and the Naples city council agreed to let him build his wall. The mansion is understated and elegant. It's a modern take on a classic English manor designed by one of the region's finest architects. The house is nicely situated on a $6.5 million lot on the prestigious Gulf Shore Drive in a town where address matters.

Thomas White was quietly sacked as secretary of the Army by Donald Rumsfeld immediately after Gulf War II. We'd be amazed if you even heard about it, the media were so focused on our great victory. In the meantime, White sold his Florida house for $13.9 million — picking up a tidy profit of $3.4 million. For a guy whose division at Enron never made a dime, he's done awfully well. But it would have been a nice gesture if the Whites had invited the Ramseys down to visit before they sold the house. Just because Tim Ramsey lost a million dollars in the Enron debacle doesn't mean he actually paid for 20 percent of White's $5 million house. Of course not. Not really. But he's one of the somebodies who paid. Ramsey put in thirty-five years and is still testing circuits and climbing power poles in Oregon, trying to figure out how he can retire. Hey, you know, just a couple of Vietnam-era vets at Enron, and the stories came out a little differently. Not that the system is rigged or anything.

• 13 •

GOD IN THE WHITE HOUSE

*I appreciate that question because I,
in the state of Texas, had heard a lot
of discussion about a faith-based
initiative eroding the important
bridge between church and state.*
— GEORGE W. BUSH,
WASHINGTON, D.C., JANUARY 29, 2001

Dubya Bush may not have noticed, but the Texas Legislature began rebuilding the important "bridge" that separates church and state about the time he started selling his "faith-based" social-welfare program to the U.S. Congress. To be precise, the second week of his administration.

In Washington Bush was announcing a plan to direct billions in federal funds to faith-based social-service organizations, setting up a White House Office of Faith Based and Community Initiatives, and giving his cabinet six months to eliminate regulations that discourage faith-based service providers from participating in federal programs.

In Austin legislators were preparing to kill off a Bush program that exempted faith-based programs from state regulation. Among the first Bush programs to go was his deregulation of "faith-based" youth homes. In 2001 Texas lawmakers killed the faith-based alternative-accreditation agency for good reason. They were afraid that if they didn't kill the program, the program was going to kill the kids.

Four years after Governor Dubya Bush freed Christian residential child-care facilities from state supervision, an emergency-room physician examined an eighteen-year-old boy rescued from a South Texas boys' home by his mother. The doctor told her her son had been "tortured." The doctor obeyed state law and called the sheriff. Bible-based discipline notwithstanding, torturing children is still against the law in Texas. We're sentimental that way.

We saw this one coming (and wrote about it) when Governor Bush persuaded the Legislature to change a state law so that a Christian home that had been forced to leave the state quite literally under cover of darkness fourteen years earlier, could come home to Corpus Christi. (At the same time the governor kept a "Christian discipleship" drug-treatment program in business, after state-welfare agencies tried to close it because of risks to its residential clients.) The story behind the criminal conviction that sent the unregulated Christian boys' home packing for Montana is another cautionary tale for senators who have wisely slowed Bush's faith-based program.* It's not likely that bad public policy in Texas is going to get any better if we make it federal law.

None of this sordid history of beating the devil out of children and Christ into them should have surprised Bush. Lester Roloff's Anchor Home for Boys and George W. Bush are related through Bush's political marriage to Karl Rove.** Roloff,

*For the complete story, see Pamela Colloff's "Remembering the Christian Alamo" in the December 2001 *Texas Monthly* and Chris Womack's "Taking Deregulation on Faith" in the September 28, 2001, issue of *The Texas Observer. The Washington Post*'s exceptional religion reporter, Hanna Rosin, also has been following this story since faith-based de-reg got under way in Texas in 1997.
**Readers should know that the late Brother Roloff sued one of the authors of this book for libel in 1975.

the fundamentalist preacher, delivered the votes that gave Rove his first big political win. In 1978 Rove worked for Bill Clements, a crusty Dallas oilman who decided he wanted to be governor and had enough money to make it happen. Roloff, in addition to his radio ministry, operated homes for wayward boys, girls, and women. The Roloff homes were under investigation by attorney general John Hill, the Democratic candidate for governor.

Brother Roloff was a Texas original. The self-made hellfire-and-brimstone come-to-Jesus preacher took his Jersey cow, Marie, with him to college in Waco and sold milk to pay for his education — while he preached. (He polished up his first sermon by reciting it to Marie, making her one of the few born-again Jerseys in the history of evangelical Christianity.) Roloff graduated, worked as a pastor for small churches, and settled in Corpus Christi. There he leveraged his pastor's gig and a daily radio program into Roloff Evangelistic Enterprises. By the sixties, his daily *Family Altar* radio program was bringing in hundreds of thousands of dollars for Christian homes built on Roloff's biblical model of discipline: "Withhold not correction from the child, for if thou beatest him with the rod, he shall not die."

Nobody died, but there were some spectacular beatings, enough to attract the attention of lawmakers in Austin — and later of the attorney general. The Legislature invited girls from Roloff's Rebekah Home to Austin to testify, and after hearing their stories, passed the Child Care Licensing Act. But Roloff was a "render nothing unto Caesar" kind of guy, and refused to submit to any secular authority. Brother Roloff used his daily radio program to openly pray for the success of "Brother Bill" Clements in the 1978 gubernatorial race against John Hill. Roloff also barnstormed around the state in his single-engine Cessna, preaching and stumping for Karl Rove's first big-league candidate. Clements won by eighteen thousand votes. Roloff claimed he had delivered a quarter of a million of them. The headlines should have read: ROLOFF AND ROVE DELIVER REPUBLICANS FROM 100 YEARS OF WANDERING IN THE DESERT.

Four years later, on the same November day Bill Clements lost to another Democratic attorney general, Brother Roloff piloted his Cessna into the hereafter. Roloff was often a reckless flier who believed "the touch of an unseen hand" would bring him back to earth. He often flew into bad weather and crowded airports without fear, because God was his copilot. When his plane went down in East Texas, he took with him four of the "Singing Honeybees" from his Rebekah Home choir.

In 1985, three years after Roloff's death, the state caught up with his schools. The U.S. Supreme Court refused to hear the appeal of a state court ruling that the schools had to be licensed. Roloff's heir, the Reverend Wiley Cameron, loaded the kids onto a bus late at night and started a trip that would take them to a new Roloff home in Missouri. Years later they would flee farther north, to Montana.

There it is. Roloff, Rove, Clements, and Bush all working together in the Republican takeover of Texas. Even if Rove didn't much care for the ardent Christianity practiced by Roloff and Bush, he did all the policy-and-politics thinking for his boss. So Rove and Bush knew what they were getting into when they pressed the Legislature to pass a 1997 law that liberated the Lester Roloffs of the world from state licensing. No more criminal background checks for counselors. No more standards and professional-training requirements for counselors. No more bureaucrats bringing vanloads of whining, wayward girls to

Austin to tell tales of beatings with belts and days locked alone in stark rooms where Brother Roloff's taped sermons played around the clock. State senator Carlos Truan of Corpus Christi pleaded with his colleagues and the governor not to drag the state back into the regulatory dark ages.

The Roloff schools returned to Texas in 1999, after Bush's faith-based bill passed the Texas Lege and the new Christian alternative-oversight agency was created. By the time the boys from Roloff's Anchor Home were spirited out of Texas for a second time, Bush was preaching faith-based social services to Congress. This time Roloff's successors left because Anchor's Corpus Christi headmaster was convicted of abusing two boys, including the one described as "tortured." The headmaster's wife was permanently banned from working in any child-care facility in the state because of her treatment of a girl at the Rebekah Home, which closed its doors rather than apply for a state license. (The girl, DeAnne Dawsey, was bound with duct tape, kicked in the ribs, and locked in solitary for thirty-two straight hours of taped Roloff sermons.) What was once the Anchor Home for Boys in Corpus Christi is now the Anchor Academy for Boys in Maiden, Montana. The new headmaster is a twenty-six-year-old who learned the ropes at the Anchor school in Corpus Christi. The Texas Association for Christian Child Care Agencies — the model for one of Bush's federal faith-based programs — died a quiet death in the Texas Legislature.

These lessons — and there are more — are ignored by President Bush, who seems hell-bent on imposing a failed Texas model on the nation. When he orders federal agencies to eliminate barriers that bar or discourage faith-based groups from getting federal funds, he's beginning the deregulation process that failed when he was governor.

So what's this all about? It is in part Karl Rove's project to reelect his boss. Rove admits he doesn't share the faith that makes White House Bible-study groups almost compulsory. ("I'm an Episcopalian. Faith is not a requirement.") But the political consultant who made Bush our governor and your president understands that today's Republican Party wins elections only if Christian conservatives are accommodated.

So they get accommodated.

When Bush proposed former Montana governor Marc Racicot as attorney general,

Rove vetoed the choice and made the case for John Ashcroft — certain to please extremist Christians. Rove also choreographed Bush's elaborate, public soul-searching over the use of stem cells in medical research. Bush then announced a stem-cell decision that pleased the Christian right. Two years later that decision was such an impediment to medical research that American Ph.D.'s have fled to England and Utah. Senator Orrin Hatch has challenged his own president's policy. Rove's vetting of court appointments to pack the federal appellate bench with anti-abortion judges brings us Texas Supreme Court judge Priscilla Owen, Mississippi judge Charles Pickering, and Antonin Scalia clerk and clone Miguel Estrada.

Judicial appointments, faith-based social-welfare programs, and restrictions on stem-cell research all fall into the category that one watchdog of the religious right in Austin calls "throwing red meat and green dollars to the wolves in the fundamentalist Christian pack." It keeps them in line, said Samantha Smoot of the Texas Freedom Network. "But it's dangerous because they can never be satisfied."

Rove hasn't satisfied the evangelical Christians, who rightly complain that no substantial faith-based bill has passed both houses of Congress. Even the father of compassionate conservatism, University of Texas professor Marvin Olasky, said the faith-based bill that finally passed in April 2003 is "a shadow of what was hoped for." But add George Bush's religious beliefs to Rove's pragmatic courtship of the Christian right, and you whip up enough religious fervor to keep the evangelicals writing checks and casting votes through 2004.

No modern American president has been as public about his personal religious beliefs as George W. Bush.* No modern president has tried so hard to impose his own religious beliefs on the American public, and no American president was ever so fluent in the language of the Christian right. To the evangelical extreme right, Dubya Bush is the real deal — a godly man who believes God made him president — not in the big "Divine Providence made me President" way, but in the sincere belief that God saved him from a life of drunken-

*Although President Jimmy Carter was a born-again Christian, who often displayed his faith, he did not base public policy on it. Unless you count emphasizing human rights as specifically Christian.

ness and dissolution. (And by "God," Dubya Bush means Jesus Christ — as Franklin Graham made clear when he prayed "in Jesus' name" at Bush's inauguration.) Bush "witnessed" or related his saved-from-the-bottle story to Christian social workers in Nashville in February 2003. "I would not be president today," Bush said, "if I hadn't stopped drinking seventeen years ago. And I could not have done that without the grace of God."

Bush found that grace in a small Bible-study group for men in Midland, Texas. He began with socials and services at Laura Bush's Methodist congregation, but he found Jesus at a Community Bible Study men's group. CBS was started by a group of suburban Christian women in Bethesda, Maryland, in 1957. The Bible-study/self-realization groups spread across the country and arrived in Midland in 1979, several years before Bush and his childhood friend and now secretary of commerce Don Evans signed on together.

All this (as we observed in *Shrub*) would normally be off limits to journalists, but Bush's private beliefs are gradually becoming our public policy. Had Bush found salvation through mainstream Protestantism, his religion's relation to our policy would be less important. How to discreetly say that a Christian religious extremist has seized control of the White House? We're not alone in this reading. Two years into his presidency, even the staid and steady team *Newsweek* assigned to divine Bush's religious beliefs warned us that Dubya Bush didn't find his faith in your father's (or his father's) Protestant church. In a men's Bible-study group in Midland, the guy who dodged the Western canon at Yale finally read and explicated one of its greatest works — the Bible.

Since then, Bush has been a sheep in the flock of some odd pastors. He's still praying with the Reverend James Robison — the Fort Worth anti-abortion-rights fanatic given to quoting both sides of the conversations between him and God. According to what Robison told Jane Little of the BBC, he and Bush prayed together in the Oval Office before the Iraq war. "I know that whenever we have visited him in the White House he says before . . . let's pray. He says you never know who's gonna call, bang on that door," Robison said. "He kept one president waiting for twenty minutes outside while we continued to pray together." OK, so it was probably the president of Cameroon or one of the members of the Coalition of the Willing who signed the pledge card to support the U.S. invasion of Iraq. Hundreds of preachers have prayed with presidents in the White House. Billy Graham himself has prayed there hundreds of times.

But James Robison? The guy who lives and prays on the fringe of the religious mainstream in Texas. In the White House? It's enough to make you miss Billy Graham holding Dick Nixon's hand. You always had the sense that Nixon was worldly enough to know where to draw the line when it came to biblical apocalypse and foreign policy.

Rove's road to Damascus was more political than spiritual. It led straight through Fort Worth, where in 1994 evangelical extremists seized control of the Texas Republican Party just as Rove was previewing Bush's first statewide campaign. Rove is a secular Republican, a Barry Goldwater disciple converted to the pragmatic politics of Richard Nixon, but he quickly realized that his candidate's religious beliefs were an asset, not a liability.

Rove was right. By the time Bush was invoking God's name to order troops into Iraq, *The New York Times* reported that 46 percent of Americans had identified themselves in a Gallup poll as born-again evangelical Christians; 48 percent of Americans believe in creationism, while 28 percent believe in evolution; and Americans are twice as likely to believe in the devil as in the theory of evolution. Laura Bush has said her husband always had good timing. The recent polling on religious belief in America suggests she's right again. The first nonsecular presidency coincides with what looks like yet another Great Awakening in America.

It's painfully obvious to us — and to the foreign press and foreign leaders who worry constantly about it — that President Bush's religious beliefs have shaped his foreign policy. It is a policy often defined in the Old Testament language favored by fundamentalists. Saddam Hussein was not a tyrant but an "evildoer," like that evildoer in the Fifth Psalm, "Break thou the arm of the wicked and evildoer." Or those evildoers in the 125th Psalm: "But those who turn aside upon their crooked ways the Lord will lead away with evildoers. Peace be in Israel!" Odd how one line from a psalm reads as though it had been lifted from Douglas Feith and Richard Perle's blueprint for preemptive wars in the Middle East — on the literal road to Damascus.

Bush and the administration's resident war council seem to be developing the first overtly biblical foreign policy the country has ever known.

It's also a foreign policy that has produced alliances as peculiar as the Michael Jackson–Lisa Marie Presley union. Consider this outline of Middle East policy. "Jerusalem belongs to Israel; the West Bank belongs to Israel; the Temple Mount belongs to Israel; the U.S. Embassy should be in Jerusalem, not Tel Aviv; Yasir Arafat is a terrorist with whom one cannot negotiate; and unconditional support for Israel is the only foreign policy option." Toss in the plan to invade Iraq and topple Saddam Hussein, and you have an exact summary of the position paper written in 1996 by Richard Perle, Douglas Feith, Charles Fairbanks, Jr., et al. for Israel's Likud Party in 1996. Perle and others wrote the report on how to break with Israel's previous foreign policy for the newly elected Bibi Netanyahu. The paper pushes the idea of regime change in Syria and suggests a major way to achieve that is by going after Saddam Hussein in Iraq. The same group of hawks pushed Clinton to invade Iraq in 1998, but he declined. Rejected by Clinton, the "Clean Break" for Israel report became Bush's blueprint for his invasion of Iraq. Here you have it outlined by the Reverend James Hagee of the Cornerstone Church in San Antonio, one of Texas' foremost fundamentalist preachers.

In November 2002 Hagee addressed his congregation of four thousand, outlining a foreign policy weirdly similar to what Bush is pursuing from Washington. Joining Hagee at the pulpit was Republican House majority leader Tom DeLay. Benjamin Netanyahu had been scheduled to appear but canceled because of campaign obligations in Israel. Netanyahu has spoken at Cornerstone Church in the past. On this night he sent along a videotaped message and his apologies.

Netanyahu's taped message mentioned the end piece to the policy Perle and Feith had written for him six years earlier. "The first order, the first duty, is to destroy the regime of Yasir Arafat," the former prime minister of Israel said. "He is the same evil you will face with Saddam Hussein." Hagee agreed and closed out the sermon by looking at evil in the camera's eye. "Listen, Saddam," Hagee warned, staring into the camera. "There's a Texan in the White House, and he's going to take you down."

Maybe we're overcome with premillennial-dispensationalism sensationalism, but it worries us when the secretary of defense and a reluctant secretary of state fall in line behind the likes of the Reverend James Hagee. Faith-based domestic policy is scary. Faith-based foreign policy is terrifying — in an apocalyptic way.

Hagee is part of a virulent strain of Christianity Michael Lind traces back to an Anglican priest who abandoned his church in 1820 to found his own sect. John Nelson Darby cooked up the premillennial-dispensationalism theory Hagee serves up to his local congregation and to a world-wide TV audience he claims includes 120 million homes. Israel is central to the theory. As Lind describes the theory in *Made in Texas*, Israel is re-created as a nation-state. God intervenes repeatedly to save Israel. Then Israel is destroyed in the battle of Armageddon, where an international con-federation like the U.N. or the European Union is led by the Antichrist — probably an apostate Jew. Most Jews are killed, except for the 144,000 who convert to Christianity. Jesus returns to deal with the Antichrist. Then the Temple on the Mount is rebuilt (after they clear away one of Islam's most sacred sites, the al-Aska Mosque). Once all that's in place, Jesus establishes a theocratic world government and rules for one thousand years.

That's it in a nutshell.

This "end times theology" requires Christians to cooperate with Israelis — to hasten along the events that must occur before the prophecies are fulfilled. It all has Hagee, Netanyahu, Perle, Bush, and Rove working for the same end — or at least the same temporal end.

If this is not end times, it's at least strange times.

There is another, less visible war you won't see on Fox or CNN. It's the evangelical crusade Bush is waging against women. At home it's most visible in his anti–abortion-rights appointments to the federal bench and in his support of laws restricting reproductive rights. As we report in Chapter 15 on foreign policy, when you pull all the bits and pieces together, Bush looks like a fanatic Christian warrior laying siege to the reproductive rights of women around the globe.

From the global gag rule to cutting funding for the U.N. Population Fund to sending a former Vatican negotiator and a woman from the National Right to Life Committee to represent our country at an international conference on reproductive-health issues, it just gets weirder and weirder.

In May 2002 Dubya dispatched Health and Human Services secretary Tommy Thompson to a U.N. session on children in New York. There Thompson and the U.S. delegation engaged in a brief moment of tactical and ecumenical solidarity with the Islamic world. We joined Iran, Syria, Libya, and Iraq in a fight against sex education for adolescents. The Vatican was the other Christian nation joining us in our campaign to deny sex education to adolescents, restrict contraceptive instruction for married couples, and ensure that abortion is not included in reproductive-health services connected to the U.N. The U.S. delegation even managed to block a consensus opposition to state executions of minors.

Are we surprised that Secretary Thompson was booed?

Six months later at an international population-policy conference in Bangkok, the U.S. delegate advocated a birth control method that might have been endorsed by Pius XII's College of Cardinals. There was U.S. State Department officer Elaine Jones telling delegates about her personal experience with the Billings birth control method

— that's the one that involves checking the viscosity of one's own cervical mucus. An Iranian delegate who was also an OB-GYN physician responded that "natural family-planning methods have a very high failure rate." The sources cited by the doctor/delegate were "all the textbooks that come from the United States."

This would be funny were it not so deadly serious. It is most serious in the developing world, where contraception is a lifesaving measure because medical care is all but unavailable, and where high fertility rates drive high poverty rates. The Bush twins, Dick Cheney's daughters, Laura Bush, and Lynne Cheney would never subject themselves to these primitive reproductive regimens. It's unlikely that they would even sit with a group of friends and listen to such nonsense. Yet the president of the United States imposes it on women living in developing countries. It's an easy way to please American fundamentalist Christians. All it requires is putting at risk the health of women who lack the financial resources to defend themselves and the health-care resources to meet their most basic needs.

When Samantha Smoot read that Henry Lozano was sitting behind Laura Bush during the 2003 State of the Union speech, she experienced one of those "déjà vu all over again" moments so common to Texans since Bush moved on to Washington.

Smoot is executive director of the Texas Freedom Network, an advocacy group that monitors the policy initiatives of evangelical extremists. The TFN lobbied and opposed many of Bush's faith-based programs in Austin, much as Americans United for Separation of Church and State and the Baptist Joint Committee on Public Affairs do in Washington. Lozano is not from Texas, but the Teen Challenge drug-treatment program he ran in Southern California is the same program — along with the Roloff schools — that inspired Bush's deregulation of faith-based organizations.

Smoot pulls a two-inch-thick Teen Challenge folder from a file cabinet in her small office. The largest single document in the folder is the licensure-inspection report the Texas Commission on Alcohol and Drug Abuse prepared in 1995.

The forty-nine-page report documents an almost complete lack of compliance with requirements that fall into ninety-nine categories, from counselor qualifications to staff training in CPR and first aid, on to electrical outlets and gas lines. Even clients looking for Bible-centered drug treatment can benefit from smoke alarms, emergency-exit lights in dorms, and functioning gas lines, all of which the state found lacking at Teen Challenge's San Antonio campus. (Despite the name, Teen Challenge treats adults, not minors.)

It's unlikely that Bush read the agency's report, or its order to Teen Challenge to comply or surrender its license. However, he did respond. "Teen Challenge should view itself as a pioneer in how Texas approaches faith-based programs," Bush told Marvin Olasky's *World Magazine*. "Teen Challenge is going to exist. And licensing standards are going to be different than what they are today."

He was right. Teen Challenge continues to operate today — unlicensed and without state supervision.

Two years into his presidency, Bush has failed to pass most of his compassionate-conservative agenda. The pared-down bill that finally made it through the Senate in early April 2003 had lost most of its religion and included only 15 percent of the tax incentives the White House wanted. Bush's first faith-based program czar, John DiIulio, predicted the failure and returned to teaching at the University of Pennsylvania.

He blamed the political arm in the West Wing, telling *Esquire* writer Ron Suskind they were "Mayberry Machiavellis." Their leader, of course, is Rove. They might be from Mayberry, but they learn from their mistakes. They'll be back with their faith-based bill. Meanwhile, Bush has directed $600 million in federal voucher money to drug treatment programs like the one run by Teen Challenge. They've got to keep the Christian radicals working for the party.

• 14 •

DUBYA BUSH'S BENCH

The law is a ass, a idiot.
— MR. BUMBLE, CHARLES DICKENS'
OLIVER TWIST

*The trial lawyers are very politically
powerful. . . . But here in Texas we
took them on and got some good
medical — medical malpractice.*
— GEORGE W. BUSH, WACO, TEXAS,
AUGUST 13, 2002

We're foursquare in favor of a Texas House resolution that would confer honorary Texanhood upon associate Supreme Court justice Antonin Scalia.

Even though Bush stumbled over Scalia's name when he had him over the Sunday after the inauguration — mangling it twice in one sentence by calling him first Antonio and then Anthony — the two men have a lot in common. Like Bush, who pre-

383

sided over more executions than any governor in the history of Texas, Scalia is an enthusiast of executions. "The choice for the judge who believes the death penalty to be immoral is resignation," pronounced Scalia. Even though he was not speaking ex cathedra, Scalia added a religious coda: "Any Catholic jurist [with moral or religious concerns about the death penalty] . . . would have to resign." (Do they issue black hoods to go with those robes?) Scalia doesn't like affirmative action. He's opposed to abortion rights — but apparently doesn't consider his moral and religious concerns on that issue grounds for resignation. He has problems with gays and lesbians. Doesn't care much for workers' rights. As we reported in Chapter 4, his son Eugene is so anti-worker, Bush appointed him chief litigator at the Department of Labor.

If executions, religion, nepotism, and the strong anti-worker career credentials of Scalia *père et fils* do not a Texan make, then Dubya Bush should sell the ranch and move back to New Haven.

But he could have got the man's name right. After all, Antonin did cast one of five votes in the 5–4 decision that made Bush president.

At least Bush got it right when he promised high-court justices from the extreme right of American jurisprudence. During the campaign he cited Scalia and Clarence Thomas as the two judges he most admires. Bush didn't get to fill a Supreme Court vacancy during his first two years in office. He did, however, make a lot of appointments to the thirteen federal circuit courts of appeal created by Congress late in the nineteenth century to relieve the crowded Supreme Court docket. Courts where opinions matter. Nine justices on the Supreme Court decide about seventy-five cases each year. One hundred seventy-nine justices on the federal circuit courts of appeal decide about twenty-eight thousand cases. For most plaintiffs or defendants in the federal system, the district courts of appeal are the Supreme Court.

We're not saying the Supremes aren't supreme. It took a shitload of Article 3 supremacy to make Dubya Bush the forty-third president of the United States. But a lot of that supreme authority is shared with 179 (when all thirteen courts are fully staffed) judges on the appeals bench.

That's why the fight over Texas Supreme Court justice Priscilla Owen, nominated to a seat on the Fifth Circuit Court of Appeals in New Orleans while the ink was drying on the Supreme Court decision that made Bush president, is so important. If Bush had muscled the Owen appointment through the Senate at the beginning of his first year in office, he could have begun to remake the federal appeals bench in the image of right-wing Southern circuit courts he admires: the Fifth in New Orleans and the Fourth in Richmond.

Or in the image of the Texas supreme courts. We have two, the Texas Court of Criminal Appeals, known as "the Rocket Docket to the Death Chamber," and the Texas Supreme Court, nine justices beloved for their canine fidelity to corporations and to the law firms that pay for their political campaigns. Sam Kinch, Jr., a veteran *Dallas Morning News* reporter, recently wrote a book about the system entitled *Crapshoot Justice: Politics, Money and the Texas Judiciary*, and that pretty well sums it up. As we write, Owen is so far over the top of the Texas Supreme Court bench that she often can only agree to disagree. Before her colleagues reined her in, she was defining a jurisprudence so pro-business and pro-church it was unacceptable even in Texas. (Not only is she enamored of big bidness, she's an evangelical Christian, never shy about rewriting abortion law from the bench.)

She's forty-seven. Smart but not cerebral. A bit lazy. A fundamentalist Episcopalian (which is sort of a walking oxymoron). In short, the perfect Dubya Bush candidate for a lifetime appointment to the federal bench. Good as "Nino" Scalia. Maybe better. Scalia is at least partial to open government; Owen is responsible for the most restrictive open-records ruling imposed on Texans since Santa Anna seized the diaries of the defenders of the Alamo. Born in Palacios. Educated in Waco. Top score on the Texas Bar Exam. Good hair. Priscilla Owen is more Texas than the Dixie Chicks.

But do we want her on the Fifth Circuit Court of Appeals?

Did we miss something?

Was there a 2000 election mandate to remake the federal courts in the image of the Texas bench?

Hell no.

Hanging chads, absentee military votes, and intimidated African-American voters notwithstanding, the 2000 election was a mandate for centrism. If you take into account the Gore-Nader majority, we might have actually delivered a center-left mandate. Gore won the election. Gore and Nader swept it. Bush won by a plurality, then began to govern as if he had a mandate.

When it comes to judicial appointments, the Bush "mandate" is something we should all be watching. The federal judiciary is a BFD — a really big deal. A lot of progressive Democratic voters voted for Gore rather than Nader only because they feared Bush would win and pack the courts with right-wing ideologues.

Well, he won. And he's packin'.

There's a lot to pack. Eight of the thirteen circuit courts of appeal Bush inherited when he took the oath of office were already controlled by Republican judges. There were twenty-five vacant seats scattered around those thirteen appeals courts, in part because the Senate stonewalled many of the centrist judges Bill Clinton appointed while the R's ran the show during his last four years in office. Bush political operative Karl Rove looked at those courts and saw the future. Just as he had in Texas. Packing courts with right-wing judges is one of Rove's many talents.

Prissy Owen was Rove's candidate from the git-go. She was a workaday commercial litigator at a Houston law firm when Rove made her candidacy, campaign, and election happen. His firm earned $250,000 from the big corporations and law firms (like Baker Botts) that paid for the campaign he ran for her. In four months he turned an unremarkable young lawyer into a dissenting Texas Supreme Court justice.

At the time Rove got Owen elected, every justice on the Texas Supreme Court had been a Karl Rove candidate, among them John Cornyn, whom Rove advanced from a San Antonio state district court to the high court to the office of state attorney general and then to the U.S. Senate. Kay Bailey Hutchison is another of Rove's successful candidates, first for state treasurer and then for the U.S. Senate. In fact, all the statewide elected officials today in Texas were Karl's candidates, with the exception of the lieutenant governor. Although Rove didn't have a dog in that hunt, he chased one out of it. In an anyone-but-him campaign, a Rove surrogate (and candidate) bullied a principled Republican statesman out of the 2002 primary race for lieutenant governor.

If you like Texas government, you'll love what this country will look like after two terms of GeeDubya Bush and the man Bush calls "Boy Genius" — or "Turdblossom" when Rove gets uppity. ("Wherever he goes, something is bound to pop up.")

Rove presided over a complete makeover of Texas government. By 2000, everyone from the ag commissioner to the governor was a Karl Rove candidate. But the Texas Supreme Court was his designer bench. Rove hates trial lawyers. He recites from memory stories of malingering plaintiffs shaking down honest corporate citizens for millions of dollars. And he understands that while you are rewriting the rules governing lawsuits, you need to take over the high court so you can stop them at the top before you shut them out at the bottom. So he did. If the Texas Supreme Court isn't the most anti-consumer, anti-plaintiff, anti-environment, anti–open-government court in the country, it's damn close.

Priscilla Owen was so far out of line with her fellow justices on the bench that she often seemed like the court jester. It's hard to imagine a better bellwether Bush appointee to the federal bench. He may have struggled with Antonin's name, but he knows how to pronounce *Priscilla*. Bush didn't know Charles Pickering, Miguel Estrada, or Michael McConnell, but he knows Priscilla Owen. He knows her record. He knows the grandees at the law firms who picked up the tab to get her elected. He knows the court she served on. And he knows what kind of opinions it handed down — even if the details are a little sketchy to him.

Owen is the compleat Texas jurist: a business-community whore who sings in the church choir. Trust us. If we're wrong on this one, to borrow a line from a Dallas lawyer whose client's life was destroyed by a decision written by Justice Owen, we'll "kiss your ass on the courthouse steps."

Since there are few businesses as big as Ford and few law firms as badass as Baker Botts, we might as well start examining the record of Justice Owen with the lawsuit filed on behalf of Willie Searcy. It shows what Bush looks for in a judge, and it sheds a little light on an issue at the top of the Bush agenda — tort reform. Tort reform in the Queen's English is imposing limitations on the rights of individuals to file suit when they are injured or suffer a financial loss at the hands of another party. Corporate immunity, corporate impunity. So we'll start with big bidness.

In April 1993 fourteen-year-old Willie Searcy was a passenger in a 1988 Ford pickup truck traveling south, in the rain, on Interstate 35. He leaned forward to pick up a piece of trash on the floor of the truck, pulling the slack out of his shoulder belt. His timing couldn't have been worse. A Mercury Cougar crossed the median just ahead, and Willie, his twelve-year-old brother, Jermaine, and their stepfather, Kenneth Miles, plowed into it. Restrained by his seat belt and hanging on to the wheel, Willie's stepfather was badly banged up, as was Jermaine, but both recovered. Willie didn't fare so well. The tension eliminator — the little mechanism that allows for slack in the shoulder belt — didn't take up the slack when he sat back up with the trash in his hand. The boy's chest hit the dashboard, tearing all the posterior ligaments that keep the skull in its proper place in relation to the spinal column. A former Army paramedic who learned his trade in Vietnam was in the first car to arrive on the scene. He's credited with saving Willie's life.

He could not save him from complete quadriplegic paralysis. Willie Searcy would spend the rest of his life in bed. He could not breathe without a ventilator. He required nursing care — or at least attendance twenty-four hours a day — in order to stay alive. It was a terrible prognosis for a fourteen-year-old who played running back on his YMCA league football team. The emotional costs to Willie's mother and stepfather were impossible to calculate.

The financial burden was easier to figure. Medical and nursing care would cost millions.

The lawsuit filed on Willie's behalf was about as straightforward as his prognosis. His attorneys alleged that his injury was a result of the failure of the tension eliminator that provides for the give and take in the shoulder belt. Since Texas law at the time allowed a plaintiff to file suit in any county where a defendant did business, the lawyers filed Willie's case in a nearby rural county where the docket was short. The rules of law would later change under Bush's tort-reform program. But in 1994, when the suit was filed, the injured party had more to say about where the suit would be tried. The faster Willie's lawyer got his client's money, the easier it would be for his family to provide for his nursing care.

Suing a big company like Ford is never easy. They retain the best legal counsel and hire the best expert witnesses. They bury the judge in motions. That's their job. But Ford's last-minute motion for continuance — to delay the trial — when a kid was gasping for life on a ventilator was more than district court judge Donald Ross could accept. Ross, now on the state appeals court bench, denied Ford's motion and told the attorneys to get ready to pick a jury.

Then there was another eleventh-hour delay.

Willie Searcy's biological father, a convict in a Texas prison, decided to join the case and filed a motion to intervene in his son's trial. To Willie's lawyers, his father's involvement didn't pass the smell test.* How did a man

---

*There are literal smell tests in Texas courts. In 2001 a federal judge appointed to the bench by the more reasonable George H. W. Bush ruled that a meatpacker's failure to pass the USDA's new scientific tests for *Salmonella* is not a justification to close down the plant — a decision upheld by the Fifth Circuit bench to which George W. Bush named Owen. As federal judge Joe Fish and the Fifth Circuit see it, USDA inspectors can "poke and sniff" to determine if meat is safe to eat. By the time the second Bush administration was up and running, federal case law in Texas had spread to Nebraska. Bush's USDA was embarrassed by record meat recalls in 2001–2002 and threatened to withdraw government inspectors from an Omaha slaughterhouse that repeatedly failed to meet new

serving time in a Texas prison come up with the idea that he should join a case his ex-wife was filing on behalf of their son? Ford claimed they had nothing to do with it but wanted the father to join the case because they didn't want to face another lawsuit when he got out of prison. Willie's lawyers traveled to the prison where Franklin Knight was incarcerated to check out the story told by Ford's lawyers — that they had nothing to do with Knight's attempt to join the case. The prison keeps a visitor's log. One of Knight's visitors on the eve of his decision to intervene in the case was Margaret Keliher, a member of Ford's defense team who was later elected Dallas County judge. When he was told that his intervention would slow a court case that could mean life and death for his son, Knight withdrew from the suit.

The jury needed less than four hours to

---

standards to protect against bacterial contamination of ground meat. Hamburger meat contaminated with *E. coli* O157:H7 had been traced to the plant, but a federal judge in Nebraska ruled that the company's economic interests outweighed the government's attempts to clean up the plant. Unfortunately that means their economic interests also outweigh the lives of their customers.

reach a verdict at the end of a four-week trial in the Rusk County Courthouse. Willie's attorney, Jack Ayres, had opened his argument with a $27 million estimate of lifetime health-care costs for Willie. The jury found Ford liable and awarded Willie Searcy $30 million in actual damages. On the following day it took the jurors ninety-three minutes to assess $10 million in punitive damages against Ford.

Ford appealed and the case bogged down in an odd fight over which of two appeals courts would hear the case. A year later the Texas Supreme Court ruled that the Texarkana court of appeals had authority. "It was horrible," said Ayres. "We were trying to save this kid's life. And we lost a year." The appeals court in Texarkana upheld the $30 million in actual damages but overturned the $10 million punitive-damage award. Ford appealed again. Willie Searcy and his mother, Susan Miles, would have to wait for the Texas Supreme Court to hear the case.

Each party filed its briefs and listed the points of error it wanted the justices to consider. Each party prepared for oral arguments before the nine justices in a courtroom in an unremarkable building behind the Texas Capitol. Ford hired

Baker Botts to handle the appeal. That's Baker as in the old family firm of James Baker III: Ronald Reagan's Treasury secretary, Poppy Bush's secretary of state, and director of the legal and public relations campaign that got George Bush out of the 2000 Florida recount and into the White House. At the counsel's table with the boys from Baker Botts was a former Texas Supreme Court justice, and William Powers, dean of the University of Texas Law School. (Powers later accepted an assignment from Enron to investigate the company's collapse, even though Enron was a major donor to the law school.) Enron also had an equity position in the Texas Supreme Court. Ken Lay and Co. had invested $134,558 in the campaigns of the nine justices on the bench since Owen won her first election in 1994. Owen herself got $7,000 even though she had no opponent. She also got $24,450 from Baker Botts.

It's hard to find better legal counsel than the team Ford put together, yet in the points of error Ford's lawyers raised, little attention was paid to venue. It was a question that would later occur to Justice Owen.

By 1996, more than three years had passed since Willie Searcy slammed into the dashboard of his mother's pickup. His attorney, Jack Ayres, begged the justices to act as quickly as possible. "We filed a motion to expedite," Ayres said. "We may not have had a right to that preference under the rules of law, but we wanted them to consider the child's condition."

Ford joined Willie's lawyers in the request to expedite.

The court took the motion into consideration.

Two years later Priscilla Owen wrote the court's opinion.

The court decided that the venue was improper — that Willie's attorneys had filed in the wrong court. The whole case would have to be retried — in Dallas. Searcy's family and lawyers were stunned. The supreme court had given the defense team something it hadn't even asked for. Under the "writ of error" system in the Texas appeals process, the supreme court tells lawyers what points of error the court will consider. Nowhere had the court mentioned venue. Yet that's what Priscilla Owen gave Ford. And more.

Owen wrote a long opinion, steeped in legal history and precedent, laying out the court's venue argument. It's the sort of opinion justices prepare when they want to build on precedent and define law for future litigants. But it was completely moot. In the years the case had languished in court, Governor George W. Bush had pushed the Legislature to pass a new venue law that is much more restrictive to injured parties suing corporations. The law Owen elaborated upon no longer existed.

"Why write a historical, precedent-setting opinion on a Texas law when it is moot?" asked an attorney who had watched the case. Another justice on the court, also a Bush appointee to a vacant seat, answered that question in her dissent: Justice Owen was trying to preordain the outcome of the case.

George W. Bush was preparing to run for governor of Texas when Willie Searcy lost the use of his limbs in April 1993. Bush was president of the United States when Willie Searcy finally got as close to justice as the Texas courts would ever allow him. After Justice Owen sent the skinny kid and his lawsuit to a district court in Dallas, the judge immediately granted Ford's motion to dismiss. The Dallas appeals court didn't have the stomach to uphold that decision. On June 29, 2001, it reversed the judge's decision and wrote an opinion that almost guaranteed Willie's family the tens of millions needed to care for him.

Finally Susan Miles would get the money she'd asked for to pay for full-time nursing care and a better ventilator for her son. Too late. Four days after the appeals-court ruling, Willie Searcy died at home in bed sometime between four and five in the morning. Susan Miles has a pretty good fix on the hour of her son's death. Unable to hire full-time care because she was waiting for the judgment the court had awarded her, Susan Miles had patched together a complicated schedule of practical nurses and caregivers covered by Medicaid, supplemented by neighbors. On this particular July morning, one of the patches gave way. The attendant Susan paid to sit with Willie left at four. She had been doing routine work on the young man's ventilator when her cell phone rang and her shift ended. When Susan walked in at five, the ventilator was not working.

While they had struggled to keep Willie alive, Susan and Ken Miles' marriage also failed — or collapsed under the pressure of eight years balancing litigation and nursing care. Baker Botts got a million-dollar contingency fee for reversing the first decision. Their general counsel had told Willie's attorney he would never get a dime out of

Ford, that if Willie's lawyers couldn't come up with a settlement offer Ford found acceptable, they would string the case out until the boy died. After he did, a Dallas probate court awarded Willie Searcy's estate $5,635,000. Ford is preparing to appeal.

"I failed," Jack Ayres said. "This is the biggest failure of my life. I kept telling that kid and his mother that we would get them their money. I told them the system was straight. It wasn't. And I failed them both."

"That case is a national disgrace," said an East Texas attorney who requested his name not be used (in case he has to appear before either the Texas Supreme Court or the Fifth Circuit). "And it's Priscilla Owen's disgrace. Now they want to put her on the Fifth Circuit Court?"

There's more.

In a case involving a medical-malpractice lawsuit, Justice Owen defended a statute that required the injured party to file suit while he was still a minor. Because he sued after he was eighteen, the suit should be thrown out, she said. But the statute Owen defended had been unanimously declared unconstitutional by a previous court. Her dissent jolted John Cornyn, a conservative member of the court who was elected to the U.S. Senate in 2002.

"If we did not follow our own decisions," Cornyn wrote of the previous unanimous vote, "no issue could ever be considered resolved." Cornyn lectured Owen about the practice of stare decisis, by which judges stand on previous decisions. He worried about speculative suits that follow when judges ignore earlier decisions and justice becomes a roll of the dice. Although he's never joined the Sisters of Mercy, Cornyn was bothered that Owen would change the rules of the game and stiff the young man filing suit: "We should give due consideration to the settled expectations of litigants . . . who have justifiably relied on the principles articulated in the previous case."

Owen seems to prefer the World Wrestling Federation model of civil jurisprudence: decide who is going to win, then choreograph the moves that make it happen.

Justice Owen was exceedingly imaginative in her efforts to shape and rewrite a new Texas law, one that requires minors to get the consent of a parent — or a judge — to get an abortion. Owen went thirteen for fourteen against minors getting an abortion through the "judicial bypass" provision of the parental-consent law. She remained committed to religious conviction — over law — until Bush nominated her for the Fifth Circuit. Her first vote on behalf of a minor seeking an abortion came after her nomination was submitted to the Senate.

Funny how things work out sometimes.

In case after case, Owen followed her own logic to the same conclusion: a minor requesting a judge to approve an abortion should not have one, even though the stated purpose of the "judicial bypass" provision of the law is to protect minors from abusive or nonsupportive parents.

Jane Doe 4 was a seventeen-year-old who told the lower court that when her older sister got pregnant their parents kicked her out of the house and cut off all contact. Concerned that her parents would treat her the same way, Jane 4 went to a district judge and asked him to authorize an abortion without notifying her parents. The majority ruled that "not only did [Jane Doe's] parents banish her sister from their home, but they have not spoken to her ever since. This type of potential disruption to Doe's family relationship may weigh against notifying her parents."

Owen disagreed. She found nothing in the record to prove that Jane Doe's parents would "withdraw their emotional or financial support after she turns eighteen and graduates from high school." Then she set a standard that made the law — written to allow a judge to make the decision in place of the parents — unworkable. "I cannot countenance a rule of law that would permit a minor to deceive her parents in order to avoid their expression of disapproval." For minors requesting a judge to rule in their parents' place, "disapproval" can be physical abuse or estrangement and abandonment. "Deceit" by keeping potentially abusive parents in the dark is the law's purpose.

The law was amended to protect kids from parents who would become abusive if they learn their daughter is pregnant and from incestuous fathers whose sexual abuse required the kid to get an abortion in the first place. Lucky "emancipated" teenagers — such as the fifteen-year-old hooker with AIDS and a heroin habit who never knew her father and lost track of which Texas prison her mother is in — are also required to get a judicial bypass.

Each of these sad and resolute Janes appearing before the supreme court to ask the justices to compel local judges to apply the law of the state of Texas got the same answer from Priscilla Owen: no.

Owen told Jane Doe 2 that under the "best interest" language of the law she failed to establish an abortion was in her "best interest." The law, as Mr. Bumble said, "is a ass." But it doesn't require proof of anything so subjective as whether an abortion is in the best interest of a minor. The language of the law required months of angry haggling in the Texas Legislature and reads: "If the court finds that the minor is mature and sufficiently well informed, that notification would not be in the minor's best interest, or that notification may lead to physical, sexual, or emotional abuse of the minor, the court shall allow a bypass."

The law requires minors to prove that "notification would not be in the minor's best interest." Owen demanded the young woman prove that "abortion is in her best interest." Talk about rewriting law.

Jane Doe 1 spent months in a state district court, while she held down a part-time job, attended school, and took her college boards. She feared that her parents, who had strong anti-abortion convictions, would stop supporting her financially if they learned she had had an abortion. "There is some evidence," Owen wrote, "that Doe is not mature enough to accept responsibility for her actions or her future.

She intends to continue to seek and take support from her parents in virtually all aspects of her life, but not with regard to her decision to have an abortion."

How could Jane 1 win? By using the law as it was intended she only proved she was not mature enough to use the law as it was intended.

Owen even established a religious standard that exists nowhere in the Texas law. Before another Jane could get a judge to approve of an abortion, "she should also indicate to the court that she is aware of and has considered that there are philosophic, social, moral, and religious arguments that can be brought to bear when considering an abortion." Owen used her judicial robes to cover her ass on this one, adding that requiring a minor to be aware of religious prohibition of abortion is "not prohibited by the Establishment Clause."

Just as day follows night and just as Willie Searcy was not going to get a dime from Ford, Jane Does 1–13 were not going to get an abortion if Priscilla Owen had any say in it. Her opinions have the feel of something lifted from Margaret Atwood's *The Handmaid's Tale*. Like the matrons who regulated reproduction in Atwood's 1986 futuristic novel, Justice Owen was aiming for results. If she had to make law rather than interpret it, so be it.

Disturbed by his colleague's opinions, Justice Albert Gonzáles responded: "The United States Supreme Court has observed that abortion is a divisive and highly charged issue. Thus, we recognize that judges' personal views may inspire inflammatory and irresponsible rhetoric. Nevertheless, the issue's highly charged nature does not excuse judges who impose their own personal convictions into what must be a strictly legal inquiry. . . . As judges we cannot ignore the statute or the record before us. Whatever our personal feelings may be, we must 'respect the rule of law.'"

Gonzáles went on to say that to "construe the Parental Notification Act so narrowly as to eliminate bypasses, or to create hurdles that simply are not to be found in the words of the statute, would be an unconscionable act of judicial activism."

Gonzáles is now Bush's White House legal counsel. But for a Texas jurist to call a colleague from the same party "a judicial activist" is like talkin' trash about somebody's mama. It just ain't done.

Associate Justice Greg Abbott didn't use the A-word [activist] when he attacked an

Owen's opinion that weakened the Texas Open Records Act, but by accusing her of rewriting the law from the bench he was accusing her of judicial activism — anathema to Republicans. Owen's ruling permitting a city government to deny a reporter access to a public document is odd. It managed to get Owen crossways with two attorneys general, who, like her, came out of Karl Rove's candidate mill. The issue was public access to public information. It boiled down to whether a city administration had to give a newspaper a copy of a report written by a private contractor at city expense about a city sewage plant.

Nothing you will ever see in an episode of *The Practice*, but it is "public" information, paid for by taxpayers, the prosaic material that allows reporters to watchdog government.

The City of Georgetown said no.[*]

[*]In the name of fair disclosure, readers should know that at the time of writing, one of the two authors of this book has a pending open-records case that has been directly and adversely affected by the opinion Justice Owen wrote in re *Georgetown*. The district-court judge in the case has cited both Justice Owen's opinion and the dissent of former Justice Greg Abbott.

U.S. senator John Cornyn, then a novice attorney general who had served for seven years on the Texas Supreme Court, suited up to go back. He argued that the *Austin American-Statesman* had a right to Georgetown's sewer report.

It was Johnny Cornyn's finest half hour. Think of it.

His first appearance before his former colleagues as attorney general of the Great State, a court appearance that got the attention of the Texas press because John Cornyn is not exactly a public-interest lawyer. (Between his Supreme and A.G. gigs, he breezed through the court to defend asbestos manufacturer Owens-Corning and a tire maker. And won both cases.) Texas attorneys general don't argue cases. They raise campaign cash, run a statewide agency, and make speeches. Cornyn could have sent an assistant A.G. to argue the Open Records Law case. But he used his gravitas — and he's doubled over with gravitas — and the authority of the state's attorney to defend a newspaper's right to public documents. "Open government is one of my priorities," he said.

He got stuffed.

Owen's opinion, written for the majority,

so stunned associate justice Greg Abbott that he rose to a rhetorical level he had never achieved. (He also later rose to the A.G.'s office, winning that race in the same 2002 election that moved Cornyn onto the U.S. Senate.)

According to Abbott, Priscilla Owen rewrote the law from the bench. The Legislature wrote that the law "shall be liberally construed in favor of granting a request for information," Abbott wrote. In Owen's opinion, he said, "the court abandons strict construction and rewrites the statute."

Dubya Bush and the political consultant he calls Boy Genius must have drunk a case of O'Doul's nonalcoholic beer (Bush's beverage of choice) to celebrate Prissy Owen's nomination. Pro-business, anti-abortion, and eager to serve the interests of the most secretive administration in the history of the modern presidency.* Here's

*No more of this Bill Clinton/Janet Reno drivel about "openness in government is essential to accountability," as the president wrote in a 1992 policy statement on the federal Freedom of Information Act. Forget Reno's October 4, 1992, Freedom of Information Act implementation directive, and her coddling the public with lines like "We must ensure the principle of open government

to a judge who goes balls-to-the-wall in defense of government secrecy!

Owen's appointment to the federal bench was defeated in committee in 2001 when the Democrats controlled the Senate. But who's surprised by Bush's unprecedented resubmission of her nomi-

---

is applied in each and every disclosure and nondisclosure." And "In determining whether or not to defend a nondisclosure decision, we will apply a presumption of disclosure."

That soft-headed, open-government sentiment doesn't stick with hard-asses like Bush, Cheney, and attorney general John Ashcroft. When Ashcroft rescinded Reno's October 4, 1992, order, he warned the heads of all federal agencies that "any discretionary decision by your agency to disclose information protected under the FOIA should be made only after full and deliberate consideration of the institutional, commercial, and personal privacy interests that could be implicated by disclosure of the information. . . . When you carefully consider FOIA requests and decide to withhold records, in whole or in part, you can be assured that the Department of Justice will defend your decisions unless they lack a sound legal basis or present an unwarranted risk of adverse impact on the ability of other agencies to protect other important records."

nation right after the R's took control in 2002?

California senator Dianne Feinstein described her first committee vote against Owen as "one of my most difficult votes I have ever taken." Feinstein, a feminist, had never voted against a woman nominee. She was personally charmed by Owen, whose nomination went down and was then re-submitted along with that of Mississippi judge Charles Pickering.

But Senator Feinstein was bothered by the obstacles Owen tried to insert in the Texas statute that clearly defines a process for a judge to grant a minor the right to an abortion without the consent of her parents. The California Democrat also seemed haunted by the sort of decision Owen could inflict on someone like Willie Searcy. She asked Owen why she took so long to decide, when the boy's life was at risk. "He did not pass away while the case was pending in my court," Owen said.

Well, as the Texas Tornados sing: "That's the way the girls are in Texas."

There are more Texas girls standing in line behind Priscilla Owen. Houstonian Edith Jones, who sits on the Fifth Circuit Court of Appeals and for years has been angling for an appointment to the U.S.

Supremes, is but one example. This darling of the right-wing Federalist Society won the admiration of the boys on the loading dock, even if she was outvoted on a 2–1 decision in a sexual-harassment appeal. (She was on the side of the harassers.) In fact, Judge Jones' conduct on the Fifth Circuit bench in 1988 recalls the unofficial motto of Sul Ross State University at Alpine, Texas: "Where the men are men and so are the women." Judge Jones got downright pissy with a lawyer representing a woman whose coworkers groped her and plastered her locker with pornography. "One of the guys pinched [my client's] breasts," the woman's lawyer said, trying to impress upon the three judges just how hostile the workplace was.

"Well," Judge Jones sniffed, "he apologized."

Some of us are still wondering if that standard can be applied to rape and murder cases. Or if the "I'm sorry defense" only works in civil suits.

We also have it on record that Judge Jones is a strict constructionist regarding a criminal defendant's right to legal counsel. She rejected an appeal of a death row inmate whose lawyer slept through much of his trial. The defendant, she reasoned, did have a lawyer. Who said he had to be awake? Jones was on Poppy Bush's shortlist for a Supreme Court appointment, and Dubya's a big fan. She's a Texas jurist on his shortlist of high court nominees.

Then there's Criminal Court of Appeals justice Sharon Keller, who also held that an attorney didn't have to be awake. At least she set a higher standard: an attorney must remain awake for the important parts of the trial. In particular when the trial can result in the execution of the defendant.

If the right-wing women on the Texas bench give you gooseflesh, you ought to see the men. We know this rough justice is not exclusive to the Great State. GeeDubya Bush and Karl Rove can find judges cut from the same coarse conservative cloth in each of the fifty states. And if they're not challenged in the Senate, they'll succeed.

As we write, the filibuster of the Miguel Estrada nomination continues, and the filibuster of Priscilla Owen has begun. From where we sit it looks as though only Ted Kennedy, Patrick Leahy, and Dianne Feinstein have drawn a line in the sand — somewhere between Washington and the Red River.

We hold out some small hope that judges

like Owen, Charles Pickering, Estrada —
and later perhaps Edith Jones — will finally engage the gag reflex of moderate Republicans such as Olympia Snowe, Lincoln
Chaffee, and Susan Collins.

It's a small hope. But it's all we've got.

• 15 •

SHRUB II: THE EMPIRE STRIKES BACK

The president believes that
Ariel Sharon is a man of peace.
— ARI FLEISCHER, APRIL 11, 2002

Foreign policy was not George W. Bush's forte, as you may recall from the 2000 presidential campaign. As he stumbled through the Grecians and the Kosovians, his own campaign staffers winced and rolled their eyes. Most of us thought it was pretty funny but not terribly important. After eight years of peace* and adultery, rumors of war were not high on anyone's list. We had won the cold war, and globalization with its discontents was the hot topic du jour. We were the only

---

*The Pentagon lists one American soldier killed by hostile fire in the eight years of Clinton's presidency, but another seventy-six are listed as killed by terrorists, presumably including the eighteen who were killed in Somalia.

superpower, Number One, and the last thing we worried about was being attacked.

Dubya Bush campaigned as a rather mild-mannered international citizen, saying, "I think the United States must be humble, and must be proud and confident of our values, but humble in how we treat nations that are figuring out for themselves how to chart their own course." During the presidential debate on foreign policy, when expectations of Bush were so low all he had to do was clear a matchbox, he addressed anti-Americanism: "It really depends on how our nation conducts itself in foreign policy. If we're an arrogant nation, they'll resent us. If we're a humble nation, but strong, they'll welcome us."

One of Bush's major foreign-policy differences with Al Gore during the campaign was over nation building, a concept Bush clearly held in contempt. He said he would not allow American military forces to be used in converting countries to stable democracies — that was not their job. He wanted to get the U.S. peacekeepers out of Bosnia and Kosovo — 20 percent of the forces there — as soon as possible.

Everybody knew Bush's daddy had been an experienced diplomat and a skilled international player (except for the time he accidentally barfed on the prime minister of Japan — not his fault but still a foreign-policy low). Even those with doubts about Dubya figured at least he'd have his father's advisers around him. (Foreign-policy experts noted an early warning flag in the selection, or self-selection, of Dick Cheney as vice president. In *A World Transformed* by Brent Scowcroft and George H. W. Bush, it is clear that Cheney, then secretary of defense, was the most hawkish of all Bush the Elder's advisers.) A big believer in prudence and caution was Poppy Bush. Dubya's handlers began home-schooling him in foreign policy in early 1999. He got foreign-policy tutorials from former secretary of state George Shultz, Condoleezza Rice, and even Carl Bildt, a former prime minister of Sweden, among others.

Beyond that, a credulous press kept reporting that he could speak Spanish (always says the same two sentences and then they cue the mariachis), and at least he appeared to be interested in Mexico. It could probably be proved by any decent historian that we've had presidents more ignorant about the rest of the world than that.

Until September 11, 2001, George Bush's foreign policy was pretty simple — whatever Bill Clinton was for, he was against.

Bush's first action, on his first day in office, was to reinstate the "global gag rule," a ban against giving American foreign aid to any family-planning clinic that mentions — not performs but mentions — the word *abortion*. The ban applies even in countries where abortion is legal, and even when abortion services are paid for by non–United States funds. This was not the payoff of a long-promised campaign pledge; Bush had never even mentioned it. As a result, clinics in Eastern Europe, Asia, and Africa have been closed, leaving women without any health care, thus leading to a further spread of AIDS and, of course, the greatest irony, causing even more abortions because of more unwanted pregnancies.

The first inkling anyone had of what we were in for was on March 28, 2001, when Bush called off America's participation in the Kyoto Protocol on global warming. He didn't try to renegotiate or change what he didn't like about the treaty, he simply pulled out and then tried to scuttle the whole thing. Since the United States, with 5 percent of the world's population, produces 30 percent of the emissions that cause global warming, more than any other country, our withdrawal was devastating to the treaty. It's usually silly to generalize about something as complex as world opinion, but there was no mistaking the global outrage over that decision. It set up Dubya Bush's reputation as a unilateralist who doesn't give a damn what the rest of the world thinks. His subsequent actions only sealed that impression.

In May 2001 Bush's delegates to the U.N. Commission on Human Rights were so obstreperous and uncooperative that the Europeans refused to reelect the United States to the commission for the first time ever. In July Bush replaced the usual contingent from the American Medical Association and the American Public Health Association who normally represent our country at the World Health Assembly. Instead, he dispatched Jeanne Head, a professional anti-abortion activist with the National Right to Life Committee, Janice Crouse of Concerned Women for America — the outfit founded by Beverly LaHaye, wife of the apocalyptic evangelist and author Tim LaHaye — and John Klink, a former chief negotiator for the Vatican. None of them is an expert on public health. The U.N.'s World Health Organization is widely credited with doing terrific work, including wiping out smallpox and other diseases. That Bush would have sent such an eccentric delegation to an international conference is indicative of the contempt with which the administration views such efforts.

Next, Bush officials called a halt to negotiations with North Korea and withdrew from attempts to negotiate peace between Israelis and Palestinians. Both decisions have had consequences somewhere between serious and disastrous. Continuing the go-it-alone policy, the administration blocked a series of international arms-control treaties and decided to scrap the Anti-Ballistic Missile Treaty. The United States promised to make cuts in its own nuclear arsenal but initially refused to make an agreement with Russia on mutual reductions, which seemed rather an odd course.

The decision to go ahead with Star Wars, now called National Missile Defense (NMD) or the nuclear umbrella, further upset allies and enemies alike. NMD is not only notoriously expensive, but many scientists believe it is barely plausible, the equivalent of trying to hit a bullet with a bullet. Theoretically, if we stay at it long enough and spend enough money, it may work, but this is one project that was never submitted to the cost-benefit analysis of

White House efficiency expert John D. Graham.

The drawback, as far as the rest of the world is concerned, is that NMD appears to be not a defensive weapon but instead a way to let the United States use nuclear weapons in a first strike without fear of retaliation. The balance of terror (appropriately called MAD, for "mutual assured destruction") may be perfectly loony, but it did stave off nuclear war for fifty years. The administration's 2002 talk of using "tactical nuclear weapons" in Iraq further appalled at least European public opinion. Bush also withdrew from the START II Treaty, which required both the United States and Russia to reduce strategic nuclear weapons from 6,000 to a range between 3,000 and 5,000 by 2007. The Senate had actually ratified the treaty, but the Russian Duma conditioned its ratification on Senate approval of minor changes. Bush decided not to seek approval of the changes.

Bush also backed out of the Comprehensive Test Ban Treaty to ban all nuclear tests. The White House decided not to submit the treaty to the Senate for ratification, saying it would "limit U.S. research."

In one week in August 2001 Bush backed

out of the 1995 draft accord on a Biological Weapons Convention to rid the world of biological weapons and then moved to weaken the Small Arms Control Treaty. The enforcement protocol on biological weapons had been developed over ten years of negotiation. Bush refused to sign it, saying that the spot checks on medical-research facilities authorized by the convention would be "too intrusive" and would "expose American companies to industrial espionage." The Small Arms Control Treaty was to stem the illegal flow of small arms; the United States rejected two key provisions that called for regulation of civilian ownership of military weapons and for restrictions on trade to rebel movements. That same week, the United States became the lone holdout, as 178 other nations agreed to implement the Kyoto Treaty. Kind of a banner week for foreign policy there.

Bush actually followed Clinton's lead in rejecting the land mine ban, which calls for the destruction of antipersonnel mines. So much for Princess Diana's legacy.

In a little noted move, in the summer of 2001, the Bushies also dropped a Clinton initiative to go after international money laundering. This is the system of offshore banks used by Osama bin Laden and other terrorists, as well as by drug dealers, tax evaders, kleptomaniac dictators, nasty husbands, and American corporations. Clinton had committed us to working with the Organization for Economic Cooperation and Development (OECD), thirty of the world's strongest economies, to start putting pressure on the offshore banks. The Clinton administration pushed a tough bill that would have given law-enforcement authorities more legal tools to go after terrorist money, but Senator Phil Gramm of Texas killed it by refusing to let it come up for a vote in his committee. The Bushies then dropped the OECD effort at the urging of right-wing groups such as the Heritage Foundation and the Center for Freedom and Prosperity. Texas-border bankers, generous contributors to the Republican Party, were also opposed to going after the system that protects terrorists and drug dealers.

All this was before September 11. In both Europe and Canada the media pay far more attention to world affairs than do the American media. As a result, Bush's reputation as a unilateralist and even an obstructionist was set in cement before the attacks. As the British *Guardian* put it, Bush's foreign-policy vision "has largely amounted to trashing existing agreements without any clear idea of what to put in their place."

Then September 11 changed everything. For a while.

Following September 11 the administration appeared to reverse much of its earlier policy. Unilateralism was suddenly replaced by multilateralism, as Colin Powell put together the coalition to topple the Taliban and other partnerships to chase al-Qaeda around the world. The whole world was with us. WE ARE ALL AMERICANS NOW was the headline in France's *Le Monde* on September 12. French citizens covered the American Embassy in Paris with flowers, often accompanied by touching notes with references to World Wars I and II. At the changing of the guard at Buckingham Palace, the band played "The Star-Spangled Banner." People all over the world collected money to send to the families of the victims in New York and Washington. For the first time, NATO invoked Article V of its charter, committing all members to side with the United States under attack. New possibilities for breaking down old enmities surfaced, as Iran, China, and others with whom we had less-than-cordial relations expressed outrage and sympathy. Nation building was suddenly off the shit list and back in vogue.

France, Germany, Italy, Denmark, the Netherlands, Belgium, Turkey, the United Kingdom, Canada, Spain, Norway, Albania, Bulgaria, Lithuania, and Romania all sent troops to Afghanistan and helped pay for the war there.

On September 20, George W. Bush made the speech of his life, his post-attack address to Congress. The allies were quiet about Bush's "you're either with us or for the terrorists" doctrine (countries, like people, prefer to make up their own minds, without threat of coercion), but secretary of state Colin Powell worked adroitly to keep the coalition together. As of November 1, 2001, we reversed our earlier stand on the biological-weapons treaty and came up with a tough new enforcement plan for the once-abandoned pact. The Clinton administration's plan to go after offshore banks was reintroduced as part of the PATRIOT Act. House Republicans, led by Dick Armey and Tom DeLay, tried to remove it, but Tom Daschle announced that the Senate would not vote for the bill without the anti–money-laundering provision. *Time* magazine did a devastating story on the lobbyists who came out of the woodwork to protect the offshore-banking system, and with that House Republicans began asking their leadership, "Why are we fighting this?" Hard to defend tax dodgers in a time of national crisis. It was included in the bill.

Bush ignored the doubters, waded into Afghanistan, and won. The military victory was no surprise,* but was nonetheless gratifying. Bush had redefined himself as a war president, and a successful one at that.

Five months after September 11 and the defeat of the Taliban, we were back to the antebellum status quo.

In his 2002 State of the Union address, Bush praised President Musharraf of Pakistan, perhaps our most problematic ally, but failed to thank the other coalition partners. By his account, America had struggled alone against the evildoers, against the forces of darkness. Not to use what Bush once called the language of "diplomatic nuanced circles," the allies were royally pissed-off by this. Big-time. (In the Afghan

---

*Barry Bearak's famous lede in *The New York Times* was: "If there are Americans clamoring to bomb Afghanistan back to the Stone Age, they ought to know that this nation does not have so far to go."

war, seventeen non-American allied troops died.) Powell had announced a Middle East peace plan in November, but that was gone by February and the rhetorical offensive against "rogue states" was back with the memorable "Axis of Evil" line. According to Bush speechwriter David Frum in his book *The Right Man*, the phrase was not the result of well-thought-out policy. Instead, North Korea was thrown in at the last minute to give the thing the right triumvirate ring, triples being a famous rhetorical device.

From a diplomatic point of view, the problem with the Axis of Evil is that it pretty much precludes negotiation, in addition to the risk of setting off paranoid reactions by the "evildoers" named, which is apparently what happened in the case of Kim Jong Il. Putting Iran in the evil axis also undermined some promising signs of change and new pro-Western attitudes there; the allies thought it remarkably stupid. Powell began preparing the ground for "regime change" in Iraq, telling the Senate Foreign Relations Committee that we "might have to do it alone."

The general world response to the news that we were about to go after Saddam Hussein can be summarized as, "Huh? Why?"

It is always somewhat unfair to criticize anyone, including a president, for what he does not say rather than what he does. But as Frances FitzGerald observed in *The New York Review of Books* in September 2002, "In his state of the union speech, Bush did not mention any positive goals for American foreign policy, and he has mentioned none since. Indeed, apart from some vague talk about the expansion of freedom and democracy, he has never presented any clear idea of the world he would like to see emerging from the 'tectonic plate shift' of September 11. He has spoken only of threats, and in recent months, his emphasis on American autonomy and his reliance on military solutions has become even more pronounced."

As we warned three years ago, "If you think his daddy had trouble with 'the vision thing,' wait'll you meet this one." There might be a better world a-waiting — through international law, peaceful cooperation, emphasizing diplomacy rather than military action — but for all one can tell from his public statements, none of this has ever even occurred to George W. Bush. That we might consider weapons of mass construction, rather than destruction, is apparently beyond his administration's imagination.   Constructive   "weapons" would include vaccines, medicines, health interventions, emergency food aid, farming technology, and a system of microloans modeled on the Grameen Bank.* When Bush speaks on foreign policy, he speaks almost exclusively of peril, danger, threat, and risk. "It is a dangerous world," he often warns. He never even mentions positive goals. Even his commitment in the 2003 State of the Union address to spend $15 billion over five years to fight AIDS in Africa turned out to be a classic example of the Bush bait-and-switch tactic. If you go through his foreign-policy speeches underlining the words about terror, evil, and danger, you will be struck by how often they appear contrasted to the very occasional,

*The Grameen Bank of Bangladesh has reversed conventional banking practice by making loans to the poorest of the poor without collateral and by creating a banking system based on mutual trust, participation, and creativity. It has proven tremendously effective in fighting poverty: it has 2.4 million borrowers and 1,175 branches. The great majority of its customers are women who work in co-ops of all kinds. The World Bank and many other international organizations have documented its effectiveness.

very vague nod to democracy. His foreign-policy rhetoric is also free of the language of sacrifice or even simple cost. Blood, sweat, toil, and tears are never mentioned, nor even using less gasoline. Perhaps one of the greatest missed opportunities of this crisis was Bush's advice about what to do after September 11. The whole country was dying to help — ready to donate blood, money, sign up for the Marines, ride bikes, anything we could think of. Instead our president told us to shop.

The debate about unilateralism versus multilateralism is not about realism versus idealism; it is about pragmatism; is international cooperation merely desirable, or is it necessary? Of the major problems that confront the world — AIDS, population control, water shortage, and global warming — it is difficult to see how any of them can be solved without international cooperation. Multilateralists see international cooperation not as some vaguely nice thing but as a necessity.

One interesting development in the ensuing months was that Osama bin Laden fell off the map. According to the polls, most Americans still thought tracking down bin Laden was essential to the success of the Afghan campaign. Sixty percent said they were willing to risk large numbers of U.S. casualties in order to kill or capture him. By March, one Defense Department official was quoted as saying, "Everybody wants to know where Osama bin Laden is. The next question is, 'Who cares?' Osama bin Laden as a center of gravity is gone."

Another Defense official said, "Osama bin Laden is a poor measure of effectiveness."

The chairman of the Joint Chiefs of Staff, General Richard Myers, said, "I wouldn't call [getting bin Laden] a prime mission." In April Myers said, "The goal has never been to get bin Laden." Donald Rumsfeld said, "He could walk in here tomorrow and al-Qaeda would go on functioning."

In July Bush said, "Osama bin Laden, he may be alive. If he is, we'll get him. If he's not alive, we got him. We haven't heard from him in a long time. I don't know if the man's living or the man's dead. But one thing is for certain: the war on terrorists is a lot bigger than one person." This from the man who said bin Laden was "wanted, dead or alive." When bin Laden did finally reappear, the administration greeted the news with all the excitement normally reserved for the Hula Bowl.

In May 2002 the Bush administration

"unsigned" the Rome treaty establishing an International Criminal Court and announced we would provide neither information nor cooperation. The court took jurisdiction over cases of genocide, crimes against humanity, and war crimes on July 1, 2002. Our withdrawal particularly shocked European public opinion but, as usual, went almost unreported here. The court is an outgrowth of the International Criminal Tribunal for the Former Yugoslavia at The Hague in which Slobodan Milosevic is being tried; the irony is that the United States paid Belgrade millions — some would call it a bribe — to turn Milosevic over to that court. The court was established with generous input from the United States. Bush then attempted to destroy the court not only by refusing to sign but also by threatening to veto all U.N. peacekeeping missions unless the Security Council overrode the treaty and gave blanket immunity to all Americans engaged in peacekeeping. This did not go down well with the allies. There are only 700 American peacekeepers, of the 45,000 total currently on duty, and the ICC had already made numerous concessions to American sensitivities. After a huge international brouhaha — which got almost no attention here because the American media are engaged in serious investigative reporting, such as the television special about Michael Jackson — Bush agreed to put off the decision for a year.

The folly of the move is self-evident: we need international cooperation in the pursuit and prosecution of terrorists and other political criminals. The move also had weird consequences, since later the same year the administration was talking about the possibility of trying Saddam Hussein, and/or his top echelon, for their various heinous crimes against humanity. Unfortunately, we cannot have them tried in the court created for this purpose since we have already announced we will provide neither cooperation nor information to that court. Our fall-back position then became that Hussein et al. could be tried under the same kind of ad hoc tribunal for crimes against humanity set up by the United Nations in Sierra Leone, site of some truly horrific crimes in the course of a civil war. But the United States, under the Bush administration, has urged that similar tribunals for Rwanda and the former Yugoslavia be disbanded. This was the point at which the word incoherent began to be used about our foreign policy.

At the same time we reneged on the International Criminal Court, we announced that we were no longer bound by the Vienna Convention on the Law of Treaties, which sets out the obligations of states to abide by treaties they have signed but not yet ratified. This means we are no longer bound by several, including the 1989 Convention on Children's Rights. The Pentagon has stalled that one because they want to continue to induct seventeen-year-olds, only a minuscule proportion of military to begin with.

Later in May 2002 the United States did sign a treaty with Russia's Vladimir Putin to reduce nuclear warheads, but many believe the treaty actually increases potential dangers, since we have no way of verifying what happens to the decommissioned warheads. Russia's nuclear stockpiles are notoriously poorly guarded and are an obvious source of weapons and potential weapons for terrorists. The administration has paid so little attention to the problem that in August 2002 a private foundation, Ted Turner's Nuclear Threat Initiative, paid $5 million to secure from a poorly guarded reactor in Belgrade enough highly enriched uranium to make two and half nuclear bombs. Warren Buffett later contributed $2.5 million for the same purpose. The Bushies seem to be privatizing nonproliferation efforts.

Also in May, at the U.N. Special Session on Children, the behavior of the U.S. delegation again appalled the rest of the world. Siding with Iran, Syria, Libya, Sudan, and Iraq, the United States objected to sex education for adolescents, tried to restrict information on sexually transmitted infections and contraception to heterosexual married couples, and fought to redefine "reproductive-health services" to exclude abortion. The United States also blocked a move opposing capital punishment for adolescents. Then we objected to a section calling for services to children in "post-conflict situations," meaning children injured and traumatized by war, because our delegates were afraid that might include girls who had been raped and who could be offered an abortion or even emergency contraception (which is entirely legal in the United States).

Meanwhile, the Bushies continued their pattern of sending career ideologues rather than career diplomats to international conferences. They stripped $34 million out of the United Nations Population Fund and withheld $3 million from the World Health Organization's Human Reproduction

Program. The United Nations estimates that this will eventually result in 800,000 additional abortions around the globe, since it cuts money for family planning.

The move against the Population Fund has become the focus of a rather extraordinary effort among American women to replace the money dollar by dollar. Two women, Lois Abraham, a lawyer in New Mexico, and Jane Roberts, a retired schoolteacher in California, decided that American women needed to act to replace the money. They announced, starting by e-mail to their own friends, that they wanted 34 million women to send a dollar each to the fund.* As Jennifer Block noted in *The Nation*, Bush has since earmarked almost exactly that amount — $33 million — to encourage abstinence-only sex education here at home. At the World Summit on Sustainable Development (Bush was the only major leader who did not attend) and at the Fifth Asian and Pacific Population Conference American delegates again

*The address for 34 Million Friends Campaign is 220 East 42nd Street, New York, NY 10017. The message has been passed on, via book clubs, soccer moms, PTAs, groups of all kinds. As of March 2003, they had raised almost $828,000.

and again gave the impression they thought it was "my way or the highway."

On June 1, 2002, in a speech at West Point, Bush announced the doctrine of "preemptive war." "Unilaterally determined preemptive self-defense" is indeed a concept. As Tony Judt wrote in August 2002, "It paints once more the picture of an American leadership deaf to criticism or advice. It is a leadership that seems all too often contemptuous and bellicose, and, in the words of *El Pais*, fuels 'public alarm' by its obsessions and self-serving warnings of imminent Armageddon."

The speech was based on something called the National Security Strategy, one of the most radical and chilling foreign-policy statements ever made by this country. It commits the country to spend untold billions to dissuade any and all other countries from "a military buildup in hopes of surpassing or equaling the power of the United States." We are also committed to "rid the world of evil." That could take a while. This is frankly ridiculous and has already led to glaringly inconsistent policies. Quite a shift from John Quincy Adams' "We go not abroad in search of monsters to destroy."

On June 24, after making and breaking a

promise to intervene in the Israeli-Palestinian conflict, Bush simply withdrew from the whole mess. Then, in a memorably inept move, he revived the idea on the eve of Gulf War II, promising "a road map" to peace to be unveiled later, in the manner of Richard Nixon's "secret plan" to end the Vietnam War.

In September 2002, at the World Summit on Sustainable Development, the U.S. delegates again threw the by-now normal monkey wrenches into the works, including trying to kill language that would have included female genital mutilation, forced child marriage, and "honor" killings as human-rights violations. That's us: in favor of female genital mutilation, forced child marriage, and "honor" killings. We deadlocked negotiations at the eleventh hour, siding once again with the Vatican and various Islamic fundamentalists. We finally acceded, but only after we had further alienated other nations.

The crisis with Korea had been building since Bush first broke off talks at the beginning of his administration. He has thoroughly alienated not only North Korea but South Korea — there's a feat. He chose the occasion of an early visit to Washington by the South's President Kim

Dae Jung to announce his opposition to Jung's "sunshine policy," which was creating real cooperation across the DMZ. Jung won the Nobel Peace Prize for his policy in 2000. Bush went on to describe North Korea's leader, Kim Jong Il, as "a pygmy," saying, "I loathe him" and "I want to topple him." In October 2002, at the first high-level meeting between the Bush administration and North Korea, the United States presented evidence that North Korea had a uranium-enrichment program. To our astonishment, the North Koreans confirmed it — yeah, we do, and what do you plan to do about it? The administration promptly announced that the 1994 Agreed Framework was defunct. Under that agreement, North Korea froze its plutonium-based reactor at Yongbyon in return for help with two light-water reactors for power and a promise of U.S. diplomatic and economic relations. Unfortunately, we did not quite live up to our part of that bargain. The North Koreans said they would stop the uranium-enrichment program and accept new inspections, if the United States promised not to launch a preemptive attack (not hard to see why they were concerned about that) and to normalize relations. Bush refused, and cut off the shipments of oil agreed to under the 1994 framework. A few months later Kim Jong Il restarted the Yongbyon reactor and kicked out the U.N. weapons inspectors. The United States had never lived up to its commitments under the '94 agreement — neither the light reactors nor the promise to lift economic sanctions were ever followed through on. Republicans took over Congress shortly after the agreement was signed and began denouncing the '94 agreement as a Clinton sellout. This in turn strengthened the hard-liners in North Korea.

After the October announcement, Bush flatly refused to negotiate with the North Koreans, then, in January 2003, he changed his mind and said we would not negotiate, but we would "talk." The word *incoherent* began to be replaced by the word *silly* to describe our foreign policy.

In November the United States announced it wanted to withdraw its support for the treaty signed at the 1994 International Conference on Population and Development. We threatened to drop out unless all references to "reproductive-health services" and "reproductive rights" were eliminated. One of our delegates insisted that "natural family-planning methods" work perfectly and should be substituted. She was corrected by the delegate from Iran, of all places, who happened to be an OB-GYN. We lost the contested votes 31–1 and 32–1. The U.S. delegation then appended a "general reservation" to the final document that is perilously close to completely nutty. "Because the United States supports innocent life from conception to natural death, the United States does not support, promote or endorse abortions, abortion-related services or the use of abortifacients." This from a country where abortion is still legal, as is the birth control pill, an "abortifacient" by that definition.

The most serious split between ourselves and our allies was over the war in Iraq. As White House chief of staff Andrew Card observed, "You don't roll out a new product in August," so it was September 2002 before the administration officially announced it planned to attack a country that had not attacked us or anyone else. The administration initially maintained that it needed approval from neither the United States Congress nor the United Nations. Public opinion forced them to get both. Democrats were perfectly inert, but respected Republicans, including Brent Scowcroft, James Baker, and to some extent Henry Kissinger, began raising questions. The impetus for war came from a small group of neoconservative hawks, including Deputy defense secretary Paul Wolfowitz, Richard Perle, chairman of the Pentagon's Defense Advisory Board,* and Douglas Feith, undersecretary of defense for policy. This is a dicey subject, but these gentlemen, along with a posse of neoconservative hawks in the pundit corps, including William Kristol, Charles Krauthammer, and Marty Peretz, are not only Jewish but also the American equivalent of Israel's Likud Party. To say that we have Likudniks in the administration is not to endorse the Protocols of the Elders of Zion. Get a grip, people. This is not a plot, it's a situation.

In 1996 Feith and Perle were among

---

*Perle resigned the chairmanship but not from the board in March 2003 following questions from the media (led by Sy Hersh) about conflicts of interest. Perle got a $125,000 retainer fee from Global Crossing to help get Pentagon approval for the sale of the company to a Hong Kong billionaire. Both the Pentagon and the FBI had objected to the sale on national security grounds. If Perle could get them to change their minds, he would receive another $600,000, national security be damned.

those who wrote a foreign-policy/strategy paper for Likud's Benjamin Netanyahu. In it they recommend abandoning the Oslo peace process for a much tougher line. Their primary concern at the time appeared to be Syria: "Israel can shape its strategic environment, in cooperation with Turkey and Jordan, by weakening, containing and even rolling back Syria. This effort can focus on removing Saddam Hussein from power in Iraq — an important Israeli strategic objective in its own right — as a means of foiling Syria." (In midwar with Iraq, Rumsfeld accused Syria of shipping sensitive military technology to Iraq, specifically, night-vision goggles. "We consider such trafficking as hostile acts and will hold the Syrian government responsible," said Rumsfeld.) In 1998 Wolfowitz and Donald Rumsfeld started a full-scale lobbying campaign to get President Clinton to start a war with Iraq to topple Saddam Hussein. Both were then in the private sector and connected to a right-wing think tank, Project for a New American Century, established by William Kristol, editor of *The Weekly Standard*. In a letter dated January 26, 1998, Rumsfeld and Wolfowitz state that a war with Iraq should be initiated even if the United

States could not muster support from its allies. "We believe the U.S. has the authority under existing U.N. resolutions to take the necessary steps, including military steps, to protect our vital interests in the Gulf. In any case, American policy cannot continue to be crippled by a misguided insistence on unanimity in the Security Council."

Feith, Perle, Wolfowitz, Dick Cheney, and Donald Rumsfeld had been agitating for a second Gulf War for years. Their long-held view that America was somehow chained and crippled by international agreements is reflected in their later foreign policy. That Americans had not signed up for this program or even been informed of it seemed to make no difference.

According to Josh Marshall writing in *The Washington Monthly*, the plan stretches far beyond Iraq and envisions a complete remaking of the Middle East. That such an ambitious undertaking is fraught with risk seems to be of little concern to these rather cavalier gentlemen. In an April 6, 2003, interview on *Meet the Press*, Wolfowitz repeatedly referred to Hussein's contempt for "the international community" and warned Syria that it too must respect "the international community." Since much of the "international community" was by then united against the United States, it was a masterpiece of chutzpah. Despite months of pledges to bring democracy to Iraq and despite promising that Iraqi oil would be used only for the Iraqi people, Rumsfeld said in congressional testimony in late March, "I don't believe that the United States had the responsibility for reconstruction."

Among the skeptics and critics on the Iraq venture were several retired generals, including Anthony Zinni, Norman Schwarzkopf, Wesley Clark, and Barry McCaffrey. Zinni, former commander at Centcom of the Middle East, said he believes Iraq is about fifth on the list of things that need to be done in order to arrive at peace in the Middle East. The first, blindingly obvious, is to settle the Israeli-Palestinian conflict.

Conservatives are fond of observing that there are some problems that cannot be solved by throwing money at them. There are even more that cannot be solved by dropping bombs on them.

Bush got a blank check from Congress, one of the most curiously passive performances by our elected representatives anyone could remember. Gulf War I, a far more defensible proposition, set off a pip of a debate in the Senate. Members have since maintained they were misled by the administration, which was then touting "evidence" that Hussein had tried to acquire uranium for his alleged nuclear program from Niger in Africa. The evidence turned out to have been forged, and U.N. inspectors later announced flatly they had found no evidence of any nuclear program. "Evidence" of biological and chemical weapons was vague, and the claimed connections to al-Qaeda embarrassingly thin.

The United Nations preferred trying to disarm Hussein without war. Throughout the weapons-inspection process, the administration remained bellicose. Everybody else thought war should be a last resort, but the Bushies appeared to be champing at the bit, posting with unseemly haste to blow the smithereens out of Baghdad. When Germany and France joined Russia in the "whoa, slow down" camp, a truly nasty spate of Frog-bashing ensued. Richard Perle said in January in England that we would go to war whether the weapons inspectors found anything or not. The egregious Mr. Perle later described the elected leader of Germany as "a discredited chancellor" and announced that France is no longer our ally, that it has lost its "moral compass" and "moral fiber." Donald Rumsfeld first described France and Germany as "old Europe" and then lumped Germany in with Cuba and Libya.

The armchair generals in the punditocracy, none of whom has ever served in the military, were even tougher: Jonah Goldberg of the *National Review* popularized the phrase "cheese-eating surrender monkeys" to describe the French, while right-wing commentators launched a perfect jihad over the news that the French had *dared* to disagree with *us*. Phrases like "Euroweenies" and "EUnuchs" were flung about with fine abandon as the Europeans were charged with being envious, hypocritical, petulant, anti-Semitic, philosophy-reading, wine-sipping, limp-wristed pansies. The House of Representatives, in a moment of breathtaking gravitas, decided to rechristen the French fries served in the House cafeterias as "Freedom fries," a ringing blow against the perfidious Frogs. To say the least, the case was not argued on its merits. Timothy Garton Ash, the British writer, put his finger on an interesting feature of this new anti-Europeanism: "The most outspoken American Euro-bashers are neoconservatives using the same sort of combative rhetoric they have habitually deployed against American liberals." That the ugly and contemptuous rhetoric of right-wing radio talk shows is not normally employed in "diplomatic nuanced circles" and might, indeed, have serious long-term consequences did not seem to occur to the Euro bashers. As Nicholas Kristof of *The New York Times* pointed out, "Every time Rumsfeld insults Europe, it costs us another $20 billion." (Ninety percent of the first Gulf War was paid for by our allies.)

By February, public opinion across Europe was running 80 percent against a war with Iraq, putting those governments that did support the United States in considerable electoral peril. Why American jihadists hell-bent on democracy in Iraq thought democracy elsewhere should not matter remains a mystery. They got a bellyful of democracy from Turkey, where public opinion was running 90 percent against the war. The diplomacy with Turkey was so badly handled that according to *The Washington Post*, "One senior U.S. official acknowledged that U.S. pressure in recent months had backfired, saying that at one point Pentagon officials insinuated to Turkish politicians that they could get the Turkish military to back the request for

U.S. troop deployments in Turkey. 'It was stupid stuff. These are proud people,' he said. 'Speaking loudly and carrying a big stick wins you tactical victories from time to time, but not a strategic victory.'"

The background on the "insinuation" is that the Turkish and American military are very tight, and a few years back the Turkish military had pushed out an Islamist government there. We were implicitly threatening a democratic ally with a military coup — so we could bring democracy to Iraq, of course. No opposition was greeted with anything but contempt and derision, as though anybody who dared to say, "You know, this might not be a good idea" was stabbing us in the back. NATO was fraying. President Bush warned the United Nations to "show backbone and courage," to stand up to Iraq or "be seen as an ineffective, irrelevant debating society."

Since the United Nations is in business to prevent war, not promote it, there seemed to be a failure to communicate. Our shifting rationale for taking out Saddam Hussein — first it was "regime change," then disarmament, then he had a nuclear program, next he was suddenly in bed with al-Qaeda and about to hand off anthrax to terrorists, then it was because

Iraq was in violation of Resolution 1441 (as though Israel had not been in violation of dozens of U.N. resolutions for decades), then it was weapons of mass destruction, then we couldn't back down because it would destroy our "credibility," then it was regime change again — led to further confusion. As Paul Freundlich put it at the start of the war: "All right, let me see if I understand the logic of this correctly. We are going to ignore the United Nations in order to make clear to Saddam Hussein that the United Nations cannot be ignored. We're going to wage war to preserve the U.N.'s ability to avert war. The paramount principle is that the U.N.'s word must be taken seriously, and if we have to subvert its word to guarantee that it is, then, by gum, we will. Peace is too important not to take up arms to defend. Am I getting this right?"

The discussion veered off into cuckooland, with the left screaming, "No blood for oil!" and the right screaming that anyone who had doubts about invading Iraq was a Saddam sympathizer. Osama bin Laden popped back up to add to the festivities. By the time the United States went to war on March 19, 42 percent of Americans believed Saddam Hussein was personally responsible for the attacks on the World Trade Center, something that had never even been claimed by the Bush administration. According to a poll conducted by ABC News, 55 percent believed Hussein had given direct support to al-Qaeda, for which there was no evidence. Doesn't speak well of American media.

Foreign affairs was not supposed to be George W. Bush's "thing." September 11 presented him with some appalling choices. In the ensuing days, he spoke several times of his "mission" to confront terrorism, that this is what he had been "chosen" for, that he had found his "destiny." Given his deep religious streak, that should be taken literally. The catch-22 is that in going after Saddam Hussein, there is considerable risk of creating more terrorists. On February 5, 2003, a deputy director in the North Korean foreign ministry told *The Guardian* that North Korea is entitled to launch a preemptive strike against the United States. "The United States says that after Iraq, we are next," said Ri Pyong-gap, "but we have our own countermeasures. Preemptive attacks are not the exclusive right of the U.S." Oops. This rather ominous indication that the notion of "preemptive war" might be catching is not encouraging.

The administration's diplomacy in the lead-up to Gulf War II was frankly disastrous. At the end of it, we had the majority of public opinion in exactly two countries on our side — the United States and Israel. Our "coalition of the willing" was thirty, including Ethiopia, Eritrea, and other countries afraid of having their foreign aid cut off. Only Britain and Australia agreed to commit troops (45,000 and 2,000, respectively). In every nation where people were free to demonstrate, they did so against this war, approximately 10 million from every continent.

The administration was repeatedly caught dissembling. In early December 2002 they leaked a painfully obvious fake story that Saddam Hussein had given chemical weapons to al-Qaeda. That one was shot down so fast — from within the administration — it didn't even last a full news cycle. Meanwhile, Rumsfeld revived his dandy scheme for a Pentagon Office of Strategic Disinformation, in other words, a Department of Lies. The neocon hawks on the Pentagon Defense Advisory Board, including Kenneth Adelman and Eliot Cohen, took to attacking the entire religion of Islam directly. "The more you examine the religion, the more militaristic it seems,"

453

announced Adelman. Cohen said, "Nobody would like to think that a major world religion has a deeply aggressive and dangerous strain in it — a strain often excused or misrepresented in the name of good feelings. But uttering uncomfortable and unpleasant truths is one of the things that define leadership." We, of course, were the ones launching an unprovoked war.

Many, many chickens came home to roost. Fareed Zakaria reported in *Newsweek*, "I've been all over the world in the last year, and almost every country I've visited has felt humiliated by this administration. Jorge Castañeda, the recently resigned foreign minister of Mexico, said, 'Most officials in Latin American countries today are not anti-American types. We have studied in the United States or worked there. We like and understand America. But we find it extremely irritating to be treated with utter contempt.' " Most people do. It turned out the reason we couldn't get some African countries to go along with us rather than the French is because they get more foreign aid from the French. America ranks dead last among wealthy countries in foreign aid as a percentage of the economy.

Looking at the "legislative history" of

1441, as judges do when trying to interpret law, it is clear the other members of the Security Council believed they were signing off on a two-part process, that if inspectors found Saddam Hussein in (endlessly overworked meaningless phrase) material breach, the problem would be brought back to the council for further decision. Our ambassador, John Negroponte, told the council as 1441 was debated, "There is not 'automaticity' and this is a two-stage process, and in that regard, we have met the principal concerns that have been expressed for the resolution. Whatever violation there is, or is judged to exist, will be dealt with in the council, and the council will have an opportunity to consider the matter before any other action is taken." Thus the bitter resentment of other nations that felt the United States dealt in bad faith.

The war itself brought an almost surreal disjuncture between what Americans saw of the war and what the rest of the world saw. A pop-eyed young reporter for Fox News, assigned to watch Arab television, announced indignantly, "They are reporting about a *completely* different war. They say this is a war of unprovoked aggression in order to get the Iraqi oil fields and control the whole region." As they say in Sweetwater, no shit?

The United States spends $398 billion a year on its military; Iraq spends $1.4 billion. Thus we had every right to expect a short, easy war, if not the "cakewalk" predicted by the neocon enthusiasts. Our only real worry was that Saddam Hussein, cornered like a rat, would finally use his weapons of mass destruction. As the war began, American troops met unexpectedly heavy resistance in southern Iraq, and our long supply line appeared dangerously vulnerable. Pundits who know absolutely nothing about military logistics weighed in on the issue with great certitude.

A wartime moment I particularly relished was hearing Senator Ted Stevens of Alaska suggest on April 1 that New York's cops and firefighters should work overtime without pay as a wartime sacrifice. "I really feel strongly that we ought to find some way to convince the people that there ought to be some volunteerism at home," quoth this worthy. "Those people overseas in the desert, they're not getting paid overtime. . . . I don't know why the people working for the cities and counties ought to be paid overtime when they're responding to matters of national security."

He had just voted for a tax plan that would give $92,000 in tax cuts to our friend B Rapoport, who is worth a couple hundred million. Some must sacrifice more than others.

While the war itself went as well as could be expected, we are still faced with the peace from hell. A million Iraqi Shiites made pilgrimmage to Karbalā' a week after the war, screaming, "No to Saddam and no to America!" Our troops are a magnet for every terrorist in the Middle East and continue to get picked off in apparently random incidents.

As we advanced on Baghdad, the unwelcome news arrived that many on the Christian right were aflame with enthusiasm for going to Iraq and converting the hapless heathen to Christianity.

This is guaranteed to make us as popular as the clap.

In terms of the "real people" affected by all this, the United States sent 250,000 American soldiers to fight this war. They were the Americans most seriously affected, yanked away from their homes and families. There was a clear class division between those who were related to someone serving in Iraq, or who even knew someone there, and those who didn't. It was hard to find anyone at a country club or on an elite college campus or in a boardroom with a connection, but at the Las Vegas convention of the Service Employees International Union in mid-March, parent after parent stood to express the rending conflict they felt over the war. This was the first war fought by the United States without support from the AFL-CIO.

Meanwhile, no weapons of mass destruction, Bush's most often cited reason for the invasion, have been found. This presents a monumental credibility problem for the Bush administration. As the weeks passed with no sign of WMDs, a perfect festival of backpedaling and spin ensued. If Iraq had no WMDs, this was not a spinnable situation. Either the government had lied to us and to the rest of the world to get us into an unnecessary war, or its own intelligence was insanely inaccurate.

One of the postwar issues you will want to keep an eye on is the health effects of using depleted uranium weapons. Depleted uranium (DU) is the low-level radioactive waste left over from manufacturing nuclear fuel and bombs. It is used in weapons and missiles by the United States, Britain, Russia, and several other nations —

though not by Iraq. According to the *San Francisco Chronicle* — and numerous other sources — "Military experts regard DU as an almost magically effective material. DU is 1.7 times denser than lead, and when a weapon made with a DU tip or core strikes the side of a tank or bunker, it slices straight through and erupts in a burning radioactive cloud. In addition, armor made of DU appears to make tanks far less vulnerable on the battlefield." It plays offense, it plays defense: who could ask for anything more? During Gulf War I, U.S. planes and tanks unloaded 320 tons of munitions made with DU on the people of Iraq. In exactly the areas most heavily hit, health problems have been especially severe. Nationwide in Iraq, the number of cancer cases in children has risen fivefold, and congenital birth defects and leukemia have tripled, according to Iraqi health officials. Many health authorities here have concluded that DU is the origin of Gulf War syndrome, the puzzling concatenation of maladies that have hit Gulf I vets. The Pentagon denies any connection to either Iraqi civilian illness or to Gulf War vets — but then, it took the military quite a while to get around to admitting that Agent Orange kills people. Although branches of the European Parliament and the United Nations have already condemned DU, the fact is that it will take larger and longer epidemiological studies to track its effects to a scientific conclusion.

Among other things, the Gulf War II produced a remarkably peppy peace movement in practically no time. The signs carried by the protesters seem to us to represent some of the best about America — a loud, noisy, irreverent explosion of dissent and free speech. Here is what some of your fellow citizens had to say:

DRUNKEN FRAT BOY DRIVES COUNTRY
INTO DITCH
WHO WOULD JESUS BOMB?
WAR BEGINS WITH "DUBYA"
BUSH IS PROOF THAT EMPTY WARHEADS
CAN BE DANGEROUS
LET'S BOMB TEXAS, THEY HAVE OIL TOO
HOW DID OUR OIL GET UNDER THEIR
SAND?
IF YOU CAN'T PRONOUNCE IT, DON'T
BOMB IT
ONE THOUSAND POINTS OF LIGHT AND
ONE DIM BULB
PREEMPTIVE IMPEACHMENT
FRODO HAS FAILED. BUSH HAS THE RING.
EMPIRES FALL

MAINSTREAM WHITE GUYS FOR PEACE
WE CAN'T AFFORD TO RULE THE WORLD
9-11-01: 15 SAUDIS, 0 IRAQIS
I ASKED FOR UNIVERSAL HEALTH CARE AND
ALL I GOT WAS A LOUSY STEALTH BOMBER
WAR IS NOT A FAMILY VALUE
DRAFT RICHARD PERLE
(Picture of a peace symbol) BACK BY
POPULAR DEMAND
(Picture of Bush) WHY SHOULD I CARE
WHAT THE AMERICAN PEOPLE THINK?
THEY DIDN'T VOTE FOR ME.
YOU DON'T HAVE TO LIKE BUSH TO LOVE
AMERICA
ANOTHER SADDAM-HATER FOR INSPEC-
TIONS
$1 BILLION A DAY TO KILL PEOPLE —
WHAT A BARGAIN
STOP THE EXCESS OF EVIL — $396 BIL-
LION DEFENSE BILL
WHAT'S THE DIFFERENCE BETWEEN ME
AND GOD? HE MIGHT FORGIVE BUSH, BUT
I WON'T.
(Beneath a picture of a menacing soldier
pointing his bayonet toward the viewer)
SAY IT! ONE NATION UNDER GOD. SAY IT!
THE ASSES OF EVIL
SMART WEAPONS, DUMB PRESIDENT
THE ONLY THING WE HAVE TO FEAR IS
BUSH HIMSELF

PEACE TAKES BRAINS
HOW MANY LIVES PER GALLON?
ANOTHER PATRIOT FOR PEACE
DON'T DO IT, GEORGE. POPPY WILL STILL
LOVE YOU.
TO THE PEOPLE OF THE EARTH: DON'T
BLAME US. WE VOTED FOR THE OTHER
GUY.
ONE NATION UNDER SURVEILLANCE
GO SOLAR, NOT BALLISTIC
(On a five-year-old) MORE CANDY, LESS
WAR
ONE GOOSE-STEP, TWO GOOSE-STEPS. . . .
IT'S NUCLEAR, NOT NUCULAR, YOU IDIOT!

Still alive, still well, still raising hell in the home of the free and the land of the brave. God grant it goes right.

•16•

STATE OF THE UNION

The Constitution of the United States is a law for rulers and people equally in war and peace. And covers with the shield of its protection all classes of men at all times and under all circumstances.
— THE UNITED STATES SUPREME COURT IN *EX PARTE MILLIGAN*, ITS DECISION ON THE LEGALITY OF ABRAHAM LINCOLN'S SUSPENSION OF HABEAS CORPUS DURING THE CIVIL WAR

I'm the commander — see, I don't need to explain — I do not need to explain why I say things. That's the interesting thing about being the president. Maybe somebody needs to explain to me why they say something, but I don't feel like I owe anybody an explanation.
— GEORGE W. BUSH, QUOTED BY BOB WOODWARD IN *BUSH AT WAR*

The late John Henry Faulk, a Texas humorist and folklorist, also had a career in the Texas

Rangers. In fact, he was a captain. He was six at the time, and his friend Boots Cooper, who was seven, was the sheriff. The two of them used to do a lot of serious law enforcement work out behind Johnny's home in South Austin. One day Johnny's momma, havin' two such fine law-enforcement officers on the premises, decided to put 'em to work. "I want you men to go down to the henhouse and roust that chicken snake out of there," she said. All excited, the boys hopped onto their brooms, galloped down to the henhouse, tethered their brooms, and went inside. They searched through all the nests on the bottom shelf of the henhouse but found no snake. They were of a size and an age where they had to stand on tiptoe to see if there was a snake on the top shelf. There was.

I myself have never been nose to nose with a chicken snake, but I always took John Henry's word for it that it will just scare the living shit out of you. Scared the boys so bad they both tried to get out of the henhouse at the same time, doing considerable damage to both themselves and the henhouse door in the process. They came trailing back up to the porch all shamefaced, and Miz Faulk said, "Boys, boys, what is wrong with you? You know perfectly well a chicken snake will not hurt you." That's when Boots Cooper made this semi-immortal observation: "Yes, ma'am, but there's some things'll scare you so bad that you'll hurt yourself."

And that's what we do in this country, over and over. Get so scared of some dread menace — of communism or crime or drugs or illegal aliens or terrorists — that we hurt ourselves. We think we can make ourselves safer by making ourselves less free. It never works. When we make ourselves less free, we're not safer, we're only less free. When the PATRIOT Act (one thing this country needs is a good truth-in-captioning law) was passed in the wake of September 11, the country was good and scared, and so we hurt ourselves, doing real damage to the First and Fourth Amendments. Most Americans shrugged and said, "Well, it only applies to some Arab immigrants." As Pastor Niemoller put it in the most quoted Holocaust text: "First they came for the Communists, but I was not a Communist — so I said nothing. Then they came for the Social Democrats, but I was not a Social Democrat — so I did nothing. Then they came for the trade unionists, but I was not a trade unionist. And then they came for the

465

Jews, but I was not a Jew — so I did little. Then when they came for me, there was no one left who could stand up for me."

I'm not implying that attorney general John Ashcroft is a Nazi; I just think the "It's only happening to them" principle is the same. In 2002 General Ashcroft announced his desire to set up camps for U.S. citizens he deems "enemy combatants." This country is now holding American citizens in custody, without trial, without charges, without right to confront accusers, and without right to counsel, in direct violation of the Constitution of the United States of America. The government may now monitor religious and political groups without suspecting criminal activity. The government has closed once public immigration hearings, has secretly detained hundreds of people without charges, and has encouraged bureaucrats to resist public-records requests. Despite the hundreds of arrests by Ashcroft, the only person found who may be associated with September 11 is Zaccarias Moussaoui, who was already in custody before the attacks.

Government may prosecute librarians or keepers of any other records if they tell anyone that the government subpoenaed information related to a terror investigation. Government may monitor federal-prison jailhouse conversations between attorneys and clients and deny lawyers to Americans accused of crimes. Government may search and seize Americans' papers and effects without probable cause to assist a terror investigation. Government may jail Americans indefinitely without a trial. Americans may be jailed without being charged or being able to confront witnesses against them.

None of this has made us any safer.

On March 18, 2003, in a speech at the Cleveland City Club, Supreme Court justice Antonin Scalia said the government can scale back individual rights during war. "The Constitution just sets minimums," he said. "Most of the rights that you enjoy go way beyond the Constitution."

Justice Scalia is wrong. The only amendment in the Bill of Rights that is affected by war is III: "No soldier shall, in time of peace be quartered in any house, without the consent of the owner, nor in time of war, but in a manner to be prescribed by law." Amendment IX specifically makes it clear that the Bill of Rights is not a set of minimums: "The enumeration in the Constitution of certain rights shall not be construed to deny or disparage others retained by the people."

This country is going to be attacked by terrorists again. Everyone from the Bush administration to the most dedicated doves agrees that we will get whacked again. And when that happens, the administration has PATRIOT II waiting.

The Department of Justice secretly drafted a sweeping sequel to the PATRIOT Act. The draft was discovered on February 2, 2003, by the Center for Public Integrity, which posted the plan on its website. This plan was prepared by Ashcroft's staff and has not been officially released; elected officials were not informed. Among its provisions, PATRIOT II would

- empower the government to strip Americans of their citizenship if they participate in the lawful activities of any group the attorney general labels "terrorist."

- no longer require the government to disclose the identity of anyone, even an American citizen, detained in connection with a terror investigation — until criminal charges are filed, no matter how long that takes. Thus, an American suspected of being part of a terrorist conspiracy could be held by investigators without anyone being notified. He could simply disappear.

- repeal current limits on local police spying on religious and political activity, reactivating the old Red Squads that used to do such useful things as spying on Unitarians in Dallas. (Unitarians are such a menace.)
- allow government to obtain credit records and library records without a warrant.
- permit wiretaps without any court order for up to fifteen days after a terror attack.
- restrict release of information about health or safety hazards posed by chemical and other plants.
- expand the reach of the already overbroad definition of terrorism — individuals engaged in civil disobedience could lose their citizenship, and their organizations could be subjected to wiretapping.
- permit the extradition, search, and wiretapping of Americans at the behest of foreign nations, whether or not treaties allow it.
- strip lawful immigrants of the right to a fair deportation hearing, and bar

federal courts from reviewing immigration rulings.

- authorize a DNA database of "suspected terrorists" — a group so broadly defined it could include anyone associated with "suspected" groups, and any "noncitizens suspected of certain crimes or of having supported any group designated as terrorist."*

Those are the grand themes of the GeeDubya years, but we mustn't neglect the little things. As Robert Earl Keen sings, "It's those little things, those itty-bitty things, that really piss me off."

- On the day a major earthquake struck the Northwest in February 2001 Bush killed a federal program designed to help communities deal with the effects of natural disasters.
- In June 2002 Bush made an Ohio commencement address about "a new ethic of responsibility" and "a culture of service," which his advisers claimed had been inspired by his

*List provided by the American Civil Liberties Union and the Center for Public Integrity.

470

reading from Aristotle, Adam Smith, James Madison, George Eliot, Emily Dickinson, William Wordsworth, Cicero, Lincoln, and the founding fathers. In his new ethic, Bush called upon us all to reject "a culture of self-ishness" and to embrace "some cause larger than his or her own profit."

The day before that speech, Dick Cheney and Karl Rove went to speak at a conference of business leaders in Washington. "This is a war," said Rove, "and we need to make an on-going commitment to winning the effort to repeal the death tax." Under current law, the estate tax applies only to estates of over $1 million, and that is set to rise to $3.5 million in 2009. The gross campaign of disinformation claiming the estate tax causes people to lose family farms and small businesses has repeatedly been shown to be false.

• On October 12, 2001, General Ashcroft sent out a memo instructing federal agencies to stall on all Freedom of Information Act (FOIA) requests for documents. Such requests should be subject to "full and deliberate consideration." FOIA has been in effect since 1966, and its acronym has become a verb, as in, "I just FOIAed the guy." Janet Reno's 1993 FOIA policy was to put the burden on federal agencies to justify any withholding of "FOIAed" documents.

- John Snow, Bush's new secretary of the treasury, was CEO of CSX Corporation, where he earned $10.1 million in his last year. CSX paid zero in federal income tax in 2000 and 2001. CSX received $122 million in tax rebates from the federal government in 2000 and 2001. Just the man we want in charge of the federal treasury.

- The Christian right, which seems to be somewhat sex-obsessed, is running a campaign against condoms, including radio spots and disinformation saying condoms do not prevent the spread of AIDS. In December 2002 the Bush administration apparently signed on to that nutty notion. At an international conference in Bangkok, the U.S. delegation demanded the deletion of a reference to "consistent condom use" to fight AIDS and other sexually transmitted infections.

- In January 2002 Bush invoked "security concerns" to outlaw union representation at United States attorneys offices and at four other agencies in the Justice Department. Federal law bans strikes by federal employees, but Bush still maintained he had issued the order "out of concern that union contracts could restrict the ability of workers in the Justice Department to protect Americans and national security."

- In March 2003, on the first day of Gulf War II, deputy defense secretary Paul Wolfowitz ordered military-service chiefs to provide information that would help President Bush invoke national-security exemptions to environmental laws. Can you say, "Using national security for political purposes"?

- One of Bush's earliest executive orders required federal contractors to post notices telling workers they do not have to join unions. It was overturned by a federal judge in January 2002.

- While playing golf in the summer of 2002, Bush said, "I call upon all nations to do everything they can to stop these terrorist killers. Thank you.

Now watch this drive."

- Also that summer, he told *Runner's World* magazine, "You tend to forget everything that's going on in your mind. It's sad that I can't run longer. It's one of the saddest things about the presidency."
- As of September 3, 2002, Bush had spent 42 percent of his time at Camp David, Kennebunkport, or the Crawford ranch, according to the meticulous records of Mark Knoller of CBS News.
- In November 2002 the administration was upset with Al-Jazeera, the Arab television network, for having interviewed the noted racist David Duke. *Newsweek* reported, "An administration official said Al-Jazeera would be subject to the same kind of 'message discipline' — reduced access for hostile coverage — that the White House uses to goad American media."

The state of the union is that money talks and bullshit walks. Public policy is sold to the highest bidder. Less than one tenth of 1 percent of Americans gave 83 percent of all campaign contributions in the 2002 elections. The big donors are getting back billions in tax breaks, subsidies, and the right to exploit public land at ridiculously low prices. The corporations that paid zero taxes from 1996 to 1998 include AT&T, Bristol-Myers Squibb, Chase Manhattan, Enron, General Electric, Microsoft, Pfizer, and Philip Morris. Those same companies gave $150.1 million to campaigns from 1991 to 2001. Public Campaign (www.publiccampaign.org) reports those same companies got $55 billion in tax breaks from 1996 to 1998 alone and perennial legislation to gut the alternative minimum tax. There has been a huge shift in the tax burden from corporations to ordinary citizens. Three times as much money now comes into the federal treasury from working people's payroll taxes as from corporate tax payments.

Conservatives are fond of claiming that "rich people pay more taxes." Actually, they don't. The conservatives are counting only our increasingly unprogressive "progressive" income tax. The Consumer Expenditure Survey prepared by the Bureau of Labor Statistics counts all taxes — income, excise, sales, property, and payroll. The majority of Americans pay more in payroll taxes than they do in income tax. The poorest quintile has a cumulative tax rate of 18 percent; those are the people *The Wall Street Journal*'s op-ed page (always to be distinguished from the excellent reporting in the *Journal* itself) called "lucky duckies." The middle quintiles pay 14, 16, and 17 percent respectively, while the top fifth pays 19 percent.

The big winners in our cash-and-carry system of government are corporate special interests. Public Campaign reports that for a mere $48.9 million in political campaign contributions, from 1989 to the present, the managed health-care and health-insurance companies got protection from lawsuits by patients who have been denied medical care, defeat of proposed laws that would make it easier for patients to choose their own doctors and to get emergency-room visits reimbursed. We pay with over 41 million Americans lacking health insurance, billions in wasted premiums spent on advertising, duplicative paperwork, and insurance company bureaucracies, including multimillion-dollar salaries for executives — and with unnecessary death and suffering when HMOs overrule doctors.

The health-care crisis is now a middle-class phenomenon. The entire health-care system is being robbed blind by hospital chains, HMOs, insurance companies, and drug companies. In March 2003 researchers for the Foundation for Taxpayer and Consumer Rights reported in the *Los Angeles Times* that in 2002 the cost of health care increased 250 percent more than the rate of medical inflation.

PacificCare reported a $37 million profit in the fourth quarter of 2002 after raising premiums. The profits of Wellpoint, the parent company of Blue Cross, jumped 64 percent in the fourth quarter from the previous year: HMO stocks are up 23 percent, compared with the S&P index's loss of 21 percent. What the HMOs want the public to forget is that 12 percent to 33 percent of every premium dollar they collect is eaten by their increasing profits and overhead. Who is responsible for runaway costs if not the companies charging them? Analysts say that less of the premium dollar is going to patient care than ever before because of added levels of administration and profiteering. In addition to the HMOs, there are large physician-run medical groups, hospital chains with the power to demand higher profits and profit-hungry pharmaceutical markets and managers.

Had it not been for Gulf War II, the cratering of HealthSouth Corporation would have ranked right up there with Enron and Global Crossing. HealthSouth systematically overstated its earnings by at least $1.4 billion since 1999, "a massive accounting fraud," according to the SEC. "HealthSouth's fraud represents an appalling betrayal of investors," said the SEC's director of enforcement, Stephen Cutler.

What we have here is an interesting instance of what the weblog writer Mickey Kaus calls "the Jo Moore factor." Jo Moore was the British civil servant who wrote a memo on September 11, 2001, saying to her colleagues, "If you have any bad news to put out there, today would be a good day to do it." Interestingly enough, Ms. Moore, an embarrassment to Tony Blair's government ever since that famous memo, was herself fired on the third day of Gulf War II.

For a lousy $318.7 million in contributions from 1991 to 2001, the resource-extracting industries (oil, gas, mining, electric utilities, chemical manufacturers, and timber) got $33 *billion* in tax breaks *in the pending energy legislation alone.* They also got a weakened Superfund toxic-cleanup law; freedom to remove the tops off mountains and dump the waste into valleys and streams; lax regulation of energy markets and other regulatory relief, such as not having to close high-pollution smokestacks. We pay with dirtier air and water; despoiled national parks, forests, and wilderness; high rates of childhood asthma; millions in price gouging; and heavily polluted toxic-waste sites. You have to pay to play. *Ka-ching, ka-ching.*

And so it goes.

A specialty of the Bush style of governance is the old con man's bait-and-switch tactic. Among the more notorious examples of this is his treatment of New York City's firemen. When he went to Ground Zero shortly after September 11, Bush threw his arm around a tired, retired firefighter at the scene and assured him and the other rescue workers he was with them. In August 2002, he pocket-vetoed $150 million in emergency first-responder grants. Bush touted the $3.5 billion in "new" funding for first responders, but *Congressional Quarterly* reports, "According to the administration's own budget documents, the Bush plan for funding first responders amounts to double-entry bookkeeping: changes in the ledger that would result in no net increase in the amount of money flowing to cities, counties and states." New York City was supposed to get $90 million in federal aid to monitor the health of workers at Ground Zero. That money was to have been included in the overall post–September 11 aid package for New York but was shifted to a separate $5.1 billion spending plan that Bush rejected. Bob Beckwith, the tired fireman Bush hugged at Ground Zero, considered attending the 2003 State of the Union address as a silent protest but later decided not to.

The No Child Left Behind funding is examined in an earlier chapter — a cut of $90 million below the previous year's funding and $7 billion less than Congress had authorized. Under Title I, to help the poorest children, Bush proposed only 18 percent of the increase that was in his own bill. After-school centers were frozen in his budget, so 50,000 fewer children can be served. English-language training also got a freeze despite an estimated increase of 300,000 students who need assistance. Bush proposed 95 percent less than was in his own bill for school libraries.

We have also looked at his record on corporate reform. The rhetoric is great: "Employees who have worked hard and saved all their lives should not have to risk losing everything if their company fails. Through stricter accounting standards and tougher disclosure requirements, corporate America must be made more accountable to employees and shareholders, and held to the highest standards of conduct." Then he proposed 40 percent less than authorized for the SEC, and when that wouldn't fly, he coughed up 26 percent less than authorized. The SEC has accomplished no significant corporate reforms.

Meanwhile, the Commodity Futures Trading Commission (formerly graced by Mrs. Phil Gramm) distinguished itself in a true "Jo Moore moment" in midwar. The CFTC was set up to protect investors from abusive practices in commodities trading, and to that end this alert guardian watchdog of the public interest proposed three new rules in March 2003 that would, according to *The New York Times*, "reduce the quality of disclosure required in reports of past performance, increase the opportunity for advisers to put some clients' or their own interests ahead of others' and curtail the already lax regulation on operators of hedge funds. Using language that could have come straight out of an Enron annual report, the commission said the rules would streamline regulation, allowing 'greater flexibility and innovation.' " For those of you who are a little vague about these advanced vehicles of capitalist gambling, Muriel (Mickie) Siebert, head of Muriel Siebert & Company, Inc., speaks our language. The first woman to own a seat on the New York Stock Exchange, Siebert calls hedge funds "derivatives on steroids" and has been advocating their regulation for years.

Just to remind you of exactly how risky these funds are, the *International Herald Tribune* reported on September 26, 1998, "The near-collapse of one of Wall Street's most highly respected hedge funds sent shudders through global financial markets for a second day as more banks warned of losses, share prices tumbled in Asia and Europe, and regulators questioned why some investors roam so free of oversight.

"On Wall Street and in other financial centers, shock competed with a growing fear that the near-death experience of Long-Term Capital Management LP, one of the most aggressive but respected of the so-called hedge funds, would trigger a spiral of damage through international financial markets." Basically, this thing was so close to blowing — the financial equivalent of "the China syndrome" — you don't even want to think about it. Alan Greenspan and the Federal Reserve banks stepped in to shore up (that would be your taxpayer money there) Long-Term Capital Management, which was about to sell off about $100 billion in market bets, triggering a wave of losses and forced sales of assets by other institutions. According to the *Herald Tribune*, "One banker involved in the rescue talks told *The Washington Post* that many of the banks and investment houses had agreed to join the rescue only after Fed officials had warned that failure would result in 'chaos' in financial markets and could damage economic growth worldwide."

This is what government regulators now decide needs even less regulation? One single hedge fund has already come close to wiping out the entire world financial system. We should let them get away with even more?

Bush called for "fair and balanced election and campaign reforms" in his 2001 address, then vetoed $400 million passed by Congress for that purpose, meaning no money is going to election reform in the wake of the Florida mess. In 2002 he promised to "expand patrols at our borders." He held a photo op to sign legislation for more staff and facilities, but his budget provides no money for this, and he also vetoed $6.25 million in pay increases for the agents.

How proudly we hailed his announcement in his 2003 State of the Union address (what else was there to hail?) that we would spend a magnificent $15 billion to fight AIDS in Africa. Oops, turns out that wasn't $15 billion in *new* dollars; that was just the money we were already contributing (far less than the usual suspects in Europe, of course) switched from multilateral to unilateral efforts, to no one's benefit. And the dying children of Africa thank the highly Christian President George W. Bush for that particular sleight of hand.

Here's one of my favorites. When he came into office, Bush proposed a package of charitable-giving tax cuts that would cost $90 billion over ten years. In the 2004 budget, even as huge new tax windfalls for the rich are proposed, the charitable-giving component has been whittled down to a mere $20 billion. We wouldn't want B Rapoport, the generous capitalist, giving away too much of his tax cut.

The mess in the country's visa system actually had more to do with September 11 than did failures by the FBI or the CIA. The folks at Immigration and Naturalization sent a student visa to Mohammad

Atta and another hijacker six months *after* September 11. Bush promised to use new technology to track arrivals to and departures from the country. Immigration and Naturalization asked for an increase of $52 million to pay 441 more agents to pursue foreigners who overstay their visas. The request was refused. In August 2002 Bush vetoed $25 million for the same purpose. In January 2003 the Justice Department issued a report highly critical of the INS, stating that the agency had failed to initiate needed security reforms largely because it had not made airport safety a top priority but had instead bowed to pressure from the airline industry.

Here's a dandy. In January 2002 Bush visited the Youth Opportunity Center, a job-training program in Portland, Oregon. He spent a half hour visit and photo op talking with unemployed workers, visiting a class of students working to get GEDs, and looking over the shoulders of people checking out job listings at computer terminals. He praised the center and its staff. A month later he cut it out of the budget.

One of the great applause lines of his 2001 speech was "No senior in America should have to choose between buying food and buying prescriptions." Under Bush's plan, a widow living on $15,000 a year would get no help until she had already paid $6,000 for prescription drugs.

In his 2002 address Bush promised to work for broader home ownership, "especially among minorities." His 2003 budget proposes eliminating low-income housing programs in HUD, including Empowerment Zone programs and the rural Housing and Economic Development Program. He also cut $400 million (15 percent) from the public-housing capital fund.

We have already covered the weaseling and underfunding on unemployment: his 2002 budget cut $541 million (10 percent) from job-training programs, and his 2003 budget proposes a $476 million cut (9 percent) from 2002.

His 2001 promise to review and reform the military is deader than an armadillo on I-35. The *Los Angeles Times* reported, "He seems unwilling to invest the time or political capital required to force radical change on the Pentagon."

In a refreshing reversal, there's a little-noted instance of switch and bait. In August 2002 Bush met with the Quecreek Nine, the miners whose rescue from a Pennsylvania coal mine collapse had captivated the nation in July. It was a great photo op. Except in January 2001, Bush's administration had started cutting the mine safety budget, halted regulatory improvements, and reduced enforcement of safety standards. Last year, forty-two workers died in U.S. coal mines, up for the third straight year. The Department of Labor has halted work on more than a dozen mine safety regulations, all made during the Clinton administration. In February 2002 Bush proposed cutting the Mine Safety and Health Administration's overall budget and slashing money for safety enforcement. But hey, the president was really glad the nine miners made it out alive.

Now, this one's a doozy. In his 2002 speech Bush said, "A good job should lead to security in retirement. I ask Congress to enact new safeguards for 401(k) and pension plans." The six most fatal words in the language are rapidly becoming "The Bush administration has a plan . . ." The Bush plan allows companies to switch from traditional fixed-benefit retirement to what's called the cash-balance plan. It saves corporations millions a year, in the case of huge companies as much as $100 million. Under fixed-benefit plans, retirement is based on the employee's salary and years of work at the company. This gives older workers a chance to rack up benefits. Under cash-balance plans, older workers can lose up to 50 percent of their pensions. When companies started switching to cash-balance plans in the late nineties, the Association for the Advancement of Retired People, the Pension Rights Center, the AFL-CIO, and other groups set up a mighty holler. The Equal Employment Opportunity Commission received more than eight hundred age-discrimination complaints. As a result, the IRS stopped approving these conversions in 1999. The Bush rules not only permit the conversions but also give cash-balance plans a tax advantage, as well as protection from age-discrimination lawsuits. It's the perfect Bush plan: they get to screw workers and get a tax break, and nobody can sue.

There is absolutely nothing he has promised about the environment that can be trusted, but there is one particularly touching item in the Bush tax plan that would triple the size of the tax loophole allowing business owners to write off the purchase of large SUVs. A business gets no break for buying a car but does get an $87,135 deduction for buying a Hummer H1.

We have already reviewed the Superfund situation, but even a specific promise in 2001 to accelerate the cleanup of toxic brownfields turns out to mean 20 percent less than full funding for that purpose. On the other hand, with Bush's environmental initiatives, we get particularly creative names. The Clean Skies Act will make the air dirtier, the Healthy Forest initiative is a giveaway to the timber companies, and most charming of all, we have Climate VISION. That stands for "voluntary innovative sector initiatives: Options Now," and is this administration's response to global warming — voluntary, optional controls on the production of greenhouse gases. It's a vision, all right. We assume Rove is to be congratulated.

The greatest bait and switch of the administration's record thus far was the aforementioned substitution of Saddam Hussein for Osama bin Laden. As we went to war, 42 percent of Americans believed Saddam Hussein was personally responsible for the attacks on September 11, and 55 percent believed he was providing direct support to al-Qaeda. There is no evidence for either thesis. The role of the American media in that disgraceful degree of misinformation cannot be ignored.

Well, as Bush himself once said, "There's an old saying in Tennessee — I know it's in Texas, probably in Tennessee — that says, fool me once, shame on — shame on you. Fool me — you can't get fooled again."

Shame on him. Shame on us.

• 17 •

WHAT IS TO BE DONE?

No fair, we think, to sit around taking pot-
shots at the people trying to govern the joint,
unless you can present better ideas. It's one
thing to point out that the great majority of
Americans under Bush are not doing well —
are in fact losing by every economic and
quality-of-life measurement known to man
— and that this country no longer works for
the benefit of most of the people in it — but
it's another to come up with a better plan.

We do have some ideas — plenty of them,
in fact — we think are solid, sensible, and
worthy of consideration. We concentrate on
two areas because they are the essentials
without which nothing else can proceed —
political reform and economic reform.

If there were one thing we could change
about this country by the wave of a wand,
it would be to end the legalized bribery
that has rotted the democratic political
system. We know we don't have to sell you

on this one. Never met an American yet who is not perfectly well aware that the political system is stacked in favor of those with money. You can't amaze an American with that news — they know politicians get bought. "Our" elected officials answer to "them," the ones who give big campaign contributions, not to "us" the people. Bullshit us no bullshit about how money "only buys access," it doesn't buy votes. It buys votes. Time after time after time after time. This is open corruption. It reeks, it is rot, and it is rampant. It is killing this country.

There is a cure. It's called public campaign financing. Right away the conservatives fire back, "That's socialism for politicians!" (thus cleverly marrying two things Americans hate — socialism and politicians). We've actually had public campaign financing in America for over thirty years, and it worked damned well for most of them. The major reform after the 1972 Watergate scandal — when millions of dollars in cash went sloshing around the country in briefcases to get dumped into Richard Nixon's CREEPy Committee to Reelect the President campaign — was a form of public campaign financing. Every year, when you get to the bottom of your

IRS 1040, there are two little boxes at the end before you sign the thing. One says, "Check here if you want to kick in a couple of your tax dollars to keep the presidential campaign honest," and the other one says: "Check here if you don't give a shit."

Actually, the boxes don't say that, but they should. And it worked, for at least three cycles, 1974 to 1986, then the Supreme Court gummed it up. In 1988 the Court made an absurd decision in a case called *Buckley* v. *Valeo*. The Court held that money is the same thing as free speech. Actually, money is the green stuff you use to buy things with; free speech is what comes out of your mouth, hopefully after some thought. Money ain't free speech, and someday the Supremes will get around to reconsidering that one. In the meantime, the wall, the dam that had been built against special-interest money in presidential elections, commenced to leak something fierce. In 1988 the money was spurting through a couple of cracks in the dam; by 1992 it was gushing through huge holes; by 1996 it was pouring over the top of the dam like Niagara; and by 2000, the dam was gone. (In 2000 George W. Bush was able to raise such vast sums from corporate America that he turned down the public money available for his campaign so he wouldn't have to observe the limits on spending that come with the public money.) Now, you could take this as a discouraging word, a sign that no matter how we try to fix the money in politics, the bastards will always find a way around it. Not us. We believe in Perpetual Reform.

We're not sure you can arrange any human institution so that it remains effective forever, or even much longer than ten years. We'll probably always have to come back in and re-reform this sucker. Doesn't discourage us in the least. They figure out a way around the rules, we figure out a new way to fix them. Perpetual reform.

Every time public campaign financing has been on the ballot for the people to vote on, it has won. Both Massachusetts and Arizona, two states of no noticeable political similarity, voted for it in 1998. The more states that try this, the more experience we have with it and the better we can make it work.

Here's the way Arizona does it. If you want to run for the state legislature in Arizona, you have to raise X amount (a substantial sum) in $5 increments (one per person) from people who actually live in the district you want to represent. No lobby money, no special-interest money, just your friends and neighbors kicking in five bucks each because they know you from your work on the school board, or the park board, or the planning board — know you well enough to think you'd make a decent representative for them. Once you raise that sum in $5 amounts, you qualify for state money, taxpayer money, money kicked in by the state's voters who want to see honest elections. You agree to limit your campaign to the amount available to you from the public pool. If you're rich, you might decide not to take the state money and to self-finance your campaign instead, but naturally your opponent will call you a malefactor of great wealth and other nasty names if you do so. "My plutocratic opponent Joe Doaks, born with a silver spoon in his mouth, is using his own money like a Rockefeller to buy this election!"

In a touch we especially liked — although the courts later held it unconstitutional — Arizona initially voted to raise some of this public campaign financing by putting a special tax on lobbyists. Such a brilliant notion. We hate that it didn't fly.

Always the question with public campaign financing is where to set the bar — how much money do you have to raise on your own before you qualify for public funds? If you set the bar too high, only the designated candidates of the major political parties will ever qualify. On the other hand, if you set it too low, every nincompoop in town will be able to run for public office on the taxpayer's nickel. The more experience we have, the better we get at setting the bar.

John McCain and Russ Feingold got the first, tiny, baby step toward campaign-finance reform at the federal level through Congress in the teeth of a screaming hissy fit against it thrown by the entire establishment. That took an amazing amount of people power. People power can still beat money power, when the people get stirred up enough. McCain-Feingold may not achieve much — especially since George W. appointed a radical anti-reformer to the board that is supposed to implement the bill's reforms — but it is a beginning.

All of us are responsible for our magnificent political heritage winding up in a system of legalized bribery. Political consultants all say campaign-finance reform is a nonstarter of an issue. It certainly is if you go around calling it campaign finance instead of rank, open bribery, which is what it is. Polls show people are perfectly well aware of the stacked deck in politics, it's just that no one puts it at the top of his list. People tend to be more concerned about health care, education, privacy, whatever. We need to make the point over and over that we can't get anywhere on any other issue until we fix legalized bribery. The oldest saying in politics is: "You got to dance with them what brung you." We need to fix the system so that when politicians get elected, they've got no one to dance with — no one they owe — except us, the people. When we pay for the campaigns, the politicians work for us. When big money pays, the politicians work for them.

For starters, corporations should be prohibited from contributing funds or in-kind support to political candidates, officials, political action committees, political parties, lobbyists, ballot initiatives, political conventions, meetings of public officials, issue advertising, policy institutes, or any organization that engages in public education or advocacy on matters of public policy. Corporate officials can, of course, participate in politics as private citizens.

Since the insane cost of political campaigns is driven primarily by the cost of television time, we suggest a clear and simple rule: "No political candidate shall be permitted to buy either time or space in any news medium. Compensatory time and space shall be provided by the media." Who owns the airwaves?

We do.

We also suggest this radical, subversive, powerful notion.

Vote. Get out and register other people to vote. The Republicans "won" the 2002 congressional elections with 15 percent of the eligible voters. Given the stakes, that's ridiculous.

If everyone in this country who sees the corruption of legalized bribery goes out and registers one person to vote every month for the next year — and stays in touch with that person, talks to that person, keeps that person informed — then we win the next election. How do you do that? Get in touch with your county registrar, set up a card table on a Saturday morning outside a grocery store, and just talk to people. "Lost your job? Need health insurance? Child care? Try voting."

Another major reason American politics is so dead in the water is our current system of redistricting. Redistricting, the art of drawing a district so it favors one party or another, is now so advanced there

497

is scarcely a congressional district left in the country in which a Democrat and a Republican each have a fair chance of winning. The districts are overwhelmingly stacked in favor of one side or the other; you can barely find a dozen contested congressional races out of 435 total in any given year. Why bother to vote when the outcome is inevitable? One piece of fallout from this is the disappearing middle in politics. Washington commentators (in our opinion, the most obtuse body of nincompoops on earth) constantly deplore the lack of civility in contemporary politics. Gone are the days, they mourn, when pols could fight on the floor all day and still drink together at night, when no one ever made a permanent enemy because you might be on the same side tomorrow with your opponent of today. The commentators never seem to mention why this deplorable decline in civility has occurred. A lot of the incentive for pragmatism and compromise is lost to this increasingly polarized system of redistricting. Pols themselves, who often used to represent disparate constituencies simultaneously, no longer need to search for the win-win compromise.

But there's a solution for this too! We are practically Miss Pollyanna Sunshine when it comes to reform. Regard — Iowa!

Although square, Iowa is a splendid state. Chief among its splendors is its system of redistricting. Iowa's electoral districts are drawn by a nonpartisan state commission: the commission uses computer programs to draw, as the law instructs, compact and contiguous districts. (During a memorable redistricting fight in the Texas Lege in the 1970s, the House birthed a map that featured districts that looked like giant chickens and others that looked like coiled snakes. A disconsolate San Antonio rep rose to complain about his new district to the chair of the redistricting committee, Delwin Jones of Lubbock. "Lookahere, Dell-win," quoth he, "look at whut yew have done to mah district. It's got a great big ol' ball on the one end, and then it runs in a little-bitty ol' strip for three hundred miles, and it's got a great big ol' ball on the other end. Now, Dell-win, the courts say the districts have to be *com*-pact and *con*-tiguous. Is this your idea o' *com*-pact and *con*-tiguous?!" Jones contemplated the question at the front mike for some time before he at last allowed, "Wha-ell, in a ar-tistic sense, it is.")

In Iowa the districts are drawn without regard to partisanship or incumbency. In other states, almost all districts are drawn to protect incumbents. Iowa's system has been in place since 1981, when everybody got fed up with the inevitable lawsuits that stem from the partisan maps and cost a lot of money. The legislature can only vote a straight up or down on a proposed redistricting plan — no amendments. As a result, three of Iowa's five congresspeople faced serious electoral challenge in 2002. Three competitive districts out of five: compare that with California, which has fifty-three seats and in 2002 had only one remotely competitive race — the contest to replace Gary Condit. If we wait around for incumbents to become suspects in murder cases, change is going to take quite a while.

The guts of government are still and always: Who pays? Who benefits? Tax. And spend. It's still the economy, stupid, but more than that, our ability to solve all the other problems hinges on the economy. It's pointless to talk about fixing the schools or about health care or the environment or cities or urban sprawl or children's issues or any of dozens of other issues in a vacuum. The solutions, the improvements, are all dependent on the economy.

Normally, one can have a peppy debate about the economy — let's do this, let's try that, no, you're crazy, we need to try something else entirely. But we are at a strange point here, where before we try anything, we need the economic equivalent of the key on the computer that says "undo." Delete. The Bush tax cuts are an economic disaster. The first round was horrible, and the second is, incredibly, worse — such an overt, unconscionable, stupid redistribution of income from the bottom to the top that it alone restores class warfare to a legitimate position in American political debate.

An economic recession can be ameliorated by both tax cuts and by increased government spending, but Bush is doing the wrong kind of both. A recession, in the old example from your Economics 101 textbook, is when you own four factories and one of them is sitting idle. If you give tax cuts to working- and middle-class citizens, they will run right out and spend it, thus pushing up demand, thus enabling you to reopen your fourth factory. If you give tax cuts to the wealthy, they may invest the money in a fifth factory, which will also stand idle because of lack of demand, or they may save the money, since they don't need anything, or they may buy a polo pony with it. Giving tax cuts to working- and middle-class people is the simplest, more direct way to dig the economy out of a recession. The other way is by "priming the pump" with government spending. What you're looking for in government spending is projects that create jobs. Military spending is not the most effective way to boost the economy, despite the military-industrial complex's vast annual lobbying of Congress on the subject. True, building planes, guns, and tanks provides jobs, but then what good are they? They kill people. Whereas putting money into schools, dams, bridges, mass transit, water systems, sewage systems — the whole clump of public building known as infrastructure — not only provides jobs but also leaves us with dandy things that work to improve the general welfare — as it says we are to do in the Constitution. Bill Clinton had a pip of an idea about how to fix America's schools, almost half of which are either dilapidated or falling apart. He wanted to issue tax-free federal bonds for the purpose, an attractive investment and terrific social investment at the same time. He was shut down by the Congress.

According to the American Society of Civil Engineers and the Department of Education, cities and their metro regions now have $2 trillion of neglected physical-infrastructure needs stacked up. Their neglect causes all kinds of burdens on citizens and public employees, as well as significant energy and environmental costs. Eric Hoffer, the longshoreman philosopher who was popular in the 1950s, once observed that the real genius of Americans is maintenance, taking care of things. Although we have a reputation as a throwaway society, maintenance of public facilities is critical. During New York City's fiscal crisis in the 1970s, the desperately strapped city could prove, absolutely prove, that every week, every month that went by without spending thousands to maintain the subways would eventually cost the city millions. That's the kind of public, deficit spending that makes sense in a recession. Of course it's also the kind of spending that leads to pork-barrel abuses, with dippy projects that are a waste of the public's money going to the districts of powerful congresspeople who run important committees. Citizens have to watch them like hawks for that kind of thing. Keeping an eye on the Corps of Engineers alone is enough to occupy a citizen full-time.

But look what you can do with smart infrastructure investment. The New Growth

Initiative, a partnership between progressive think tanks and labor unions, points out, "Energy independence can be significantly advanced through smart regional infrastructure investments in energy, transportation, wastewater and other systems. These large-scale public investments create real employment, while improving services, and saving money in ongoing operations and maintenance. These investments are also good for the environment, reducing energy consumption, vehicle miles traveled and air pollution." You can improve the quality of life, provide jobs, and spur the economy simultaneously. Beats the hell out of eliminating dividend taxes for rich investors.

Also near the top of the economic list: end corporate welfare. Getting the porkers out of the creek is always a popular notion and can be backed up with a tasty array of examples of obscene misallocation of taxpayer money to well-wired corporate special interests. In political terms, this is shooting fish in a barrel.

Even more popular: outlaw offshore tax havens. Close the loopholes that permit American corporations to use mailboxes on offshore islands to avoid paying American taxes. In the meantime, prohibit all

American corporations that have offshore tax dodges from bidding on any government contract, as the late Paul Wellstone proposed.

Take the putrid Cheney National Energy Policy and bury it. Instead, we need a huge push for energy conservation. It works. Look at the record. We also need to push for renewable power sources that will diminish our dependence on Middle East oil. This is truly a no-brainer. Wind power is already competitive at market prices. The CAFE standards that require automakers to build cars with higher gas mileage might also be taken seriously.

There are myriad other areas in which change is desperately needed. One begins with political and economic reform because one can accomplish nothing else without them. Another area in which catastrophe is imminent is health care. (And we're optimists.) This will not keep. The system is not just developing cracks, huge chunks of it have already fallen out. It is not necessary to reinvent the wheel here — every other advanced country has some system of national health insurance; we can do the old blue book exercise of compare and contrast. Which system seems to work best? Which would work best in this country? As anyone who has ever studied it knows, nothing about changing the health-care system is simple: even if one opts for what sounds like a simple solution — single-payer health insurance — making it work involves untold complexities. It's quite possible the French have the best system, combining single-payer with freedom of choice for patients. (We could always call it the Freedom system.)

On corporate reform, about which nothing has been done in the wake of Enron, WorldCom, etc., the specific steps are painfully obvious:

• Treat stock options as expenses, under rigorous accounting practices, not some waffling halfway measure.
• Build an absolute wall between re-search analysts and investment banks, with heavy legal punishment for breaching it.
• Prohibit accounting firms from pro-viding consulting services while au-diting a company's books. Can you believe this is still not illegal?
• Regulate the special-purpose entities that Enron used for off-balance-sheet transactions.
• Strengthen whistleblower protections

and insure that they shield all workers.

- Overhaul current accounting standards. After a disgraceful lapse of time, in April 2003 we finally got a chairman for the new accounting standards oversight committee.
- Dump Phil Gramm's Financial Modernization Act, which repeals safeguards going back to the New Deal separating commercial and investment banking.
- Strengthen the independence of corporate boards, and use antitrust laws.

Not strictly a matter of corporate governance but still an urgent economic matter is pension reform. The Bush administration is again dragging us in exactly the wrong direction.

In thirty years of nonstop right-wing attacks on the very concept of government — government can't do anything right, privatize everything, the free market works best — we think the greatest loss may be our sense of "us-ness." Government has done great good for the people of this country over two centuries. To now pretend that it is a villain, that all institutions that have been built up so slowly over the years should be shredded in favor of some for-profit entity, strikes us as idiotic. We are now at a point when the Bush administration is proposing to end the forty-hour workweek (via some bills charmingly misentitled "Family Flexibility Act" by ending workers' right to choose time-and-a-half pay for overtime, rather than comp time, to be selected at the company's discretion).

Friends, it is time to become alarmed. This administration has gone far beyond anything they ever talked about in the 2000 campaign and far beyond anything that was ever voted for by us, or even mentioned to us. Our country, our government, our representatives, our responsibility. Government has become "them," "those people." Those people in Washington, those people at the state capitol, those people who take your money and never do anything for you. "I'm just not interested in politics." "It's boring." "Oh, they're all crooks." "There's nothing I can do."

Politics is not something you can stand off and look at as though it were a television program or a painting on a wall and decide you really don't much care for it. This is the warp and woof of your life: everything from how deep you will be buried when

508

you die, to the textbooks your kids study in school, to the qualifications of the people who prescribe your eyeglasses or contact lenses, to your health, education, home insurance — you name it, what doesn't government touch or set the rules for (or set no rules for)? It's always fun to take one of these government bashers like Phil Gramm and just start counting how many ways they've been helped by government. Started when Gramm was born in a military hospital, owes his schooling to the taxpayers, his college education, his Ph.D., never had a job that wasn't a government job, and so forth. So he dedicated his life to destroying all that, go figure.

The programs that help people are the ones being dismantled by ideological zealots. The programs that help corporations at the expense of the taxpayers are being left in place. "Un-American" is not a word we are given to tossing around, nor is "fascism" — we have spent years making fun of humorless liberals who hear the sound of jack-booted fascism around every corner. But there is something creepy about what is happening here, and the creepiest thing about it is that no one is talking about it. Mussolini said, "Fascism should more properly be called corporatism, since it is the merger of state and corporate power." That's pretty much what we're looking at here, and the results are not good for the people of this country, no matter what it is called. Jim Hightower has an old speech where he says all the reporting on the Dow Jones Average needs to be replaced with the Doug Jones Average, Doug Jones, Average American Report, how's he doin'? How's it goin' for ol' Doug?

So we went out and talked to ol' Doug. He's in big trouble. So are you. So are we all. Time to raise hell.

• ACKNOWLEDGMENTS •

We are greatly indebted to Ann Godoff, the former president, publisher, and editor in chief of Random House, who proposed this book. And to Random House vice president Jonathan Karp, for his thoughtful editorial direction and for seeing this work to its completion. Random House associate copy chief Beth Pearson carefully shepherded this book through the production process — as she did with its predecessor: *Shrub*. Margaret Wimberger provided us the same careful copyediting as she did three years ago for *Shrub*. Our steadfast agent Dan Green saw that all business matters were properly taken care of, provided us invaluable editorial commentary, and gently and persistently reminded us that books cannot be published unless writers meet deadlines. Closer to home, Betsy Moon was an invaluable researcher and fact-checker. She also held our hands and twisted our arms to ensure that we came close to meeting our deadline. The book could not have been completed without her. University of Texas journalism grad student Elizabeth Esfahani helped with database research. And Aaron Crowell of Campaign for America's Future generously provided us with a great deal of useful information. Our families — Andy and Carla Ivins, and Jeanne Goka — helped, supported, tolerated, and even indulged us while we worked on this book. Our good and generous friend Charlotte McCann improved this work with her careful proofreading and her sharp editorial suggestions.

Many of the individuals quoted herein gave generously of their time. They had nothing to gain from going public with the stories they told. They did so because they refused to remain quiet when their government failed their interests — or more important, the larger public interest. To single any one of them out would be to unfairly neglect others. They represent the best of this great nation.

• SOURCES •

CHAPTER 1: ALOHA, HARKEN

Critical investigative reporting and primary SEC source material for this chapter was drawn from the Center for Public Integrity web postings and the reporting and writing of CPI senior fellow Knut Royce. The diligent work of the nonprofit CPI refocused the attention of the public and the press on the questionable dealings involving George W. Bush and Harken Energy Corp. HarvardWatch, a nonprofit student-alumni group, provided the press with fresh and critical source material on the Harvard trust's bailout of Harken. They sourced the fall 2002 stories on Harvard's bailout of Bush and Harken. Much of the material on Harken was also drawn from the authors' previous work, *Shrub: The Short but Happy Political Life of George W. Bush.*

Allen, Mike, and George Lardner, Jr., "Harken Papers Offer Details on

Bush Knowledge," *Washington Post,* July 14, 2002.

Armstrong, David, "Global Entanglements: The Political Economy of a Texas Oil Company," *Texas Observer,* July 12, 1991.

————, "The President's Son and His Slippery Friends," *Texas Observer,* September 21, 1991.

Bergman, Lowell, and Jeff Gerth, "Power Trader Tied to Bush," *New York Times,* May 25, 2001.

Bush, George W., "A New Ethic of Corporate Responsibility," text of speech, www.whitehouse.gov/infocus.corporate responsibility, July 9, 2002.

————, "A New Ethic of Corporate Responsibility," summary, www.whitehouse.gov/news, July 9, 2002.

————, press conference, transcript, www.whitehouse.gov/news/briefings, July 9, 2002.

Bush, George, and Mikel D. Faulkner, president, Harken Energy Corp., Amendment and Extension to Consulting Agreement.

Conason, Joe, "Letter Rip," Salon.com, July 16, 2002.

————, "Lou Dobbs Downgrades President Bush," Salon.com, July 9, 2002.

Cummings, Larry, Harken Energy Corp. general counsel, letter to George W. Bush re: SEC filings, October 15, 1989.

Faulkner, Mikel, Harken Energy Corp. president, letter to George W. Bush, June 15, 1989.

————, letter to the Harken Board of Directors, February 1, 1990.

————, letter to the Harken Board of Directors, May 25, 1990.

————, letter to the Harken Board of Directors, August 27, 1990.

————, letter (with attachment) to the Harken Board of Directors, May 25, 1990.

Fineman, Howard, "Harkening Back to Texas," *Newsweek*, July 22, 2002.

Fleischer, Ari, White House briefing, Federal Document Clearing House Political Transcripts, July 3, 2002.

Harken Energy Corp., General Resolutions, March 14, 1990.

————, Minutes of the Regular Meeting of the Board of Directors, September 13, 1989.

————, Minutes of the Regular Meeting of the Board of Directors, December 6, 1989.

————, Minutes of the Regular Meeting of the Board of Directors, March 14, 1990.

————, Minutes of a Special Board of Directors Meeting, May 11, 1990.

————, Minutes of a Special Board of Directors Meeting, May 17, 1990.

————, Minutes of a Special Board of Directors Meeting, August 29, 1990.

————, Public Common Stock Offering, March 14, 1990.

————, SEC Commission Form 10-K, December 31, 1989.

————, Shareholders Notes, March 14, 1990.

————, Shareholders Notes, May 11, 1990.

Hollings, Sen. Ernest, "Time for a Special Investigator," *New York Times*, February 9, 2002.

Huff, Bruce, senior vice president, Harken Energy Corp., letter to George Bush et al., re: Special Audit Committee, May 18, 1990.

Janick, Herbert C., III, et al., SEC memo re: George W. Bush Jr.'s Filings of Forms 3 & 4 MHO-3180, April 9, 1991.

Krugman, Paul, "A Little Help from His Friends: Bush's Wheeling and Dealing in Texas Foreshadowed His Penchant for Secrecy and His Indifference to Conflicts of Interest," *New York Times*, July 17, 2002.

————, "Smoking Fat Boy," *New York*

Times, May 10, 2002.

Reidler, Jeffrey P., SEC branch chief, letter to William R. Hayes, Esq., December 14, 1990.

Royce, Knut, "Bush's Insider Connections Preceded Huge Profit on Stock Deal," *The Public i*, www.publicintegrity.org, April 4, 2002.

———, "Bush's Insider Connections," *The Public i*, May 15, 2002.

———, "Bush Violated Security Law Four Times," *The Public i*, July 3, 2002.

Simpson, Glenn R., "Harvard Was Unlikely Savior of Bush Energy Firm," *Wall Street Journal*, October 9, 2002.

Valero, Dale A., letter to Harken Energy Corp. Board of Directors, July 11, 1990.

Walker, William, "The President's New Pitch," *Toronto Star*, July 21, 2002.

York, Anthony, "Hypocrite in Chief," Salon.com, July 2, 2002.

Yost, Pete, "Bush Signed Lockup Letter," *Washington Post*, July 15, 2002.

CHAPTER 2: JULIA JEFFCOAT'S JOBLESS RECOVERY

"Before Congress Leaves," *New York Times*, editorial, October 15, 2002.

Clymer, Adam, "Congressional Democrats

Mount Offensive on Unemployment Pay," *New York Times*, January 24, 1992.

———, "President to Sign Jobless Measure but Block Money," *New York Times*, August 17, 1991.

Despeignes, Peronet, "Bush Joins Calls for Benefits Extension," *Financial Times*, December 16, 2002.

Devroy, Ann, "Bush to Drop Resistance to New Jobless Benefits: Democrats Pushing for Another Extension," *Washington Post*, January 23, 1992.

Dewar, Helen, and Kenneth J. Cooper, "Hill Again Extends Jobless Benefits," *Washington Post*, February 5, 1992.

Dodds, John, Philadelphia Unemployment Project, interview by LD, Philadelphia, January 23, 2003.

"George Bush Speech on the Economy," Federal News Service, January 7, 2003.

Goldberg, Jessica, Center on Budget and Policy Priorities, telephone interview by LD, January 27, 2003.

Hulse, Carl, "Bush Signs Bill to Extend Unemployment Benefits," *New York Times*, January 9, 2002.

Jeffcoat, Julia, interview by LD, Philadelphia, January 24, 2003.

Newall, Mike, "Funny Money: President Bush Finally Spoke Up for the Nation's Unemployed," *Philadelphia Weekly*, December 18, 2002.

Pianin, Eric, "Bush Signs Jobless Benefits After Senate Deal," *Washington Post*, November 16, 1991.

———, and Ann Devroy, "Bush Signals Willingness to Deal on Jobless Bill," *Washington Post*, October 30, 1991.

Primus, Wendell, Center on Budget and Policy Priorities, "One Million Workers Have Run Out of Federal Unemployment Benefits and Should Be Helped When Federal Unemployment Insurance Is Extended," January 6, 2002.

———, Isaac Shapiro, and Jessica Goldberg, Center on Budget and Policy Priorities, "Temporary Federal Unemployment Benefits Should Be Extended in All States and Strengthened," December 19, 2002.

Raum, Tom, "Bush Snubs Jobless Aid," *Philadelphia Daily News*, August 17, 1991.

Sanders, Edmund, "Bush Urges Congress to Extend Benefits to the Nation's Jobless," *Los Angeles Times*, December 15, 2002.

Staff members, Senate Committee on Health, Education, Labor, and Pensions, telephone interview by LD, February 7, 2003.

Stevenson, Richard W., "Bush Calls for an Extension of Unemployment Benefits," *New York Times*, December 15, 2002.

Strope, Leigh, "Unemployed Workers Welcome Aid, Question Delays," Associated Press, January 9, 2003.

Swindell, Bill, "Jobless Benefits Extension is 108th's Opening Act," *Congressional Quarterly Weekly*, January 10, 2003.

White House Briefing, "President Bush Remarks to Welfare-to-Work Graduates," Federal News Service, January 14, 2003.

Wicker, Tom, "Another Such Victory," *New York Times*, November 21, 1991.

Yang, John E., "Bush Won't Extend Unemployment Benefits, Aides Say," *Washington Post*, April 16, 1991.

CHAPTER 3: CLASS WAR

Center for Tax Justice, various reports, www.ctj.org.

Economic Policy Institute, various reports, www.epinet.org.

Frank, Thomas, "The God That Sucked," *The Baffler* no. 14, www.thebaffler.com.

Krugman, Paul, "For Richer," *New York Times Magazine*, October 20, 2002.

Lewis, Charles, Bill Allison, and the Center for Public Integrity, *The Cheating of America: How Tax Avoidance and Evasion by the Super Rich Are Costing the Country Billions — and What You Can Do About It* (New York: Perennial, 2002).

Phillips, Kevin, "A Tax Cut Plan Rooted in the Bush Pedigree," *Los Angeles Times*, January 12, 2003.

————, *Wealth and Democracy: A Political History of the American Rich* (New York: Broadway Books, 2002).

Rapoport, Bernard, interview by MI, Waco, Texas, January 2003.

————, and Don Carleton, *Being Rapoport* (Austin: University of Texas Press, 2002).

Renzulli, Diane, and the Center for Public Integrity, *Capitol Offenders: How Private Interests Govern Our States* (Washington, D.C.: Public Integrity Books, 2002).

Seelye, Katharine Q., "Industry Seeking Rewards From G.O.P.-Led Congress," *New York Times*, December 3, 2002.

Useem, Jerry, "Have They No Shame?," *Fortune*, April 28, 2003.

Weisman, Jonathan, "New Tax Plan May Bring Shift in Burden: Poor Could Pay a Bigger Share," *Washington Post*, December 16, 2002.

CHAPTER 4: THE BLUES IN BELZONI

Allen, Bill, Delta Pride president, interview by LD, Indianola, Mississippi, April 9, 2002.

Anderson, Johnny, interview by LD, Belzoni, Mississippi, April 6, 2002.

Anderson, Nick, "Senate Overturns Economic Rules," *Los Angeles Times*, March 7, 2001.

Clearwater Farms workers, interview by LD, Tchula, Mississippi, April 7, 2002.

Clymer, Adam, "Parties Struggle in Senate over Labor Dept. Nominee," *New York Times*, October 3, 2001.

Dine, Philip, "Catfish Workers Beat Odds," *St. Louis Post-Dispatch*, July 7, 1991.

———, "Catfish Workers Lauded at Rally," *St. Louis Post-Dispatch*,

December 16, 1990.

Dodd, Sen. Christopher, Senate Debate on Ergonomic Standards, March 6, 2001.

Durst, Sherry, interview by LD, Belzoni, Mississippi, April 11, 2002.

Kennedy, Sen. Edward, Statement at Senate Committee on Health, Education, Labor, and Pensions, Washington Hearing on Nomination of Eugene Scalia as Solicitor of Labor, April 14, 2002.

LaSalle, Denise, interview by LD, Belzoni, Mississippi, April 6, 2002.

Lewis, Carrie Ann, interview by LD, Belzoni, Mississippi, April 10, 2002.

Lewis, Rita, interview by LD, Tchula, Mississippi, April 7, 2002.

Miller, Rep. George, et al., letter to President George W. Bush, March 20, 2002.

Myers, Dr. Ron, interview by LD, Belzoni, Mississippi, April 12, 2002.

Nowell, Jackie, United Food and Commercial Workers, interview by LD, Washington, D.C., April 18, 2002.

Scalia, Eugene, Government Ergonomic Regulation of Repetitive Strain Injuries, October 1997.

————, letter to Jennie Hays, Department

of Labor and Industries, Tumwater, Washington, February 23, 2000.

———, National Legal Center for the Public Interest, White Paper, "Ergonomics: OSHA's Strange Campaign to Run American Business," August 1994.

———, "OSHA Backs Its Ergonomics Rule with Mysterious Science," *San Francisco Daily Journal*, July 10, 2000.

———, "OSHA to Business: Slow Down, You Work Too Fast," *Wall Street Journal*, January 13, 1994.

———, Policy Analysis (the Cato Institute), "Osha's Ergonomics Litigation: Three Strikes and It's Out," May 15, 2000.

———, Testimony, Confirmation Hearing, Senate Committee on Health, Education, Labor, and Pensions, October 2, 2001.

Scalia, Eugene, Esq., for Gibson Dunn & Crutcher LLP, before the House Committee on Education and the Workforce Subcommittee on Workforce Protections Regarding OSHA's Proposed Record-keeping Rule, July 20, 2000.

Scalia, Eugene, et al., Comments of Rubber Manufacturers Association on Proposed Ergonomics Standard, July 1, 1999.

————, Comments of United Postal Service on the Ergonomics Advanced Notice of Proposed Rule-making; 1998 OSHRC Docket No. 98-265 Amicus Brief on Behalf of United Postal Service, 1998.

————, re: Pepperidge Farm, Pleadings, March 4, 1993.

Schweid, Richard, "Delta Strike: Civil Rights or Just Plain Economics," *Los Angeles Times*, November 18, 1990.

Seminario, Peg, AFL-CIO, interview by LD, Washington, D.C., April 19, 2002.

Senate Committee on Health, Education, Labor, and Pensions, Hearing, Washington, D.C., April 18, 2002.

ShamsidDeen, Ali, "Workers Calling for Boycott Against Freshwater Farms," *Jackson Advocate*, January 6, 1999.

Staff member for Senate Committee on Health, Education, Labor, and Pensions, background interview by LD, Washington, D.C., April 25, 2002.

Staff member for Senator Paul Wellstone, background interview by LD, Washington, D.C., April 24, 2002.

White, Ernest, interview by LD, Belzoni,

Mississippi, April 6, 2002.

White, Sarah, interview by LD, Indianola, Mississippi, April 8, 2002.

"Workplace Solutions for Repetitive Stress Injuries," *CTDNEWS*, October 30, 2000, and February 19, 2002.

CHAPTER 5: LEAVE NO CHILD BEHIND

Balta, Victor, "End Creative Teaching, Says Assistant Secretary," *Record* (Stockton), October 25, 2002.

Broder, David S., "Long Road to Reform: Negotiators Forge Education Legislation," *Washington Post*, December 17, 2001.

Edley, Christopher, "Statement on President Bush's FY2004 Funding Under the No Child Left Behind Act," The Civil Rights Project at Harvard, January 4, 2003.

Edwards, Odell, interview by LD, Houston, February 13, 2003.

Hobbs, Tawnell D., "Moses Wants DISD Trustees to Voice Concerns About Test, Superintendent Citing Field Results, Says TAKS Is Too Difficult," *Dallas Morning News*, January 23, 2003.

Houston, Paul, telephone interview by LD, March 4, 2003.

Khanna, Roma, "Bush Affirms Commitment to Education: Critics Say Reforms in American Schools Took a Back Seat to War and Enron," *Houston Chronicle*, March 6, 2002.

Kress, Sandy, telephone interview by LD, March 5, 2003.

McGraw-Hill Companies Earnings Conference Call, Federal Document Clearing House, January 28, 2003.

McNeil, Linda M., *Contradictions of School Reform* (New York: Routledge, 2000).

———, telephone interview by LD, March 4, 2003.

———, and Angela Valenzuela, "The Harmful Impact of the TAAS System of Testing in Texas: Beneath the Accountability Rhetoric," in *Raising Standards or Raising Barriers? Inequity and High-Stakes Testing in Public Education*, ed. Gary Orfield and Mindy L. Kornhaber (New York: Century Foundation Press, 2001).

Metcalf, Stephen, "Reading Between the Lines," *Nation*, January 28, 2002.

Michelau, Demaree K., and David Shreve, "Education Reform from the Top Down," *State Legislatures Magazine*, December 2002.

Mollison, Andrea, "New Law Will Spread

Bad Reforms," Cox News Service, March 15, 2002.

Murray, Mark, "Calling on the States: Interview with Rod Paige," *National Journal*, August 10, 2002.

Scharrer, Gary, "Lawmakers Feel Pinch of Budget Cuts, Protest Rallies," *El Paso Times*, March 16, 2003.

Staff member, Senate Committee on Health, Education, Labor, and Pensions, background telephone interview by LD, February 26, 2003.

"State of the Schools: Measurable Progress, High Hurdles for Houston District," *Houston Chronicle*, editorial, March 7, 2002.

Sylvan Learning Companies, Inc., Earnings Conference Call, Federal Document Clearing House, February 20, 2003.

Tavis Smiley Show, The, "Bush's Proposed Education Budget Doesn't Make Good on the Promise of the Leave No Child Behind Act," National Public Radio, February 17, 2003.

———, "Tony Cox, Sandy Kress, and Monty Neill Discuss a Recent Study Suggesting That Standardized Tests Are Lowering Academic Achievement," interview, National Public

Radio, January 2, 2003.

Traub, James, "No Child Left Behind: Success for Some," *New York Times Educational Supplement,* November 10, 2002.

Valenzuela, Angela, "High-Stakes Testing and U.S.-Mexican Youth in Texas: The Taste for Multiple Compensatory Criteria in Assessment," *Harvard Journal of Hispanic Policy,* vol. 14, 2002.

————, telephone interview by LD, February 28, 2003.

Wilkins, Amy, "No Child Left Behind," interview, *Frontline,* WGBH, 2002.

CHAPTER 6: GREEN RABBITS AND
YELLOW STREAMS

Berhrmann, Marcy, "EPA Wants to Dig, Remove Toxic Soil," *Home News Tribune* (New Jersey), August 4, 2000.

Chemical Insecticide Corporation, Bankruptcy Affidavit, Section A, February 13, 1973.

————, Products List, June 25, 1962.

Dames & Moore, Cranford, New Jersey, Geohydrological Investigation of the Edison, Metroplex, December 1983.

Gallotto, Anthony A., "Edison Homeowners Alerted on Pollution," *Star-Ledger* (New Jersey), September, 6, 1991.

———, "Edison Insecticide Plant Labeled Health Hazard," *Star-Ledger* (New Jersey), August 4, 1992.

Govelitz, Gary, "Edison Wetlands Association Receives $50,000 Grant for Superfund Project," *Metuchen-Edison Review*, September 17, 1999.

Greenberg, Eric J., "Edison Faults EPA," *News Tribune* (New Jersey), April 29, 1993.

Hackler, James S., United States Environmental Protection Agency, letter to Robert Spiegel, January 6, 1997.

Herman, Edward, Esq., interview by LD, Princeton, New Jersey, September 3, 2002.

Horvath, Gail, interview by LD, Edison, New Jersey, September 5, 2002.

Humphreys, Sharon L., and Joseph Vitale, "Information Search Concerning . . . Chemical Insecticide Corporation in Edison, New Jersey," EPA Region II Draft Final Report, March 1985.

Josephs, Jonathan, Environmental Protection Agency Region II project manager, Chemical Insecticide Corporation, Site Inspection Report, July 31, 1991.

Lacik, Fred, Investigation Report, Edison, New Jersey, Police Department, November 28, 1969.

Livingston, Arnold, In the Matter of Chemical Insecticide Corporation Chapter XI, Testimony Transcript, Bankruptcy Hearing, Trenton, New Jersey, June 23, 1970.

————, and Tom Burke, Director of Office of Cancer and Toxic Substances Research, Deposition Transcript, Trenton, New Jersey, July 11, 1983.

Livio, Susan K., "Arsenic Tainting Yards in Edison," *Home News* (New Jersey), April 28, 1993.

————, "EPA Downplays Risk of 'Missing' Toxic Pit," *Home News* (New Jersey), July 31, 1992.

————, "EPA's Warnings to Be Explained," *News Tribune* (New Jersey), Sepember 5, 1991.

Livingston, Arnold, Deposition, New Jersey Department of Environmental Protection, July 19, 1983.

————, Testimony, New Jersey Department of Environmental Protection, July 5, 1983.

New Jersey Department of Health, Health Assessment, Chemical Insecticide Corporation (Draft), July 11, 1991.

Olenick, Walter, senior industrial hygienist, Air Pollution Evaluation, Chemical Insecticides, Inc., March 25, 1966.

Picard, Joseph, "Cleanup Fight Goes On," *Home News Tribune* (New Jersey), September 12, 1999.

Seelye, Katharine Q., "Bush Slashing Aid for EPA," *New York Times*, July 1, 2002.

Shogren, Elizabeth, "Stalled Superfund Cleanups Anger Activists, Spur Fears About Future; EPA Says Commitment to Funding Hasn't Wavered but Money Is Running Out," *Los Angeles Times*, August 14, 2002.

Spadoro, Mayor George, interview by LD, Edison, New Jersey, September 7, 2002.

Spiegel, Robert, interview by LD, Edison, New Jersey, September 3, 2002.

———, Senate Subcommittee on Superfund, Toxics, Risk and Waste Management, Testimony Transcript, April 10, 2002.

United States. Environmental Protection Agency, Draft Final Report, Volume I, "Information Search Concerning Tier 1A Facilities Associated with Chemical Insecticide Corporation in Edison, New Jersey," March 1985.

———, Office of Waste Programs, Enforcement Information Search Draft, March 1985.

———, Region II, Superfund Proposed Plan, Chemical Insecticide Corporation, November 1995.

———, Region II, Superfund Proposed Plan, Chemical Insecticide Corporation, November 2000.

CHAPTER 7: KILL THE MESSENGER

Beaudry, Kendall, "EPA Ombudsman Fights for His Job," Environmental News Network, March 15, 2002.

Brian, Danielle, Project on Government Oversight of the EPA, National Ombudsman's Office, Testimony, Senate Committee on Environment and Public Works, June 25, 2002.

Dunsky, Christopher J., "Court Allows Superfund Defendant to Renegotiate Allocated Share to Account for Cleanup Plan," Michigan Environmental Compliance Update, August 2000.

Flickinger, Marie, telephone interview by LD, January 4, 2003.

Hertsgaard, Mark, "Conflict of Interest for Christine Todd Whitman?,"

Salon.com, January 14, 2002.

Hudson, Audre, "EPA Moves to Confiscate Files in Probe of Whitman's Husband," Washington Times, April 18, 2002.

Kaufman, Hugh, "Dangers of Sludge: A Citizens Forum on Environmental and Health Concerns from Landspreading of Sewage and Paper Mill Sludges," Concord, New Hampshire, Transcript, November 15, 1997.

———, interview by LD, Washington, D.C., April 18, 2002.

———, interview by LD, Washington, D.C., April 23, 2002.

Martin, Robert, interview by LD, Washington, D.C., April 23, 2002.

Nadler, U.S. Rep. Jerrold, et al. letter to Special Counsel Elaine Kaplan, Washington, D.C., April 18, 2002.

Rachel's Environment & Health Weekly, December 18, 1991.

Robert Martin v. *EPA et al., the plaintiffs*, v. *The U.S. Environmental Protection Agency et al., the defendants*, Original Complaint and Transcripts of Oral Argument, U.S. District Court for the District of Columbia, filed January 10, 2002.

Robert Martin v. *EPA et al., the plaintiffs,* v. *The U.S. Environmental Protection Agency et al., the defendants,* Memorandum Opinion, United States District Judge Richard Roberts, U.S. District Court for the District of Columbia, 2002.

Sablatura, Bob, "Caught in the Toxic Crossfire, Residents Near Polluted Site Say They're Forgotten," *Houston Chronicle,* October 25, 1995.

Sánchez, Deb, telephone interview by LD, December 18, 2002.

Steyer, Robert, "Monsanto Wins $34 Million; Dispute Involved Superfund Site," *St. Louis Post-Dispatch,* March 9, 1995.

Texas Department of Parks and Wildlife, Advisory 3 (Upper Galveston Bay), September 19, 1990.

United States Environmental Protection Agency Region 6, Amended Record of Decision, Brio Refinery Site, May 30, 1997.

United States Environmental Protection Agency Region 6, Bulletin, Brio Refining, Inc., November 8, 2001.

United States Environmental Protection Agency, Texas Superfund Registry, Brio Refinery Site, November 29, 2002.

Becker, Elizabeth, "Critics Take Aim at Guidelines for Food Safety," *New York Times*, November 2, 2002.

"Bush Nominates Food Safety Chief," Associated Press, June 10, 2001.

Cancer Prevention Coalition, Government Accountability Project, et al., "Groups Blast Bush Administration for Plan to Buy Irradiated Meat for schools," press release, March 29, 2001.

"Doctor, Others Sue Pilgrim's Pride Over Contaminated Turkey," *Philadelphia Daily News*, November 4, 2002.

Erthal, Vincent, interview by LD, Philadelphia, December 19, 2002.

FitzGerald, Susan, "Listeriosis Cluster Turns Victims' Meals into Clues: Health Officials Are on Case. Five People Have Died," *Philadelphia Inquirer*, October 1, 2002.

"Food-Borne Illness: Listeria Outbreak, Meat Recall Spur Calls for More Regulation," *Vector & Zoonosis Week*, November 18, 2002.

Foreman, Carol Tucker, Food Policy Institute, Consumer Federation of America, telephone interview by LD,

November 4, 2002.

Frank Niemtzow, Individually and on Behalf of Others Similarly Situated v. *Wampler Foods Inc.*, Philadelphia County Court of Common Pleas, November 4, 2002.

Gale Group, Inc., "Outbreak of Listeriosis — Northeastern United States," *Morbidity and Mortality Weekly Report*, October 25, 2002.

Moll, Kenneth, Esq., interview by LD, October 24, 2002.

Murano, Elsa, Center for Food Safety, Texas A & M University, "Bringing Irradiated Food to a Grocery Store Near You," Minnesota Dept. of Public Health Conference, June 21, 1999.

National Journal's *Congress Daily*, "Veneman Discusses Status of Final Rule on Performance Standards," October 18, 2002.

Nestor, Felicia, Government Accountability Project, interview by LD, Philadelphia, November 4, 2002.

Niemtzow, Stuart, interview by LD, Lower Merion, Pennsylvania, December 16, 2002.

O'Meara, Mike, Esq., telephone interview by LD, January 2, 2003.

Philadelphia Department of Public Health et al. "Outbreak of Listeriosis — Northeastern United States," *Public Health Dispatch*, November 19, 2002.

"Pilgrim's Pride Issues Record Recall of Poultry; the Company Says 27.4 Million Pounds of Ready-to-Eat Products Could Be Contaminated with Listeria," *Los Angeles Times*, October 14, 2000.

Plaintiff's family (name withheld by request), *Frank Niemtzow, et al.* v. *Wampler Foods Inc.*, telephone interview by LD, January 13, 2003.

Prichard, Oliver, and Aparna Surendran, "Food Plant Cited Before Outbreak: Corrective Actions Were Not Taken at a Franconia Poultry Processor Linked to Seven Deaths," *Philadelphia Inquirer*, November 3, 2002.

Public Citizen et al., letter to Sen. Tom Harkin, July 16, 2001.

Rossenbaum, Donna, interview by LD, January 14, 2002.

Slosser, Eric, *Fast Food Nation: The Dark Side of the All-American Meal* (New York: Perennial, 2002).

Staff members, U.S. Senate Agriculture Committee, background interview,

Washington, D.C., December 18, 2002.

Sugarman, Carole, "FSIS Administrator McKee on Listeria, Mandatory Recalls and Life at USDA," *Food Chemical News*, November 4, 2002.

Surendran, Aparna, "Listeria Search Expands Further; the New Facilities Are Not in the Phila Area, Officials Said. A Lawsuit Targets Wampler," *Philadelphia Inquirer*, November 5, 2002.

Taylor, Karen, telephone interview by LD, December 16, 2002.

"200,000 Pounds of Poultry Recalled by N.J. Company," *Orlando Sentinel*, November 4, 2002.

USDA Food Safety and Inspection Service, Bulletin, "Pennsylvania Firm Expands Recall of Turkey and Chicken Products for Possible Listeria Contamination," October 12, 2002.

———, Field Instructions, Kansas, October 2002.

———, Noncompliance Record(s), Pilgrim's Pride, Franconia Division, January 1, 2002–October 12, 2002.

USDA Grievance Board, Listeria Summit, Transcript of Proceedings, Washington, D.C., November 18, 2002.

Bowlby, Joanne, "Coal-bed Methane Puts Powder River on Endangered List," *Wyoming Tribune-Eagle*, April 2, 2002.

"Bush Appointees Come with Biases; from Anybody but a Fox, the Explanation Would Be Almost Believable," editorial, *Atlanta Journal-Constitution*, January 20, 2002.

"Calif. Congressmen Charging Coverup, Call for Moratoria on OCS Lease Sales," *Platt's Oilgram News*, April 6, 1989.

Center for Responsive Politics, www.opensecrets.org, J. Steven Griles & Associates' total lobbying income.

Clark, Patricia, interview by LD, Pumpkin Buttes, Wyoming, May 27, 2002.

Edward Swartz v. *Gary Beach, Dennis Hemmer, and Redstone Resources*, United States District Court of Wyoming, March 2002.

"Environmentalists Fight Mining Industry Lobbyist Confirmation for Deputy Secretary of the Interior," *U.S. Newswire*, May 16, 2001.

Fineman, Howard, and Michael Isikoff, "Big Energy at the Table," *Newsweek*,

May 14, 2001.

Goldstein, Andrew, "Rocky Mountain Deep: The Next Drilling War," *Time*, May 20, 2002.

Griles, J. Steven, Assistant Secretary, Land and Minerals Management, United States Department of the Interior, memo to Bill Horn, re: Fish and Wildlife Service Comments on the Draft EIS for Northern California Lease Sale 91, 1988.

———, letter to Linda Fisher, Deputy Administrator, EPA, subject: Proposed EPA Region 8 Letter on Coal-bed Methane — EIS's [*sic*], prepared by the Department of the Interior — Wyoming and Montana, April 12, 2002.

———, United States Department of the Interior, Deputy Secretary J. Steven Griles Statement of Disqualification from Matters Involving Coal-bed Methane Environmental Impact Statements, filed with the Secretary of the Interior April 8, 2002.

———, United States Department of the Interior, Deputy Secretary J. Steven Griles Statement of Disqualification from Matters Involving His Former Employers and Clients, filed with the

Secretary of the Interior August 1, 2001.

"Interior Official Challenges EPA Report on Energy Site," *Bulletin's Frontrunner,* April 25, 2002.

Kohler, Judith, "Coal-Bed Methane Touted as Key to Building Energy Production," Associated Press, April 4, 2002.

Malone, Gillian, interview by LD, Spotted Horse, Wyoming, May 31, 2002.

Mintz, John, and Eric Pianin, "Symbol of Shift at Interior, Griles Represents Movement of Pro Industry, Anti-Regulation Conservatives," *Washington Post,* May 16, 2001.

Morrison, Jill, interview by LD, Sheridan, Wyoming, May 30, 2002.

National Energy Policy Development Group, "Reliable, Affordable, Environmentally Sound Energy For America's Future" (report commissioned by Vice President Dick Cheney), May 2001.

Panetta, U.S. Rep. Leon, et al., letter to the Honorable Sidney Yates, Chair of the Subcommittee on Interior and Related Agencies, Committee on Appropriations, April 20, 1988.

Peterson, Cass, "Interior's Giveaway Settlement: Udall Assails Agreement Transferring U.S. Land to Oil Companies," *Washington Post*, August 13, 1986.

Rankin, Adam, "In Wyoming, Gas Play Means Work; Powder River Basin Produces Huge Amounts of Methane Gas Each Year," *News-Record* (Gillette, Wyoming), Spring 2002 (Spring Tourism Supplement).

Schmollinger, Christian, "EPA Ruling on Powder River Basin Deals Blow to Coalbed Methane Expansion Hopes," *Oil Daily*, May 17, 2002.

Selden, Ron, "Pending Nomination of Rebecca Watson Raises Red Flags," *Indian Country Today (Lakota Times)*, July 14, 2001.

Shogren, Elizabeth, "Nation's Energy Needs Collide with a Way of Life: Bush Team's Push for Natural-Gas Drilling in Wyoming Is Creating Havoc with Ranchers," *Los Angeles Times*, May 19, 2002.

Simonich, Mark, Director of Montana Department of Environmental Quality, letter to Leah Krafft, Wyoming Department of Environmental Quality, re: State of Wyoming Public Notice Regarding the Proposed Issuance of the Following Coal Bed Methane Produced Water Discharge

Permits, December 18, 2000.

Soraghan, Mike, "Feds, Oil Group to Meet in Denver Amid Drill Fight," *Denver Post*, May 6, 2002.

———, "Interior Official Boosts Embattled Wyo. Gas Project," *Denver Post*, April 26, 2002.

Swartz, Edward, interview by LD, Gillette, Wyoming, May 29, 2002.

———, Testimony, House Committee on Resources Subcommittee on Energy and Mineral Resources, transcript, September 6, 2001.

———, Testimony, House Committee on Resources Subcommittee on Energy and Mineral Resources, transcript, September 20, 2001.

Wyoming Outdoor Council, "Coalbed Methane Update: 139,000 Wells for the Powder River Basin?," *Frontline Report*, fall 2001.

CHAPTER 10: WARM IN THE WHITE HOUSE

Abdur-Rahman, Sufiya, "Peoples Gas Out of Money for Poor; Free Contingency Funds, Utility's Officials Ask U.S.," *Chicago Tribune*, December 4, 2002.

Brown, Alma, interview by LD, Philadelphia, January 21, 2003.

Caruso, David, "Thousands May Be Left in Cold by Cut Utility Aid; Number of Those Seeking Help Is Rising," *Record* (Bergen, New Jersey), December 13, 2002.

Cox, Joe, ACORN organizer, interview by LD, Philadelphia, January 20, 2003.

Cruz, Luz, interview by LD, Philadelphia, January 25, 2003.

Fanjul, Juan Carlos, WGN-TV, Chicago, *WGN News at Nine*, January 7, 2003.

Hassell, Frances, interview by LD, Philadelphia, January 26, 2002.

Hemingway, Carol, interview by LD, Philadelphia, January 26, 2003.

Hill, Miriam, "Systems Shift Stalls Heat-Aid Request; a Pa. Computer Switchover Is Blamed. After Three Recent Deaths in the City, Officials Are Eager to Inform People of Their Options," *Philadelphia Inquirer*, January 30, 2003.

"Keeping the Heat On," editorial, *Boston Globe*, January 15, 2003.

Leedy, Kathy, "Don't Reduce Funds That Help Poor Stay Warm," op-ed, *Public Opinion* (Chambersburg, Pennsylvania), December 18, 2002.

LIHEAP homepage, U.S. Department of Health and Human Services, www.acf.dhhs.programs/liheap/.

LIHEAP Legal Information, Pennsylvania Department of Welfare, www.dpw.state.pa.us/oim/oimliheap.asp.

LIHEAP *Newsletter*, LIHEAP Clearinghouse, National Center for Appropriate Technology, February 2003.

LIHEAP-Penn *Newsletter*, Pennsylvania Low Income Home Energy Assistance Program, www.dpw.state.pa.us/oim/oimliheap.asp, November 2002.

"Out in the Cold," editorial, *Boston Globe*, January 23, 2003.

Parker, Akweli, "Group Lobbies to Disburse Heating Aid," *Philadelphia Inquirer*, January 24, 2003.

Presidential Debate, transcript, Boston, October 3, 2000.

Reed, Sen. Jack, interview by LD with press office for background on legislative intent on Reed-Collins appropriations amendment, February 2, 2003.

———, letter to President George W. Bush, re: Release of unspent LIHEAP funds, January 23, 2003.

———, "President Gives in to Cold, Pressure from Senate and Releases Heating Assistance Funds," press release, January 24, 2003.

"Senate Approves Amendment Boosting

Heating Aid Program," Associated Press, January 21, 2003.

"Senate Restores $300 Million to Energy Assistance Program," *Bangor Daily News*, January 22, 2003.

Swanson, David, ACORN Public Information office, interview by LD, Washington, D.C., February 6, 2003.

Talbott, Madeline, ACORN head organizer, interview by LD, Chicago, February 11, 2003.

United States Department of Health and Human Services, *FY 2003 Budget in Brief.*

Wolfe, Mark, National Energy Assistance Directors' Association *Bulletin*, December 13, 2002.

Ziner, Karen Lee, "Protestors Storm GOP Chief's Office," *Providence Journal-Bulletin*, January 10, 2003.

CHAPTER 11: THE UNITED STATES OF ENRON

Addington, David, Counsel to the Vice President, letter to U.S. Rep. Henry Waxman re: Energy Policy Development Group meetings with Enron officials, January 3, 2002.

"Another Enron–White House Connection: Enron Chairman Gave List of Favored Names to White House, President Bush Named Two as Energy Regulators," Associated Press, January 31, 2002.

Bergman, Lowell, and Jeff Gerth, "Power Trader Tied to Bush Finds Washington All Ears," *New York Times*, May 25, 2001.

Brenneman, Kristina, "Enron Stiffed State on PGE Taxes," *Portland Tribune*, March 7, 2003

Bryce, Robert, and Molly Ivins, *Pipe Dreams: Greed, Ego, and the Death of Enron Daily News* (New York: Public Affairs, 2002).

Burger, Timothy, "Cheney Tried to Aid Enron in India Debt Row," *Daily News* (New York), January 18, 2002.

Bush, Gov. George, to Ken Lay, handwritten note re: thank you for Thomas Friedman article, April 14, 1999.

————, letter re: thank you note after knee surgery, April 2, 1997.

————, letter re: tort reform, January 21, 1999.

————, letter/birthday greeting, April 14, 1997.

Cobb, Kim, "The Fall of Enron: Enron's

Failures Rippling; a Subsidiary of Energy Giant, Oregon's Largest Utility Feels Reach of Bankruptcy Filing, Caused 401(k) Losses for Portland Workers," *Houston Chronicle*, February 3, 2002.

Committee on Government Reform, U.S. House of Representatives, Minority Staff, Bush Administration Contacts with Enron, Prepared for Rep. Henry A. Waxman, May 2002.

Connell, Rich, and Robert Lopez, "Chief of Federal Energy Panel an Outspoken Southern Warrior; Curtis Hebert Jr.'s Blunt-Spoken, Brash Ways Have Been a Hallmark Since He Got into Politics," *Los Angeles Times*, March 10, 2001.

Dubose, Louis, and Carmen Coiro, "Don't Cry For Bush, Argentina," *Mother Jones*, March/April 2000.

Enron Annual Meeting, Houston, Texas, 2000 (video) www.truthout.org/ docs 01/02.27A.Lay.Skilling.htm.

"Enron Reps Met with Cheney Six Times," Associated Press, January 8, 2002.

Fleck, Tim, and Brian Wallstin, "Enron's End Run," *Houston Press*, February 7, 2002.

Krugman, Paul, "Reckonings: Enron Goes on the Road," *New York Times*, August 17, 2001.

Lazarus, David, "Memo Details Cheney-Enron Links; Company's Suggestions Resembled Elements of Administration's Energy Policy," *San Francisco Chronicle*, January 30, 2002.

Leopold, Jason, "Former Employee Says Enron Manipulated California Power Market," Dow Jones Newswires, February 20, 2002.

————, "Enron Linked to California Blackouts," CBS.MarketWatch.com, May 16, 2002.

————, "Jason, Bush and Harken," *Nation*, July 24, 2002.

Lopez, Robert, and Rich Connell, "Unyielding Approach May Imperil Chief's Job," *Los Angeles Times*, May 10, 2001.

Marquis, Christopher, "Senator Calls for Hearings into Energy Regulator's Moves," *New York Times*, May 26, 2001.

Meet the Press, "SEC Chairman Harvey Pitt Discusses Corporate Responsibility and Reform," July 14, 2002.

Murray, Ruby, "Portland General Electric Workers Lose Big on Enron Stock,"

Daily News (Longview, Washington), March 13, 2002.

Parry, Sam, "Bush Did Try to Save Enron," www.consortiumnews.com, May 29, 2002.

Ratcliffe, R. G., and Bennet Roth, " '94 Campaign Records at Odds with Bush's Claim, President Has Said That He Inherited Energy Exec's Backing from Richards," *Houston Chronicle*, January 12, 2002.

Rich, Frank, "The United States of Enron," *New York Times*, January 19, 2002.

Rivera, Nancy Brooks, Thomas Mulligan, and Tim Reiterman, "Memo Shows Enron Role in Hiking Prices," *Los Angeles Times*, May 7, 2002.

Scheer, Robert, "A Walk in the Valley of God," op-ed, *Los Angeles Times*, January 29, 2002.

Skelton, George, "Price Caps Don't Fit in Cheney's Head for Figures," *Los Angeles Times*, April 19, 2002.

Smitherman, Laura, "Bush Campaign Flew Enron, Halliburton Jets During 2000 Recount," Bloomberg News Service, August 2, 2002.

Stephens, Joe, "Bush 2000 Advisor Offered to Use Clout to Help Enron,"

Washington Post, February 17, 2002.

Tillotson, Diane, interview by LD, Longview, Washington, July 25, 2002.

Tillotson, Ed, interview by LD, Longview, Washington, July 25, 2002.

Verbitsky, Horacio, *Robo Para la Corona* (Buenos Aires: Planeta, 1995).

Waxman, U.S. Rep. Henry, letter to Attorney General John Ashcroft re: Enron contributions to Ashcroft, January 10, 2002.

———, letter to Vice President Cheney re: Enron Meetings with Energy, January 8, 2002.

Widme, Kathryn, interview by LD, Rainier, Oregon, July 14, 2004.

CHAPTER 12: ARMY SURPLUS: TWO
VETERANS AT ENRON

"Bush Is Past Champion at the Insider Game," *Financial Post* (Canada), July 12, 2002.

Chaffin, Joshua, and Steven Fidler, "In the Days When Enron Was the Envy of Corporate America, Employees Across the Company Were Troubled by a Similar Question," *Financial Times*, April 9, 2002.

Corn, David, "W's Biggest Enron Liability:

The Case Against Thomas White Grows," *Nation*, March 9, 2002.

Hendren, John, "Air Force's Roche Is Offered Army Secretary Post," *Los Angeles Times*, May 2, 2003.

Kamen, Al, "In the Loop," *Washington Post*, May 8, 2002.

Krugman, Paul, "Smoking Fat Boy," *New York Times*, May 10, 2002.

Leopold, Jason, Dow Jones Newswires, May 16, 2000.

Lyons, Julie Sevrens, "Where Blackouts Could Be Deadly, Nursing Homes Prepare for When Lights and Cool Air go Off," *San Jose Mercury News*, May 15, 2001.

Miller, Greg, "Army Chief Defends Enron Record, Stock Trades; Investigations: Secretary Thomas White's Use of a Military Plane Is Also the Subject of a Probe; He Is Still Confident, However," *Los Angeles Times*, April 25, 2002.

Nakashima, Emily, "White Made Calls Before Selling Enron Stock," *Washington Post*, May 25, 2002.

Public Citizen, "Documents Raise Questions About Army Secretary Thomas White's Senate Testimony on Energy Trades," www.citizen.org/ pressroom/

release.cfm?ID-1229, September 30, 2002.

———, "Memo Shows Enron Division Headed by Army Secretary Thomas White Manipulated California Electricity Market," www.citizen.org/pressroom/release.cfm?ID-1106, May 8 2002.

Ramsey, Tim, interview by LD, Portland, Oregon, July 17, 2002.

Smith, Dianna, "Army Secretary White Sells Naples Home for $13.9 Million," *Naples* (Florida) *Daily News*, January 30, 2002.

———, "U.S. Secretary White Allowed to Build Larger Gate, Wall," *Naples* (Florida) *Daily News*, July 20, 2002.

United States Senate Commerce, Science, and Transportation Committee Hearing, July 18, 2002.

CHAPTER 13: GOD IN THE WHITE HOUSE

Block, Jennifer, "Christian Soldiers on the March," *Nation*, February 3, 2003.

Cobb, Kim, and R. G. Ratcliffe, "Bush Urges Welfare Role for Faith-Based Groups," *Houston Chronicle*, July 23, 1999.

Colloff, Pamela, "Remember the Christian

Alamo," *Texas Monthly*, December 2001.

———, "True Believers" (online interview), www.texasmonthly.com, November 28, 2002.

DiIulio, John, to Ron Suskind, letter, re: faith-based legislative initiatives, *Esquire*, October 24, 2002.

Draper, Robert, "Beware the Grace of God," *Texas Monthly*, January 1992.

Fineman, Howard, with Tamara Lipper, Martha Brant, Suzan Smalley, and Richard Wolfe, "Bush and God," *Newsweek*, March 10, 2003.

Gibeaut, John, "Welcome to Hell: How Allegations of Child Abuse at a Texas Church Home for Problem Kids Could Threaten a Major Part of President Bush's Faith-Based Initiative," *ABA Journal*, August 2, 2001.

Jordan, Stephanie L., "Roloff Homes Allowed to Reopen," *Corpus Christi Caller-Times*, March 15, 1999.

———, "Teen Tells Deputies of Abuses; Allegations Made About Roloff Homes," *Corpus Christi Caller-Times*, April 4, 2000.

Keilman, John, "Drug War Puts Its Faith in Faith; Bush's Voucher Plan Would Boost Religious Programs," *Chicago*

Tribune, April 23, 2003.

Laceky, Tom, "Private School Brings Troubled Boys, Troubled Reputation to Montana," Associated Press, April 13, 2001.

Little, Jane, "Bush and Religion," British Broadcasting Corporation World News Service, March 4, 2003.

McIlvain, Ashley, Texas Freedom Alliance, interview by LD, Austin, April 14, 2002.

Milbank, Dana, "Bush Legislative Approach Failed in Faith Bill Battle, White House Is Faulted for Not Building a Consensus in Congress," *Washington Post*, April 23, 2003.

Moore, Evan, "Roloff Home to Reopen Doors to Troubled Youth; Founder of Facility Refused to Get Licensing in '70s," *Houston Chronicle*, March 13, 1999.

Olasky, Marvin, and Roy Maynard, "Governor Bush Backs Texas Teen Challenge," *World Magazine*, July 29/August 5, 1995.

Parker, Dan, "State Forever Bans Roloff Home Leader's Wife from Working at Facility," *Corpus Christi Caller-Times*, April 28, 2000.

Rosin, Hanna, "Faith Based Youth Homes'

'Lesson' Texas Backs Away from Unregulated Programs After Abuse
Charges," *Washington Post*, June 21,
2001.

———, "Putting Faith in a Social Service
Role: Church Based Providers Freed
from Many Rules," *Washington Post*,
May 5, 2000.

———, "Two Arrested in Child Abuse
Case," *Washington Post*, April 11,
2000.

Smoot, Samantha, Texas Freedom Alliance, interview by LD, Austin, April
18, 2003.

Suskind, Ron, "Why Are These Men
Laughing?," *Esquire*, January 2003.

Teen Challenge of South Texas, admission
staff interview, Program Application
and Contract, 2003.

Teen Challenge of South Texas, interview
by LD, April 11, 2003.

Texas Commission on Alcohol and Drug
Abuse, compliance letter, David
Morales, Southern District Super-
visor, Facility Licensure, to Reverend
James Heurich, Teen Challenge of
South Texas, Inc., March 22, 1995.

———, Consent Order: In the Matter of
Teen Challenge of South Texas, Inc.,
November 28, 1995.

————, Licensure Inspection Report: Teen Challenge of South Texas, Inc., March 22, 1995.

Weiss, Rick, "Stem Cells Strides Test Biology; Scientists Push for Use of New Cell Colonies," *Washington Post*, April 22, 2002.

Womack, Chris, "Taking Deregulation on Faith: Why Bush's Alternative Accreditation Scheme Didn't Work," *Texas Observer*, September 28, 2001.

Woodward, Kenneth L., "The White House: Gospel on the Potomac," *Newsweek*, March 10, 2003.

CHAPTER 14: DUBYA BUSH'S BENCH

Ayres, R. Jack, Esq., interview by LD, Addison, Texas, March 23, 2003.

Fisk, Margret Cronin, "Ford Thinks It Has a Better Idea: Hardball," *National Law Journal*, March 18, 1996.

Ford Motor Company v. *Susan Renae Miles, Individually and as Next of Friend of Willie Searcy et al.*, Dissenting Opinion, Justice Deborah Hankinson, Supreme Court of Texas, March 19, 1998.

Ford Motor Company v. *Susan Renae Miles, Individually and as Next of Friend of*

Willie Searcy et al., Majority Opinion, Supreme Court of Texas, March 19, 1998.

Ford Motor Company v. *Susan Renae Miles, Individually and as Next of Friend of Willie Searcy et al.*, Oral Argument/ Tape, Supreme Court of Texas, November 21, 1996.

Ford Motor Company v. *Susan Renae Miles, Individually and as Next of Friend of Willie Searcy et al.*, from Rusk County, 6th district, Orders on Causes, March 19, 1998.

Ford Motor Company and Douglas Stanley, Jr., d/b/a Stanley Ford, Relators, v. *Honorable Donald Ross*, Judge of the 4th Judicial District Court, Rusk County, Respondent, Court of Appeals of Texas, Tyler, Westlaw, October 4, 1994.

Freedman, Eric, "Texas Court Upholds $30 Million Award in Ford Belt Case Involving 1988 Ranger," *Automotive News*, April 22, 1996.

Harmon, John, Ford News, Statement: Miles vs. Ford Motor Company, March 15, 1996.

Leahey, Sen. Patrick, Opening Statement on the Nomination of Miguel Estrada to the D.C. Court of Appeals, U.S.

Senate, February 5, 2003.

National Abortion Federation Report on Priscilla Owen, www.prochoice. org, July 22, 2002.

Nickols, John, "Karl Rove's Legal Tricks," *Nation,* July 22, 2002.

Paztor, David, "Texas Jurist Sailing into U.S. Senate Storm: Death of Plaintiff Could Haunt Nominee," *Austin American-Statesman,* July 14, 2002.

People for the American Way, "The Dissents of Priscilla Owen: A Report of People for the American Way in Opposition to the Confirmation of Priscilla Owen," www.pfaw.org, 2002.

Sandifer, T. Randall, Esq., interview by LD, Addison, Texas, March 26, 2003.

Susan Renae Miles, Individually and as Next of Friend of Willie Searcy et al. v. *Ford Motor Company and Douglas Stanley, Jr., d/b/a Doug Stanley Ford,* in District Court, Rusk County, Texas, May 9, 1995.

Susan Renae Miles, Individually and as Next of Friend of Willie Searcy et al. v. *Ford Motor Company, Appellants,* Court of Appeals of Texas, Dallas, Westlaw, December 22, 1995.

Susan Renae Miles, Individually and as Next of Friend of Willie Searcy et al. v. *Ford*

Motor Company and Douglas Stanley, *Jr., d/b/a/ Doug Stanley Ford, Appellees,* Court of Appeals of Texas, Texarkana, Westlaw, March 13, 1996.

Susan Renae Miles, Individually and as Next of Friend of Willie Searcy et al. v. *Ford Motor Company, Appellees,* Court of Appeals of Texas, Dallas, June 29, 2001.

Wheat, Andrew, "Judging Prissy," *Texas Observer,* April 12, 2002.

Willie Searcy and Susan Miles v. *Texas University Health Plan System et al.,* U.S. District Court, Northern Division of Texas, Dallas Division, Memorandum Opinion and Order, May 17, 2000.

CHAPTER 15: SHRUB II: THE EMPIRE
STRIKES BACK

Bearak, Barry, "Taliban Plead for Mercy to the Miserable in a Land of Nothing," *New York Times,* September 13, 2001.

Brookman, Jay, "The President's Real Goal In Iraq," *Atlanta Journal-Constitution,* September 29, 2002.

Collier, Robert, "Iraq Links Cancers to Uranium Weapons; U.S. Likely to Use Arms Again in War," *San Francisco Chronicle,* January 13, 2003.

Fairness and Accuracy in Reporting (FAIR), "Star Witness on Iraq Said Weapons Were Destroyed: Bombshell Revelation from a Defector Cited by White House and Press," Media Advisory, www.fair.org, February 27, 2003.

FitzGerald, Frances, "George Bush and the World," *New York Review of Books*, September 2002.

Freundlich, Paul, "Logic of War," NPR, *All Things Considered*, March 13, 2003.

Lieven, Anatol, "The Push for War," *London Review of Books*, October 3, 2002.

Marshall, Joshua Micah, "Bomb Saddam?," *Washington Monthly*, June 2002.

Masland, Tom, "Interview with Nelson Mandela: The United States of America Is a Threat to World Peace," *Newsweek*, September 10, 2002.

Meller, Paul, "Europeans to Exempt U.S. from War Court," *New York Times*, October 1, 2002.

Military Toxics Project, Environmental Assessment of Depleted Uranium, www.miltoxproj.org/assessment.htm.

"Proliferator-in-chief: Bush blocks treaty;

There He Goes Again. . . ," *Guardian* (London), July 26, 2001.

Watts, Jonathan, "North Korea Threatens U.S. with First Strike," *Guardian* (London), February 6, 2003.

Worldwatch Institute, "Exportable Righteousness, Expendable Women," January 1, 2002.

Zakaria, Fareed, "The Politics of Rage," *Newsweek*, October 15, 2003.

CHAPTER 16: STATE OF THE UNION

American Civil Liberties Union (ACLU), www.aclu.org.

Armstrong, David, "Military Chiefs Will Consider Environmental Exemptions," *Wall Street Journal*, March 20, 2003.

"Brief Overview of Changes to Americans' Legal Rights Since Terror Attacks," Associated Press, August 19, 2002.

Center for Public Integrity, www.publici.org.

Center for Responsive Politics, "Money in Politics Alert," www.opensecrets. org, July 23, 2001.

Court, Jamie, and Jerry Flanagan, "Insurance 'Reform'? Consider the Source; Health-Care Profiteers Aim to Grow Fatter by Feeding Off a Crisis That Has Invaded the Middle Class," *Los*

Angeles Times, March 18, 2003.

Cullen, Lisa, *A Job to Die For: Why So Many Americans Are Killed, Injured or Made Ill at Work and What to Do About It* (Monroe, Maine: Common Courage Press, 2002).

"Devil in the Details: Seeking Men of Convictions," *American Prospect*, March 2003.

Dowd, Maureen, "Treadmills of His Mind," *New York Times*, August 25, 2002.

Gage, Jonathan, "Markets Rattled After Fund Rescue," *International Herald Tribune*, September 26, 1998.

Greenhouse, Steven, "Bush, Citing Security, Bans Some Unions at Justice Department," *New York Times*, January 16, 2002.

———, "Judge Voids a Union Rule Issued by Bush," *New York Times*, January 8, 2002.

Hertzberg, Hendrik, "Generous George," *New Yorker*, March 12, 2001.

Hosenball, Mark, "Live from America: Arab TV," *Newsweek*, November 25, 2002.

Lapham, Lewis H., "The Road to Babylon; Searching for Targets in Iraq," *Harper's Magazine*, October 1, 2002.

Milbank, Dana, "Bush by the Numbers, as Told by a Diligent Scorekeeper,"

Washington Post, September 3, 2002.

Mishel, Lawrence, Jared Bernstein, and Heather Boushey, and the Economic Policy Institute, *The State of Working America 2002/03* (Ithaca, N.Y.: Cornell University Press, 2003).

Morgenson, Gretchen, "In Commodities, It May Become Tougher to Tell Who's Who," *New York Times*, March 30, 2003.

Public Campaign, OUCH! #108, Corruption Perception Index, December, 18, 2002.

Record, Jeffrey, "Bush's Promised Pentagon Reform Remains MIA," *Los Angeles Times*, August 30, 2001.

Rich, Frank, "Sacrifice Is for Losers," *New York Times*, June 22, 2002.

CHAPTER 17: WHAT IS TO BE DONE?

Borosage, Bob, Campaign for America's Future, www.ourfuture.org.

———, "Class Warfare, Bush-Style," *American Prospect*, March 2003.

Cavanaugh, John, et al., from the International Forum on Globalization, Alternatives to Economic Globalization, Berrett-Koehler, 2002.

Huffington, Arianna, "No More Pigs at the

Trough: How to Cure Infectious Greed," *Nation*, February 3, 2003.

————, *Pigs at the Trough: How Corporate Greed and Political Corruption Are Undermining America* (New York: Crown, 2003).

• ABOUT THE AUTHORS •

MOLLY IVINS' column is syndicated to more than three hundred newspapers from Anchorage to Miami. A three-time Pulitzer Prize finalist, she is the former co-editor of *The Texas Observer* and the former Rocky Mountain bureau chief for *The New York Times*. Her freelance work has appeared in *Esquire, The Atlantic Monthly, The New York Times Magazine, The Nation, Harper's Magazine,* and other publications. She has a B.A. from Smith College and a master's in journalism from Columbia University. Her first book, *Molly Ivins Can't Say That, Can She?*, spent more than twelve months on the *New York Times* bestseller list. Her book with Lou Dubose on George W. Bush's years as governor of Texas, *Shrub*, was a national bestseller.

LOU DUBOSE has worked as a journalist in Texas for twenty years. He has been editor of *The Texas Observer* and politics editor of *The Austin Chronicle*, and is co-author of *Boy Genius: Karl Rove, the Brains*

Behind the Remarkable Political Triumph of George W. Bush. His freelance work has appeared in *The Nation*, *Texas Monthly*, *The Washington Post*, the Toronto *Globe and Mail*, the Liberty, Texas, *Vindicator*, and other publications. He lives with his wife, Jeanne Goka, in Austin.